R. H. Blyth: Haiku, Vol. III

まゆはきを俤にして紅粉の花

蠶飼する人は古代のすがた哉　　　曾良

山形領に、立石寺といふ山寺あり。慈覚大師の開基にして、殊清閑の地なり。一見すべきよし、人々のすゝむるに依て、尾花沢より、とつてかへし、其間七里ばかり也。日いまだくれず、梺の坊に宿かり置て、山上の堂にのぼる。岩に巌を重て山とし、松柏年旧、土石老て、苔滑に、岩上の院々、扉を閉て、物の音きこえず。岸をめぐり、岩を這て、佛閣を拝し、佳景寂寞として心すみ行のみ覚ゆ。

閑さや岩にしみ入蟬の声

最上川のらんと、大石田と云所に、日和を待。爰に古き俳諧の種こぼれて、忘れぬ花のむかしをしたひ、芦角一声の心をやはらげ、此道にさぐりあしして、新古ふた道にふみまよふといへども、みちしるべする人しなければとわりなき一巻残しぬ。このたびの風流爰に至れり。

(See page 975.)

尾花沢にて清風と云者を尋ぬ。かれは
富るものなれども志いやしからず。都にも折々かよひて
さすがに旅の情をも知たれば、日比とゞめて長途の
いたはり、さまぐ\にもてなし侍る。

　　涼しさを我宿にして
　　　　　　　　ねまる也

HAIKU

BY

R. H. BLYTH

Volume Three: Summer—Autumn

(Pp. 641-976)

(Reset in paperback edition)

1982
THE HOKUSEIDO PRESS
Tokyo

Haiku, Volume Three © by R. H. Blyth 1952, 1982

Paperback edition, first printing 1982
second printing 1984

Complete set   ISBN 0-89346-184-9
Vol. III   ISBN 0-89346-160-1

Published by The Hokuseido Press
3-32-4, Honkomagome, Bunkyo-ku, Tokyo

VOL. III SUMMER—AUTUMN

ILLUSTRATIONS

HAIKU

IN FOUR VOLUMES

VOL. III
SUMMER — AUTUMN

Fishing-Boat in a River, Evening

by Jasoku Soga 曾我蛇足, 15th century, an intimate friend of Ikkyū, 1394–1481, who wrote a Chinese poem on the present picture, omitted here.

THE PUBLICATION OF THIS VOLUME

WAS MADE POSSIBLE

THROUGH THE KINDNESS AND PATRIOTISM

OF

NAOTO ICHIMADA

GOVERNER OF THE BANK OF JAPAN

/

PREFACE

The nature of haiku cannot be rightly understood until it is realized that they imply a revolution of our everyday life and ways of thinking.

前念迷即凡夫、後念悟即佛。

One thought of folly makes a man an ordinary man. The next enlightened thought, and he is a Buddha.   *Rokusodangyō II*

All things around us are asking for our apprehension, working for our enlightenment. But our thoughts are of folly. What is worse, every day, and many times in the day, we are enlightened, we are Buddha, a poet, — but do not know it, and remain an ordinary man. For our sake haiku isolate, as far as it is possible, significance from the more brute fact or circumstance. It is a single finger pointing to the moon. If you say it is only a finger, and often not a very beautiful one at that, this is so. If the hand is beautiful and bejewelled, we may forget what it is pointing at. Recording a conversation with Blake, Crabb Robinson gives us an example of the indifference, or rather the cowardice of average human nature, in its failure to recognize truth, poetry, when confronted with it in its unornamented form; the lines he quotes from Wordsworth are a "haiku."

I had been in the habit, when reading this marvellous Ode to friends, to omit one or two passages, especially that beginning,

> But there's a Tree, of many, one,
> A single field
> That I have looked upon,

lest I should be rendered ridiculous, being unable to explain precisely *what* I admired. Not that I acknowledged this to be a fair test. But with Blake I could fear nothing of the kind. And it was this

very stanza which threw him almost into a hys-
terical rapture.

Consider the seven following verses, respectively of autumn,
spring, winter, spring, summer, spring, autumn.

稲妻や闇の方ゆく五位の聲   芭 蕉
Inazuma ya   yami no kata yuku   goi no koe

    A flash of lightning:
The screech of a night-heron
    Flying in the darkness.   Bashō

春雨や蜂の巣傳ふ屋根の漏   芭 蕉
Harusame ya   hachi no su tsutou   yane no mori

    Spring rain;
Water leaking through the roof
    Runs along the wasps' nest.   Bashō

埋火も消ゆや泪の烹ゆる音   芭 蕉
Uzumibi mo   kiyu ya namida no   niyuru oto

    The sound of tears
Hissing, quenching
    The banked charcoal.   Bashō

二里ほどは鳶も出て舞ふ汐干哉   太 祇
Ni ri hodo wa   tobi mo dete mau   shiohi kana

    Five miles round
The kite appears and soars,
    At the low tide.   Taigi

夕立にうたるゝ鯉のあたまかな   子 規
Yūdachi ni   utaruru koi no   atama kana

    A summer shower;
The rain beats
    On the heads of the carp.   Shiki

鶯の聲せで來けり苔の上   太 祇
Uguisu no   koe sede kikeri   koke no ue

    The uguisu has come
And stands on the moss,
    Silent.   Taigi

笠とれて雨無殘なる案山子かな　　　　　　はぎ女
Kasa torete   ame muzan naru   kakashi kana

His kasa fallen off,
The rain beats down pitilessly
On the scarecrow.						Hagi-jo

When we read these verses, we realise that haiku is a way
of living. It offers itself to mankind, not as a substitute for
Christianity or Buddhism, but as their fulfilment. It is "Love
one another" applied to all things without exception. And this
"love" is not that impossible love of repulsive and odious
things, but something far deeper, an entering into the life of
fish and reptile and bacteria through that very emotion of
aversion. It is

應無所住而生其心

Arouse the mind, without attachment to any-
thing.

Haiku at first sight may seem rather slight or thin. This is
partly because they avoid any parade of depth, and indeed
mask their profundity under a characteristic humour or apparent
simplicity; it is partly because of insufficient cooperation by the
reader. We may take the following verse of Gyōdai[1] as an
example:

我ためにとぼし遅かれ春の暮
Waga tame ni   toboshi osokare   haru no kure

For my sake,
Do not light the lamp yet,[2]
This evening of spring.

This is certainly not a masterpiece of haiku, but it is not
so flat as it looks. When we read the poet's prescript to the
verse, and enter into his feelings, we are in a realm of poetical
life that is both ideal and actual:

When it grows dark in autumn it is good to light
the lamp early. If it is lighted late in the evening,
an old man's heart is still sadder. In winter we

[1] 1732–1793. A contemporary of Buson.
[2] Literally, "light the lamp late."

feel cold until the lamp is lit. In a summer evening, it may be light enough to recognise the people passing by, but the pure light of the lamp flickering is extraordinarily cool. Spring, however, is quite different. The willow trees hanging down in the shadows, the cherry-blossoms floating whitely in the half-darkness, all else is unseen. Gradually it darkens; a soft breeze rises without, and the sound of water alone is heard. Sitting on the verandah, gazing at the distant hills, they gradually disappear in the dusk. In all this we know the deep heart of spring. To have a light brought near one, because it is dark, —this is to be far indeed from our real, our poetical nature.

> For my sake,
> Do not light the lamp yet,
> This evening of spring.

The brevity of haiku is not something different from, but a part of the poetical life ; it is not only a form of expression but a mode of living more immediately, more closely to life. This may be illustrated in the following verse by Taigi, an eighteenth century poet.

> 梅活けて月とも佗んともしかげ
> *Ume ikete   tsuki to mo wabin   tomoshikage*
>
> Arranging the plum-flowers,
> I would enjoy them in the light of the lamp,
> As if in the moonlight.

The original is even more difficult, literally: "Arranging the plum, as if the moon, I would savour, lamp-light." (*Wabiru* translated "enjoy," means "to live a life of poetry in poverty.") The poet has arranged the flowers in a vase, and wishes to see them in the light of the moon, but there being no moon, he lights the lamp instead, and adds its light to the poetry and beauty of the flowers.

The whole of the poet's life is shown in this action and the essence of the verse in 佗ん, *wabin*. This poverty, this asceticism of life and form in haiku, this absence of luxury and decoration finds its philosophical and transcendental expression

in Swedenborg's *Heaven and Hell*, §178; after he has described
the garments of the angels, some of which glow with flame,
some of which shine with light, he adds:

> But the angels of the inmost heaven are not
> clothed.

夏
SUMMER

The heat of the day and the cool of the evening are such simple, elemental things; there is an unlimited amount of poetry in them. So also with summer rain, heavy, monotonous, but changing everything, even the hearts of men. Fields and mountains have in summer a vast, overarching meaning, something of infinity and eternity in them that no other season bestows.

The hototogisu, (written in various ways) or little cuckoo, is a migratory bird that comes to Japan at the beginning of summer. It is rather smaller than a pigeon, dark grey above, whitish grey beneath. It lives deep in the mountains, laying its eggs in the nest of the uguisu, and sings at night, usually when flying, such a melancholy note that it is said to bring up blood. The inside of its mouth is actually blood-red.

Summer is the season of insects. Fireflies and cicadas are sung in the popular poetry of other countries, for example Italy, but the poetry of fleas, lice, flies, and mosquitoes is peculiar to Japan. Here the tenderness of Buddhist compassion embraces them in an atmosphere of humour. Of flowers, the peony is the flower of pride, the symbol of the glory of man and of nature. Only in this flower have the Japanese felt and expressed the magnificence and splendour that the Chinese poets portray both in the present and in retrospect.

時　候　THE SEASON

六月の海見ゆるなり寺の像　　　　　　子　規
Rokugatsu no   umi miyuru nari   tera no zō

The temple Buddhas;
In the distance,
The June sea.   Shiki

The temple stands on the side of a hill overlooking the sea.
It is early summer, warm, not hot. Out of the window at the
side, the sea glitters in the distance; the Buddhist images stand
there in the half-darkness. It is two worlds, as far apart as
possible. There is a deep contrast, but somewhere, somehow,
a feeling of the ultimate origin of both.

大蟻の疊を歩く暑さかな　　　　　　　士　朗
Ōari no   tatami wo aruku   atsusa kana

A huge ant
Walks over the *tatami*;
Ah, the heat!   Shirō

It will do no harm to say that the ant is a symbol of the
heat, provided we remember that it is so because it is felt to
be so, and in as much as it has no rationally explicable connec-
tion with that heat.

風鈴は鳴らで時計の暑さかな　　　　　也　有
Fūrin wa   narade tokei no   atsusa kana

The wind-bell is silent;
The heat
Of the clock.   Yayū

Mechanical clocks[1] were introduced into Japan as early as
1550. "Wind-bells" are small bells made of copper, suspended

---

[1] Spengler calls them,
　The dread symbol of the flow of time...the most wonderful
expression of which a historical world-feeling is capable.

from the eaves. Long strips of paper on which poems are inscribed, are hung from the tongue. They give a cool sound in the summer breeze.

The poet hears the heat in the silence of the wind-bells; he hears it in the tick-tock of the clock; there is in the ticking of a clock something that irritates, yet also appeals to our feeling of inevitability. Stevenson says:

> Quiet minds cannot be perplexed or frightened,
> but go on in fortune or misfortune at their own
> private pace, like a clock during a thunder-storm.

The silence, the heat, the ticking of the clock, these are all portions of eternity when perceived separately, but when grasped as one thing, the mind is moving "at its own private pace."

馬蠅の笠をはなれぬ暑さかな   子 規
Umabae no   kasa wo hanarenu   atsusa kana

The flies from the horse
Do not leave my *kasa*;
Oh, the heat!   Shiki

The poet has taken one of the most common experiences of summer, the irritating persistence of certain flies, on certain days, and identified it with the maddening persistence of the merciless sun that pours down upon everything. The flies do not leave the *kasa* for more than a moment; they seem to have sworn an oath never to leave him, and it is this thusness of the fly and the same inevitability of the heat which is felt.

信濃路の山が荷になる暑さ哉   一 茶
Shinanoji no   yama ga ni ni naru   atsusa kana

On the road to Shinano,
The mountain is a burden I bear,—
Oh, the heat, the heat!   Issa

If we take this as a mere thought of, "I am so hot that I feel as if I were carrying the mountain on my back," we do

not participate in the experience which produced the poem.
Compare the words of The Earth, in *Prometheus Unbound*:

> It interpenetrates my granite mass,
> Through tangled roots and trodden clay doth pass
> Into the utmost leaves and delicatest flowers;
> Upon the winds, among the clouds 'tis spread.

This "it" is love, life; and this interpenetration by Man ("Oh,
not men,") is the work of the poet. For a moment at least,
Issa and "the whole creation groaneth together," Issa and the
heat and the mountain become a single entity of pressure and
weariness. The mountain is on Issa, but Issa is also on the
mountain.

Another verse by Shiki in which confusion of mind, though
from a different cause, is felt as identical with the nature of
heat, is the following:

暑くるし亂れ心や雷をきく
Atsukurushi   midaregokoro ya   rai wo kiku

> Oppressive heat;
> My mind in a whirl
> I listen to the peals of thunder.

葉がくれをこけ出て瓜の暑さ哉   去　來
Hagakure wo   kokedete uri no   atsusa kana

> The melons are so hot,
> They have rolled
> Out of their leafy hiding.   Kyorai

This seems at first sight to belong more to fancy than imag-
ination, but through the very fancifulness and humour is
expressed something of the rotundity, heaviness, and plebeian
stupidity of melons.

風一荷擔ふ暑さや團扇うり   可　幸
Kaze ikka   ninau atsusa ya   uchiwauri

> The fan-seller;
> A load of wind he carries,—
>   Ah, the heat!   Kakō

At first sight, the attitude of Zen towards heat and cold, and that of poetry, may seem to be quite different. Take for example the case of Kaisen, 快川, of Erinji Temple, 恵林寺. When he and his monks were forced to mount the main gate of the temple and were there burnt alive by Oda Nobunaga, he quoted from the Criticism of the 43rd Case of the *Hekigan-roku*:

安禪不必須山水、
滅却心頭火自凉。

For the tranquillity of Zazen, mountains and streams are not
    necessary;
When the mind is extinguished, fire feels cool of itself.

Contrast this attitude with that of the poet, who either complains, or speaks whimsically of the heat. In the present verse, the heat of the day, and of the peddler, are contrasted with the fans, the cause of cool airs. Yet at the back of this contrast is the feeling of primordial, original unity between them. The Zen of the poet is in his eye, that of the monk is in the whole of his body.

病人の駕の蠅追ふ暑さかな   蕪 村
Byōnin no   kago no hae ou   atsusa kana

Keeping away the flies
From the sick girl in the palanquin,—
How hot it is!   Buson

One summer day, a palanquin containing a sickly-looking girl is passing along the road. The bearers set it down and rest by the way, and the mother who has been trudging along behind it, bends down and fans away the flies that come buzzing round, always attracted by calamity. The girl sits with pale, inattentive, half-averted face, eyes shut, and dishevelled hair. The heat is inexorable, like the flies, and the illness.

Shiki has a verse something like this, but the heat is felt through the pathos of animals instead of through that of human beings:

痩馬の尻ならべたる暑さかな
Yaseuma no   shiri narabetaru   atsusa kana

> Thin horses,
> Their hindquarters all in a row,—
> The heat!

These horses are to be sold in a country fair.

鍬立ててあたり人なき暑さ哉   子 規
Kuwa tatete   atari hito naki   atsusa kana

> A hoe standing there
> No one to be seen,—
> The heat!   Shiki

The idea of this is not that the man who was wielding the hoe has gone somewhere to rest out of the hot sunshine of summer, though this may be perfectly true. It is that the hoe standing there under the sun gives the poet, directly and without rational explanation, the feeling of heat, by the absence of the man. The presence of the hoe, by itself alone, gives the meaning of heat. The loneliness of summer is a very different thing from that of autumn.

負た子に髪なぶらるゝ暑哉   その女
Outa ko ni   kami naburaruru   atsusa kana

> The child on my back
> Playing with my hair,—
> The heat!   Sono-jo

When the hair is done in the Japanese style, or even when it is not, a hot child on the back, drenched with sweat, playing with his mother's hair, is something almost unendurable. But in this heat complained of is expressed through its complete lack of expression, direct or indirect, the mother's love of the child, physical, instinctive, indestructible. We might quote here Kikaku's well-known but not very poetical verse, and then one by Shiki:

夕涼みよくぞ男に生れける
Yūsuzumi   yoku zo otoko ni   umarekeru

> The evening cool;
> Lucky I am indeed
> To be born a man.

男ばかりの中に女の暑さかな
Otoko bakari no   naka ni onna no   atsusa kana

> Nothing but men;
> And a woman there,—
> How hot she is!

海士が家に干魚の匂ふ暑さかな   子 規
Amagaya ni   hizakana no niou   atsusa kana

> In the fisherman's house,
> The smell of dried fish,
> And the heat.   Shiki

A poet does not need to ask, "Is this experience a poetical one?" He only needs to know the depth, not the tumult of the soul. When we are standing in a crowded railway carriage, and the man next to us has a rubber rain-coat, the heat and the congestion and the smell of rubber, the general discomfort makes us feel frantic. This, is, or may be, a poetical experience. So with Shiki's verse. The overpowering smell of salt fish that increases and is increased by the heat, has a meaning that the moon, the flowers of spring, the song of the nightingale have not.

ずんずんと夏を流すや最上川   子 規
Zunzun to   natsu wo nagasu ya   mogamigawa

> How swiftly the Mogami River
> Washes away
> The summer.   Shiki

In his verse, space and time are combined in a remarkable yet implicit way. The river stretches out into the distance,

and the flow of the water is also that of the seasons. Summer
is cooling off into autumn, and the river and the summer are
seen as one swift, departing movement.

あの山もけふのあつさの行方哉   鬼　貫
Ano yama mo   kyō no atsusa no   yukue kana

Yonder mountain
Is where the heat of today
Has gone.   Onitsura

There is a delightfully infantile logic about this. The heat
has gone; it must have gone somewhere, somewhere in the
distance. Looking far away, the poet sees the mountains shim-
mering in the evening haze; the heat must have gone there.
This semi-rational mood is a relief from the irritating mock-
exactness of ordinary reasonable life, in which impalpable things
are weighed in the balance, invisible things described with
geometrical accuracy.

涼風の尊き森の宮居かな   橒　良
Suzukaze no   tōtoki mori no   miyai kana

The shrine
In the sacred grove:
A cool wind blows.   Chora

There is something pure and holy about the cool wind that
blows through the forest. It comes from the unknown. Its
coolness calms the spirit; the sound has a meaning beyond words
or silence.

涼しさや青田の中に一つ松   子　規
Suzushisa ya   aota no naka ni   hitotsu matsu

The coolness of it
In the middle of a green rice-field,
A single pine-tree!   Shiki

This has the simplicity in which the vast (the coolness) is perceived in one thing (the pine-tree). In the bright green rice field, the dark green pine-tree stands out against the blue sky. This is the coolness.

Shiki seems to have been peculiarly susceptible to heat and cold, and has many verses in which he expresses his visual and audible perception of temperature:

島あれば松あり風の音涼し
Shima areba　matsu ari kaze no　oto suzushi

Pine-trees on each island;
The sound of the wind
Is cool.

野も山もぬれて涼しき夜明かな
No mo yama mo　nurete suzushiki　yoake kana

Fields and mountains
Drenched with rain,—
A cool day-break.

御佛に尻むけ居れば月涼し　　　　　　　子　規
Mihotoke ni　shiri muke ireba　tsuki suzushi

Turning my back on the Buddha,
How cool
The moonlight!　　　　　　　　　　　Shiki

This was written while Shiki was staying at Mampukuji, 萬福寺, a Zen temple of the Obaku branch built in 1661 near Uji. Its architecture is in the Chinese style. Sometimes we must bow to the Buddha, and sometimes we must turn our backs on him in order to see how cool the moonlight sleeps upon the mountain side. Yet when we turn our back on him he is there, in the form of a crab:

涼しさや松はい上る雨の蟹
Suzushisa ya　matsu hainoboru　ame no kani

The coolness:
A crab climbing up a pine-tree
In the rain.

We see him through the green pine needles:

涼しさや松の葉ごしの帆かけ船
Suzushisa ya   matsu no hagoshi no   hokake-bune

> The coolness;
> Through the pine needles,
> Sailing-ships.

We see him through the aperture of the stone lantern:

涼しさや石燈籠の穴の海
Suzushisa ya   ishidōrō no   ana no umi

> The coolness;
> Through the window of the stone lantern
> The sea.

In all these verses what Shiki perceives, with absolute clarity and conviction, is the Buddha; but he calls him "a crab," "white sails," "the sea." The coolness is a kind of means to this end,—or is it also an end in itself?

涼しさは雲の大峰小峰哉　　　　　一 茶
Suzushisa wa   kumo no ōmine   komine kana

> How cool it is!
> The clouds have great peaks,
> And lesser peaks.　　　　　　Issa

In the cool of the evening we sit and gaze at the clouds towering up on the horizon, peak upon peak in the eastern sky. But what the Japanese poet sees, what no one else notices, is the small, subsidiary peaks below the main range. And when once seen, these smaller hills of cloud have even more meaning than the great masses of the highest sky.

涼しさや先づ武蔵野の流れ星　　　其 角
Suzushisa ya   mazu musashino no   nagareboshi

> The coolness;
> Above all, on Musashino Plain,
> A falling star.　　　　　　　Kikaku

This verse is typical of Kikaku, who is a "tough" poet. His masculinity, shown partly in the word *mazu*, is a contrast to Bashō's femininity. The connection between the coolness and the shooting star is of course the feeling of motion.

涼しさや行燈消えて水の音　　　　　　子　規
Suzushisa ya　andon kiete　mizu no oto

> The night-light goes out;
> The sound of water:
> The coolness.					Shiki

Shiki excels at this kind of haiku, which is however more of sensation than experience, more of psychology than poetry.

涼しさのかたまりなれや夜半の月　　　貞　室
Suzushisa no　katamari nareya　yowa no tsuki

> The midnight moon,—
> A ball
> Of coolness?					Teishitsu

This could hardly be called great poetry at all, but it is extremely interesting as an early example of the tendency everywhere in haiku to take things literally, materially. Teishitsu (1609–1673) feels the coolness, and sees the moon. The coolness is perceived by the eye; the moon is felt as a tactile sensation. This material way of looking and hearing leads on the one hand to a mixing of the sensations, a re-union of the differentiation of impressions through the five senses; and on the other hand to a physical way of apprehending intellectual, moral, and spiritual truth, to the understanding of life through the body rather than through the mind. In this sense the haiku poets are in full agreement with the attitude of D. H. Lawrence, but they combine with it the feminine sensitivity of Katharine Mansfield.

涼しさや椎の裏葉を吹かへし　　　子規

Suzushisa ya　shii no uraha wo　fukikae shi

> The coolness!
> The leaves of the pasania
> Blown over.　　　　Shiki

The leaves of the pasania are small, dark-green on the upper surface, whitish on the underside. When the wind blows, the tree changes from green to ashy white, and this gives Shiki the sensation of coolness to the eyes that comes to his body with the wind.

島あれば松あり風の音涼し　　　子規

Shima areba　matsu ari kaze no　oto suzushi

> On each island,
> There are pine-trees;
> The sound of the breeze is cool.　　　Shiki

This is written in praise of Matsushima, and its simplicity is that so hard to attain, the simplicity of hymns, of children.

涼しさや松はい上る雨の蟹　　　子規

Suzushisa ya　matsu hainoboru　ame no kani

> The coolness;
> A crab climbing the pine-tree
> In the rain.　　　　Shiki

The colour and texture and association with water of this land-crab, with its red and pink and whitish colours set against the dark trunk of the pine-tree,—all make it a picture of coolness. But in the rain, the crab is like coolness itself walking over the black bark.

壇 浦

涼しさや平家亡びし浪の音   子 規
Suzushisa ya   heike horobishi   nami no oto

The coolness:
In the sound of the waves,
The defeat of the Heike!   Shiki

This was composed at Dannoura, near Shimonoseki, where
in 1185 the naval battle was fought between the Taira and the
Minamoto. The Taira or Heike were ruined in this one battle,
and as the poet stands on the seashore, the cool washing of
the waves brings together the coolness and the great disaster
of so many hundreds of years ago.

涼風や虚空に満ちて松の聲   鬼 貫
Suzukaze ya   kokū ni michite   matsu no koe

The cool breeze
Fills the empty vault of heaven
With the voice of the pine-tree.   Onitsura

Which is it makes the sound, the pine-tree or the breeze?
Is empty space warm or cool? The region of the poem is not
different from that of these questions, the answer to them,—
not the logical or purely intellectual answer, but the answer
that willy-nilly we have to accept. If you are in the state of
mind to accept the answer *willingly*, life accomplishes its
ultimate and only object, to be lived.

釣橋に亂れて涼し雨の脚   子 規
Tsuribashi ni   midarete suzushi   ame no ashi

Over the hanging bridge,
In coufusion,
The lines of cool rain.   Shiki

Both the mind of the poet and the long lines of rain are
whirling over the bridge and below it. The coolness also

belongs to both. Contrast the following verse, in which cool-
ness and quietness are united in the mind and the scene:

のぞく目に一千年の風涼し
Nozoku me ni   issennen no   kaze suzushi

> In the beholding eye,
> A thousand years of wind
> Are cool.

野明亭にて

涼しさを繪にうつし鳬嵯峨の竹   芭 蕉
Suzushisa wo   e ni utsushi keri   saga no take

> Coolness
> Painted into a picture;
> Bamboos of Saga.   Bashō

This has the prescript, "At the house of Yamei." This man
was a pupil of Bashō, but little seems to be known about him.
He lived in Saga, famous for its bamboos. Japanese poets feel
coolness not only in touch, but in sound and sight. For example,
the following verse by Issa, which might well have been written
by Shiki:

涼しさや夜水のかかる井戸の音
Suzushisa ya   yomizu no kakaru   ido no oto

> The coolness
> Of the sound of water at night,
> Falling back into the well.

下下も下下下下の下国の涼しさよ   一 茶
Gege mo gege   gege no gekoku no   suzushisa yo

> Poor, poor, yes, poor,
> The poorest of the provinces,—and yet,
> Feel this coolness!   Issa

The original is a masterpiece, not of poetry, so-called, but
of life. The sound of *ge*, repeated seven times, is like ham-

mering Issa down in the coffin of his poverty, a poor man in
a poor village of a poor province. But from this pit of poverty
he cries, "How cool and pleasant the wandering airs come to
us!" This "*ge-ge*" had been used by Etsujin:

下々の下の客といはれん花の宿
Gege no ge no   kyaku to iwaren   hana no yado

Though I be called
Of visitors the lowest of the low,—
This flowery dwelling!

He means that even so he will praise the cherry-blossoms.
Sōkan, a hundred and fifty years before Etsujin, is said to have
written in his diary:

一、上の客人立かへり。
一、中の客人日がへり。
一、とまりの客人下の下。

Highest class, visitors who go back at once.
Middle class, those who go back the same day.
Those who stay, lowest of the low.

凉しさや鐘を離るゝ鐘の聲   蕪 村
Suzushisa ya   kane wo hanaruru   kane no koe

The voice of the bell,
As it leaves the bell,—
The coolness!   Buson

It is a warm, a sultry evening,—but not to God, to whom
hot and cold, night and day, death and life, are one. The
evening bell is suddenly heard, one resounding stroke. At that
moment of timeless time, Buson is no longer hot, he is not-hot.
But also he is not divided from the bell, whose voice is not-hot.
This state of not-hotness is expressed as "coolness." The great
difficulty in life is to catch the moment (of non-hotness) as it
flies; for the poet also, his chief work is to express this emotion
of eternity recollected in his time of tranquillity.

涼しさに大福帳を枕かな　　　　　　　　一　茶
Suzushisa ni   daifukuchō wo   makura kana

> With the coolness,
> Making a pillow
> Of the account book.

Issa

The Japanese day-book is a bulky volume, often about six inches thick. The clerk, feeling comfortable in the cool breeze, has laid on his back on the tatami, putting the book under his head. The name of the account book in Japanese, "Great Happinese Book," is a comic one. Wordsworth has the same humorous picture in *The Prelude*:

> I saw her read
> Her Bible on hot Sunday afternoons,
> And loved the book, when she had dropped asleep,
> And made of it a pillow for her head.

Another picture verse by Issa which is a variant of the same theme:

算盤に肘をもたせて昼寝かな
Soroban ni   hiji wo motasete   hirune kana

> A mid-day nap,
> Propping his elbow
> On the abacus.

涼しさをわが宿にしてねまるなり　　　　　芭　蕉
Suzushisa wo   waga yado ni shite   nemaru nari

> I sit here
> Making the coolness
> My dwelling place.

Bashō

This verse comes in *Oku no Hosomichi*. It is an expression of thanks to a man called Seifū, (Suzuki Hachiemon) a rich man who dealt in the plant from the flower of which rouge is made. In *Oku no Hosomichi* Bashō says:

Cooling in Summer by Morikage, 守景 Dates uncertain, pupil of Tanyū, 1602–1674 People cooling themselves on the hill; peasants carrying grass in baskets on the horse; a cormorant fisher (original slightly defaced).

尾花澤にて清風という者を尋ぬ、かれは富め
るものなれども志いやしからず。都にも折々
通ひて　さすがに旅の情をも知りたれば、日
比とどめて長途のいたはり、さまざまにもて
なし侍る。

    I visited a man named Seifū at Obanazawa.　He
was well-off, not vulgar in character.　He often went
to Kyōto and knew what travelling was, and having
a sympathetic feeling put me up for several days.
He was very hospitable, and soothed the pains and
vexations of my long journey.

This verse is thus a complimentary one, but the expression is
nevertheless noteworthy.　To dwell in coolness, not in a cool
place, but in the coolness itself,—this is a poetic realm in
which Milton's

          Silence was pleased,

is to be understood, and such lines as Shelley's

       And the sunlight clasps the earth,
       And the moonbeams kiss the sea.

The coolness is felt not merely as a sensation, but as a habi-
tation of the mind.

      何處見ても涼し神の灯佛の灯   子　規
      Doko mite mo　suzushi kami no hi　hotoke no hi

    Everywhere we look is cool,
  With lamps of the Buddhas,
    Lamps of the Gods.   Shiki

    This was written at Kyōto, Higashiyama.　Among the dark
pine-trees, lights from the temples and shrines gleam out.
Their meaning is "cool" and pleasant; not awe-inspiring or
imbued with religious zeal, but full of quiet piety and happiness.
This is a side of religion often perceived by the "respectable"
church-goers and neglected by the so-called religious devotees.

大佛に腸のなき涼しさよ　　　　　　　　子 規
Daibutsu ni harawata no naki suzushisa yo

The Great Buddha,
Its pitiless
Coolness!

Shiki

This involves, however faintly, however much heard as a distant echo of painful feeling, the contrast between the "Fatherhood of God" and the merciless universe in which we find ourselves. Perfection is inhuman, remote, repulsive. The Great Buddha of Kamakura sits there oblivious of everything, cool in summer, warm in winter, looking upon all things and finding them good. We also can do this, but only momentarily. Our human nature makes us cry out that the divine is ruthless, or as the verse literally says, "without bowels."

涼風の曲りくねつて來りけり　　　　　　一 茶
Suzukaze no magari-kunette kitari keri

The cool breeze;
Crooked and meandering
It comes to me.

Issa

The sardonic humour of this neutralises the subjectivity and sentimentality.

北風に不足いふなり夏座敷　　　　　　　一 茶
Kitakaze ni fusoku iu nari natsu-zashiki

This cool breeze
Through the summer room,—
But still complaining

Issa

Issa is not grumbling at the grumbler. This verse has a prescript, 無限欲有限命、"Man's desires are infinite, but his life is not." To want, to desire, is human, is thus divine, is part of our nature, is part of our Buddha nature. It is *how* we desire that decides whether we are a Buddha or an ordinary man. It is not grumbling, but *how* we grumble; it is the peevishness, querulousness, petulance that is

An expense of spirit in a waste of shame.

This verse, written when Issa was fifty seven, is his considered criticism of human life. What distinguishes man from the lower animals is the very thing that degrades him below them.

夏 の 夜 や 蚊 を 疵 に し て 五 百 両   其 角

Natsu no yo ya ka wo kizu ni shite gohyaku ryō

A summer evening;
With the drawback of the mosquitoes,
Five hundred pieces of gold.   Kikaku

This is based on a common Chinese saying, embodied in a poem of Sotōba:

春 宵 一 刻 直 千 金 。

A moment of an evening of spring is worth a thousand pieces of gold.

Kikaku says that a summer evening, because of the disadvantage of the mosquitoes, is worth only five hundred, half as much. In a sense, this is not haiku,—but is parody poetry? Perhaps not, yet if it expresses some realm of the human spirit in an unforgettable way, if it leads us to that "lightness," *karumi*, on which Bashō insisted in his later years, we cannot afford to neglect it. For this reason, following instinct, a feeling of the moment, this senryu-like haiku is included here.

何 も な い が 心 安 さ よ 涼 し さ よ   一 茶

Nani mo nai ga kokoroyasusa yo suzushisa yo

I have nothing at all,—
But this tranquillity!
This coolness!   Issa

The only difficulty here is to point out wherein lies the poetry of this verse. It consists in the fact of the identity of the "nothing at all," and the "tranquillity" and "coolness." In having and desiring nothing, he is tranquil in mind, and the coolness is not one merely of the thermometer, yet it is deeply physical.

This verse is also an example of Issa's power to express the nature of a thing without any of the usual adventitious aids. He practices what Wordsworth only preached, the employment of language commonly used among men, showing us how the general usage by mankind of certain colloquial expressions is due to their enshrining intuitions of truth afterwards forgotten. To resurrect them, with their old life, or to renew them with fresh vigour, is one of the functions of poetry. Other examples of Issa on the same subject are:

涼しさやここ極楽の這入口
Suzushisa ya   koko gokuraku no   hairiguchi

This coolness!
It is the entrance
To Paradise!

(Compare Teishitsu's verse on page 660.)

涼しさや佛陀成佛のこの方は
Suzushisa ya   mida jōbutsu no   konokata wa

The coolness!
In this direction
Amida became a Buddha.

These verses mean that the breeze blows from the west where Amida's paradise is situated. The coolness also implies the tranquillity and bliss that belong to the other world, that to say, the coolness is in some sense equated to Paradise, and becoming a Buddha. Issa was a believer of the Shin sect.

朝風の毛を吹見ゆる毛虫かな   蕪 村
Asakaze no   ke wo fukimiyuru   kemushi kana

You can see the morning breeze
Blowing the hairs
Of the caterpillar.   Buson

The secret feeling of joy that wells up in us when we see the smallest things obeying the law of their being, must come

from the perception of our safety in the arms of nature. The
wind which ruffles the hairs of the hairy caterpillar is "safe"
to overwhelm ships in the deep waters, "safe" to send the
raging fires through a great city. Every tiny seed on the
kaoliang trembles like wind-bells in the cool breeze.

短夜の闇より出でて大井川					蕪　村
Mijikayo no   yami yori ide te   ōigawa

> From out of the darkness
> Of the short night
> 　　Comes the River Ōi.					Buson

The River Ōi has begun to shine palely through the darkness
of the short summer night. The length of the river has some
kind of relation with the shortness of the night, space and
time being related in contrast.

みじか夜や毛むしの上に露の玉					蕪　村
Mijikayo ya   kemushi no ue ni   tsuyu no tama

> The short night;
> Upon the hairy caterpillar,
> 　　Beads of dew.					Buson

The association of ideas here is subtle. The shortness and
evanescence of the summer night is felt in the frail, precarious
drops of dew on the hairs of the caterpillar.

短夜や小見世明けたる町外れ					蕪　村
Mijikayo ya   komise aketaru   machihazure

> The short night;
> In the outskirts of a village
> 　　A small shop is opening.					Buson

Buson has left the inn before daybreak and walks along the
moonlit road. He is alone, but not lonely. After some time the
east begins to lighten, his shadow grows fainter, a cock crows

from the valley below. In the distance, a small cottage. The woman of the house has set out the scanty wares, dried persimmons, tobacco pipes, kites, rolls of paper. Some pairs of straw sandles dangle from the eaves. She is now lighting the fire, and smoke curls lazily up into the sky. A dog barks. Day has begun.

This is purely objective, yet portrays the whole of humanity in its instinctive urge to live, adapting itself to the unceasing changing of nature, to the length and shortness of days and nights.

みじか夜や芦間流るる蟹の泡　　　　　　蕪　村
Mijikayo ya   ashi-ma nagaruru   kani no awa

The short night;
Between the reeds flows
The froth of crabs.　　　　Buson

The bubbly froth exuded by the crabs has not yet flowed away among the reeds of the stream, so short is the night. This verse may be the result of actual observation, the froth and scum being ascribed to the crabs that scuttle to and fro in the mud; or may be the result of Buson's very powerful fancy. There is a singular pleasure in relating such remote things as the shortness of the summer night with the presence of scum on the shallow water round the reeds of the river bank. Another example of Buson's abnormally acute sensitiveness to the faintest meaning of things is the following, where the haiku is so difficult as to be a kind of puzzle:

短夜や枕にちかき銀屏風
Mijikayo ya   makura ni chikaki   ginbyōbu

The short night;
Near the pillow,
A silver screen.

What is the connection between the short night and the nearness of a screen? As the screen is white, it seems to shorten the night by causing the dawn to be brighter and earlier than without its reflection.

短夜や同心衆の川手水 蕪村

Mijikayo ya   dōshinshū no   kawachōzu

The short night;
Patrol men,
    Washing in the river. Buson

These men have been on duty all night, and in the early morning they are washing themselves in the stream near by. They have not been asleep, and the shortness of the night is felt in this. This is a scene such as we find often in Dicken's novels. Dicken's has the Japanese poets' strong feeling of the meaning of heat and cold, the length of the day and the shortness of the night.

短夜の灯火のこる港かな 子規

Mijikayo no   tomoshibi nokoru   minato kana

The short night;
Lights remaining
    In the harbour. Shiki

In the very early morning, all is quiet, the sea is calm, the sun not yet risen. In the port, lights are still gleaming along the wharf and in the streets by the sea. It is a world not of yesterday and not yet of today, a short, transitory half-world, the short night.

余命いくばくかある夜短し 子規

Waga inochi   ikubaku ka aru   yo mijikashi

My life,—
How much more of it remains?
    The night is brief. Shiki

This verse, in the mouth of a consumptive who died an early death, gives a meaning to the shortness of the summer night that is beyond all words,—but not beyond experience. When we are sick, night or day are little different. In the darkness we long for the light; when the day comes, it is so long the

light wearies the eyes and we long for night again. But not
only the length of the night fills us with grief and despair, the
shortness of it is intolerable.

行燈の消えぬ短夜四時をうつ　　　　　　子 規
Andon no　kienu mijikayo　yoji wo utsu

The night-light not yet out,
It strikes four;
　　The short night.　　　　　　　　　Shiki

　The bed-lamp not having yet gone out shows that it a short
night, for it is already getting light. The clock striking four
is still more obvious, but poetically speaking, it is the purely
accidental and intellectually unrelated *pom*, *pom*, *pom*, *pom*,
which brings out the character of the night.

短夜や淺瀬に殘る月一片　　　　　　　　蕪 村
Mijikayo ya　asase ni nokoru　tsuki ippen

The short night;
In the shallows remains
　　The crescent moon.　　　　　　　　Buson

　The night was so short that one thin slice of the moon has
not yet been washed away. The beauty of this early morning
scene is not the immediate objective of the poet. He is trying
to express the peculiar quality of the shortness of the summer
night, a subject so conventional, so unpromising, that one
would think a single verse sufficient. But Buson tries again
and again, from every point of view, to catch some aspect of
this inexhaustible phenomenon of nature:

みじか夜や二尺落ゆく大井川
Mijikayo ya　ni-shaku ochiyuku　ōigawa

The short night;
The River Ōi
　Has fallen two feet.

短夜や足跡淺き由井の濱
Mijikayo ya   ashi-ato asaki   yui no hama

The short night;
The footprints are shallow
On the beach of Yui.

短夜や浪うち際の捨箒
Mijikayo ya   namiuchigiwa no   sute-bōki

The short night;
A broom thrown away
On the beach.

天 文 SKY AND ELEMENTS

雲の峰並べて低し海の果   子 規
Kumo no mine   narabete hikushi   umi no hate

The billowing clouds,
Piled low along
The far line of the sea.   Shiki

This is a picture of sky and air, hardly anything of earth
to be seen. On the distant and low horizon clouds are piled
up, one above another, stretching out all along the line that
joins and separates the sea and the sky. We feel how much
of the world is above us.

雲の峰石臼をひく隣かな   李 由
Kumo no mine   ishiusu wo hiku   tonari kana

Billowing clouds;
Next door,
A mortar grinding.   Riyu

The summer clouds are piled up, one on another, all round
the horizon. Next door, a hand-mill, a stone mortar goes
round, grinding corn of beans. It is as if the clouds are the
froth or overflow of the stone mortar that goes on monoto-
nously and sleepily, great clouds rising ceaselessly up into the
deep sky.

野社に太鼓うちけり雲の峰   北 枝
Noyashiro ni   taiko uchi keri   kumo no mine

The drum resounds
In the shrine yonder in the fields,
White clouds piled high.   Hokushi

This hot summer afternoon there is a festival in the distant
shrine in the grove that stands in the middle of the rice-fields.
The sound of the drum overflows across the fields in perfect

harmony with the softly-swelling cumulous clouds that tower
up on the horizon. One is in sound what the other is in form.

蟒 の 住 む 沼 か れ て 雲 の 峰   子 規
Uwabami no sumu numa karete   kumo no mine

Towering clouds
Over a dried marsh
    Where a python dwells.   Shiki

This python is a kind of Grendel, and lives by a mere. It
is summer, and the water is less than normal. Over the flat
expanse, huge clouds like exhalations rise up to the very
zenith of heaven. Shiki has expressed here some of the primi-
tive terror of man at the powers of nature.

帆 の 多 き 和 蘭 陀 船 や 雲 の 峰   子 規
Ho no ōki   orandasen ya   kumo no mine

A Dutch ship
With many sails;
    The billowing clouds.   Shiki

This is a simple harmony of two white and swelling things.
The mind takes a peculiar delight in these parallels and
analogies of nature. It is the pleasure of repetition which we
find in musical form, in architecture, in verse form, in the very
5, 7, 5 of which the above haiku is made. What a marvellous
world it is in which the number of syllables of a poem, and a
sailing ship against peaks of cloud should give a profound
pleasure based on the same simple principle of symmetry!

蟻 の 道 雲 の 峰 よ り つ づ き け ん   一 茶
Ari no michi   kumo no mine yori   tsuzukiken

    This line of ants,
It continues
    From those billowing clouds?   Issa

Issa is sitting on the verandah one summer morning, watching a procession of ants. Curiosity impels him to get up and see where they come from. "They stretch in never-ending line" up to the fence and beyond it. They come Issa feels from far, far away, from beyond the peaks of white clouds that tower up on the horizon. The hyperbole arise from Issa's childlike nature. It is the fairy-tale instinct in him, and like all the best fairy tales, there is some deep truth in and behind it that can be expressed only in that form, something that appeals to young and old. The truth is in the charm, not in the facts.

夏嵐机上の白紙飛び盡す   子 規
Natsuarashi   kijō no hakushi   tobi-tsukusu

A summer storm-wind;
The white papers on the desk,
All blown off.   Shiki

There is a sudden gust of wind. Trees and bushes in the garden sway and flutter, the grasses put back their ears. The white papers on the brown Japanese table quiver, curl, move, and fly in confusion round the room and onto the verandah. The pieces of paper make a round, angular pattern on the yellow tatami.

夜水とる里人の聲や夏の月   蕪 村
Yomizu toru   satobito no koe ya   natsu no tsuki

The voices of village people
Irrigating the fields;
The Summer moon.   Buson

It is so common and yet so strange, the fact that the absence of something is more moving than its presence. Regulating the level of the water in the fields, the people of the village are making their rounds, talking to one another in the bright moonlight. The poet can see the moon and hear the voices; he cannot see the people themselves, nor the quicksilver water that falls into the indigo depths.

少年の犬走らすや夏の月　　　　　　召　波
Shōnen no　inu hashirasu ya　natsu no tsuki

A boy
Getting a dog to run
Under the summer moon. Shōha

This may seem a negligible verse, but what the poet has
done is to bring out the free-and-easy, slightly indifferent yet
friendly nature of the moon of summer. The boy is unconscious
of the moon, as he is of the nature of the dog, and yet not
entirely. All three have something innocent and childlike in
them.

砂濱や何に火をたく夏の月　　　　　　子　規
Sunahama ya　nani ni hi wo taku　natsu no tsuki

The sandy shore;
Why are they making a fire
Under the summer moon? Shiki

If the question is answered, the poetry disappears. It is
clear, then, that this question is not the ordinary demand for
information. It expresses perhaps a question-like frame of mind
towards the whole scene, the long, wide stretch of sand, the
warm evening, the summer moon, the smoke that rises straight
up into the dark sky, the dark and glittering sea bringing the
eternal note of sadness in, but pianissimo, in a whisper. There
is a similar verse by Shiki:

五月雨に人いて舟のけむりかな
Samidare ni　hito ite fune no　kemuri kana

The rains of summer;
Somebody on the boat,
Smoke rising.

Here the question is not stated. We take what we are given,
for it is all that God offers us.

蛸壺やはかなき夢を夏の月   芭 蕉
Takotsubo ya   hakanaki yume wo   natsu no tsuki

> The octopus trap:
> Fleeting dreams
>   Under the summer moon.   Bashō

The octopus lies as if asleep in the bottom of the jar which has trapped him, a float marking the place on the water above. Bashō wrote this verse while in a boat in the Bay of Akashi. Though the words do not express it, the verse seems full of light and colour; it has something of the mystery and flamboyance of *The Ancient Mariner*.   Contrast the quiet tones and subdued feeling of Issa's verse on the same subject:

魚どもが桶ともしらで夕涼
Uodomo ga   oke tomo shirade   yūsuzumi

> The fish in the butt
> Do not know that is what it is;
>   The evening cool.

橋落ちて人岸に在り夏の月   太 祇
Hashi ochite   hito kishi ni ari   natsu no tsuki

> The bridge washed away,
> People stand on the bank:
>   The summer moon.   Taigi

The haiku poet is especially susceptible to the profound meanings of what Wordsworth calls "the after-vacancy." The mind is in a state of partial solution, either divided between two alternatives, or as here, contemplating some event that though past and irrevocable, is not yet *willed*.

The moon rises over the scene of the disaster. It hangs in the sky almost unnoticed, yet of deeper, because unconscious power, sinking into the hearts of the men who stand there gazing at the waters that flow furiously by.

高岡大火

家 の な き 人 二 萬 人 夏 の 月   子 規

Ie no naki   hito niman-nin   natsu no tsuki

The Great Fire of Takaoka.

Twenty thousand people
Without a home;
The summer moon.   Shiki

This is poetry only if we keep the mind free from irony, satire, cynicism, anything anti-. If we suppose there is any contrast between the unchanged, unchanging moon that rides so calmly high in the sky, and these poor, homeless, penniless, starving thousands reduced to beggary and despair, we are making a grave mistake. All is change. Not only all is changing, moon and earth and men coming and going upon it, but all *is* change, just as God *is* love, though anguish, degradation and ruin are seen all around us. This is the paradox of Shiki's verse, the contrast, the identity, the contrast again.

釣 竿 の 糸 に さ わ る や 夏 の 月   千代尼

Tsurizao no   ito ni sawaru ya   natsu no tsuki

The summer moon
Is touched by the line
Of the fishing-rod.   Chiyo-ni

The most sensitive chords of our being are moved by this fishing-line. The reflected, and not the real moon is touched by the real line. It is a dream world, and yet it is this world. Fishing is the destruction of life, but in so doing, something is created, something happens that we feel in the verse.

夏 の 月 川 の 向 ひ の 人 は 誰   樗 良

Natsu no tsuki   kawa no mukai no   hito wa tare

The summer moon;
On the other side of the river,
Who is it?   Chora

Everything is shown up clearly as if in daylight. The river gleams like a mirror, the moon beyond it. Yet in spite of, or because of all this brightness, it is impossible to see who it is that stands on the farther bank, a black silhouette. The feeling of mystery in such brilliance of light surprises the poet himself, but the experience is unmistakable and he records it.

寝せつけし子の洗たくや夏の月 　　　　一 茶
Nesetsukeshi　ko no sentaku ya　natsu no tsuki

She has put the child to sleep,
And now washes the clothes;
The summer moon. 　　　　Issa

The mother has got the child asleep and begins to wash the clothes outside the house. Feeling an unwonted calm and freedom from the cares of the day, she gazes at the moon, not so much in poetic rapture as feeling its soft light upon her breast.

You may ask, where is the poetry here? It is a charming scene, no doubt, but is not this haiku too prosaic to be called art? If it were necessary to justify the ways of Issa to men, we could say that the sleeping child, the washing of the clothes in the water, glittering and dark by turns, the round, lovely, thoughtful moon, the soft, earnest face of the young mother, —all these are united in a higher unity, without losing their own individuality but rather having them enriched. And what is poetry if not this?

破れ鐘の響も暑し夏の月 　　　　北 枝
Waregane no　hibiki mo atsushi　natsu no tsuki

The sound of the cracked bell
Is hot too;
The summer moon. 　　　　Hokushi

There is in the sound of the cracked bell not only the hotness but the hardness and metallic meaning that the moon also has. Thus the crackedness brings the heat of the night and the hard, cold brightness of the moon into union.

蚊張を出て又障子あり夏の月 　　　丈草
Kayo wo dete　mata shōji ari　natsu no tsuki

Emerging from the mosquito net,
Still there is the paper screen,—
The summer moon! 　　　Jōsō

This is a well-known didactic verse addressed to a newly converted Buddhist devotee, (新道心におくる) and implies the gradual enlightenment, the successive stages of realization that all must pass through in order to reach the moon of perfect truth. But we may take the parable in a deeper sense, and then come back to the verse as poetry, devoid of any ulterior motive.

Pure Truth, quite apart from the fact that it does not exist, would be intolerably hideous, could it be seen or heard. In the same way it is not so much the moon itself, but the moon over the sea, on the rim of the mountains, slanting down the silent street, lying athwart the paper screen,—it is this that has meaning for us:

Couched in his kennel, like a log,
With paws of silver sleeps the dog;
From their shadowy cote the white breasts peep
Of doves in a silver-feathered sleep;
A harvest mouse goes scampering by,
With silver claws and silver eye,
And moveless fish in the water gleam,
By silver reeds in a silver stream.

Coming back to the verse; the poetry is in this combination of moon and screen, with every shadow according to the strictest law, yet the whole imbued with freedom and life. It is this sense of mystery that gives birth to poetry here, in spite of the intellectual meaning that the poet intended to convey.

夕月や涼がてらの墓参 　　　一茶
Yūzuki ya　suzumigatera no　hakamairi

Under the evening moon,
They visit the graves,
Enjoying the cool. 　　　Issa

There is a painful meaning here, but felt calmly, a cynical contrast, but perceived sweetly. The tombs of their ancestors, of relatives and friends, sad thoughts and poignant recollections which time has assuaged; and together with this the cool air of evening, and the moon shining over all with the same faint delight.

五月雨に蛙の泳ぐ戸口かな　　　　　　　　杉　風
Samidare ni   kawazu no oyogu   toguchi kana

> In the summer rains,
> The frogs are swimming
> At the very door.　　　　　　　　　　Sampū

This has a kind of Noah's ark effect, as if the poet were aboard ship. The long summer rains, which are in June by the solar calendar, and in May by the lunar, are not much less than forty days and forty nights.

五月雨の名もなき川のおそろしき　　　　　　蕪　村
Samidare no   na mo naki kawa no   osoroshiki

> The May rains:
> Even a nameless stream
> Is a thing of dread.　　　　　　　　　Buson

We are by nature earth-worshippers, fire-worshippers, water-worshippers. The elements are our teachers, our playmates, our enemies, these "dear, dangerous lords of life." They bring us into being, and receive us again at the last. No wonder that we stand in awe before even the most casual stream when it is swollen and swirling with the waters of spring.

さみだれや大河を前に家二軒　　　　　　　　蕪　村
Samidare ya   taiga wo mae ni   ie niken

> By a great stream
> In the May rain,
> Two houses.　　　　　　　　　　　　Buson

Mountains in Rain
by Baen, 馬遠 (Ma Yuan) 12th–13th centuries

The man carrying an umbrella, the moored
boat, and the whole atmosphere suggest rain.

There is something much more meaningful in two houses than in one. They have a pathos that mere loneliness cannot give. The combined strength of two houses, as against that of the mighty waters, is less even (to the poetical, not the scientific mind) than that of only one house.

五月雨を集めて早し最上川   芭 蕉
Samidare wo   atsumete hayashi   mogamigawa

Collecting all
The rains of May,
The swift Mogami River.   Bashō

The original form of this is said to have been:

五月雨を集めて涼し最上川
Samidare wo   atsumete suzushi   mogamigawa

Collecting all
The rains of May,
The cool Mogami River.

Such a complete alteration of what otherwise might have seemed a spontaneous verse, may be compared to the different versions of Blake's "Tiger, tiger." Bashō also, in this and all his mature poems, is not just sitting at his desk and improving upon his first impressions by merely substituting one word for another, like the professor in Swift's *A Voyage to Laputa*. He is delving into his own mind for the *real* Mogami River which is flowing there and nowhere else.

凧買つて子心ぞうき雨つづき   召 波
Tako katte   kogokoro zo uki   ame-tsuzuki

Buying him a kite,
The child is fretful,
In the unending rain.   Shōha

The father has bought the little boy a kite. After the first rush of happiness, he wants to fly it, but the rain continues day after day. 天地不仁, "Heaven and earth are merciless,"

says Rōshi. The father is helpless, and can do no more than
our Heavenly Father, grieve and pity in impotence.   The
impatience of the child, the compassion of the father, the calm,
inevitable rain, all are one thing together.

五月雨の竹にはさまる在所かな   一 茶
Samidare no   take ni hasamaru   zaisho kana

My native village,
Squeezed in among the bamboos,
In the summer rains.   Issa

As he looks at his native place from a distance, he sees the
bamboos overcrowding the village.   Above each house the
vigorous bamboos lean from every side; heavy rain pours down
from the sky upon it all.   There is a feeling of oppression, of
inescapable fatality, man in the close embrace of nature.

五月雨の雲吹きおとせ大井川   芭 蕉
Samidare no   kumo fukiotose   ōigawa

Ah! River Ōi!
Blow, blow away
The clouds of May rains!   Bashō

The interesting point about this verse is the fact that "Blow,
blow away," is addressed not to the wind, but to the River Ōi
itself, a vast idea in consonance with the immense expanse of
rain and river before Bashō's eyes.

五月雨の降残してや光堂   芭 蕉
Samidare no   furinokoshite ya   hikaridō

The Hall of Gold;
'Tis all that's left
In the rains of May!   Bashō

This Hall of Gold, together with the Sutra Hall, was one of
the remains of Chusonji, a temple of the Tendai sect, founded

by Jikaku-Daishi, 794 A.D. It contained many historical relics
of Yoshitsune, Benkei, etc. The Hikaridō or Konjikidō itself
was built in 1124 A.D. by Fujiwara Kiyohira as a mausoleum
for himself. This was 565 years before *Oku no Hosomichi* was
written. In this book of travel Bashō says:

かねて耳驚かしたる二堂開帳す。經堂は三将
の像を殘し光堂は三代の棺を納め、三尊の佛を
安置す。七寶散失せて珠の扉風に破れ、金の柱
霜雪に朽ちて、既に頽廢空虚の叢となるべきを、
四面あらたに圍みて甍を覆ひて、風雨をしのぐ。
暫時千載の記念とはなれり。[1]

Bashō expresses by indirect means the passage of the years.
The May rains of how many centuries have left undimmed
the gold on the pillars, though the jewel-bedecked doors are
tarnished with wind and rain.

We may compare this with the following verse by Buson:

春月や印金堂の木のまより
Shungetsu ya　inkindō no　konoma yori

The spring moon rises
Between the trees
Of the Inkin Hall.

This was a small hall,[2] eight feet square. Five-coloured silk
gauze was spread on the walls. The "*inkin*" is the printing of
a pattern on the silk by drawing the design in paste, throwing
gold leaf on it, and afterwards fixing it with laquer. Comparing
the two verses, we can see how Bashō gives the Hall of Gold
its own life, whereas Buson is simply pictorial.

[1] "From some time ago these two Halls [of the Chusonji Temple]
so wonderful, have been open. The Sutra Hall contains the statues
of the three generals [Kiyohara, Motohira and Hidehira], Hikaridō
their coffins, and the three Buddhas [Amida Nyorai, Kwannon and
Seishi]. The Seven Treasures [Gold, silver, the clam-shell, agate,
emerald, pearl and *maikai*] have disappeared, the gemmed doors are
broken, gold-coated pillars rotting in frost and snow; it will soon
become a decaying wilderness. Therefore walls are newly built
around it and it is roofed in to protect it from wind and rain. For
some time this monument of past ages will continue to exist."

[2] On a hill above Myōkōji, 妙光寺,山城葛城郡花岡村.

五月雨にかくれぬものや瀬田の橋　　　芭　蕉
Samidare ni kakurenu mono ya seta no hashi

The only thing left unhidden
In the rains of May,
The long bridge of Seta.　　　　　Bashō

It is very difficult to say what the poetical point of this verse
is. The bridge seems to have a similar value to that of the
bare space of the sky in a Chinese landscape, that leads the
mind gently on with a thought of eternity.

五月雨や佛の花を捨てに出る　　　　蕪　村
Samidare ya hotoke no hana wo sute ni deru

Going out to throw away
Flowers offered to the Buddha;
Summer rain.　　　　　　　Buson

These "flowers" may be leaves or actual flowers. Someone
comes out into the rain that falls ceaselessly, heavily, as if it
had never begun and would never end, to throw away flowers
or sprays that have been standing in vases before the image
of Buddha in the family alter. The withered leaves and flowers
have an affinity with the rain that is falling, and with the altar.
All three are meaningless, useless, tasteless, unwanted. They
belong to the darker side of life, to gloom and self-denial, to
the inevitable. Yet the verse is not so lugubrious as this, it is
only subdued, a harmony of quietness and monotony.

There is another verse by Buson in which the human
element is omitted; it gains in scope what it loses in intimacy
and depth:

冬川や佛の花の流れ來る
Fuyukawa ya hotoke no hana no nagare kuru

Flowers offered to the Buddha,
Come floating down
The winter river.

草 の 雨 祭 の 車 す ぎ て の ち   蕪 村
Kusa no ame   matsuri no kuruma   sugite nochi

>   After the festival car
> Has passed by,
>   The rain on the grasses.   Buson

Today is the day of the festival and though it is raining, the
festival car is decorated as usual, and passes by the poet as he
stands on the roadside. After it has creaked past, only the
pattering of the rain is heard, the grasses on the road side
flinch or bow or stand immovable according to their nature.
Rain-drops stand motionless on the flowers or hesitate and run
along the stems and leaves. It requires a whole village with
its remote antiquity, the festival and the car to pass ponder-
ously by, before the rain on the grasses can be properly
appreciated.

五 月 雨 の 大 井 越 し た る か し こ さ よ   蕪 村
Samidare no   ōi koshitaru   kashikosa yo

>   Crossing the River Ōi
> Swollen with the summer rains,—
>   What a feat!   Buson

If we take this verse merely as expressing, subjectively, the
fear and relief of the traveller who has crossed the foaming
river when so many are still waiting for the water to subside
without making the attempt, we get no poetry at all. If how-
ever we take it objectively, as an indirect description of the
river, something remains in our minds, as it did in Buson's,
and the turbulent waters still rush through them. They are
fully described by being completely omitted. The fear of the
poet portrays everything.

五 月 雨 や 梅 の 葉 寒 き 風 の 色   才 麿
Samidare ya   ume no ha samuki   kaze no iro

>   In the summer rain,
> The leaves of the plum-tree
>   Are the colour of the chill breeze.   Saimaro

The greenness of the leaves, the peculiar blue tinge in them, is equated to the coldness of the wind. The observation is delicate, and it is just, yet somehow or other it remains a poetical *thought*.

五月雨のうつぼ柱や老の耳　　　蕪村
Samidare no　utsubobashira ya　oi no mimi

> Ears of my old age;
> The summer rains
> Falling down the rain-pipe.　　　Buson

Outside, the rain is falling with its pattering monotone. It is gurgling down into the rain-water butt, but with musical tones and overtones, with sharps and flats, augmented and diminished intervals. Sitting there in solitude and listening to the many-sounding rain—what can be better for us in old age?

五月雨やある夜ひそかに松の月　　　蓼太
Samidare ya　aru yo hisoka ni　matsu no tsuki

> The rains of May;
> One evening in the pine-tree,
> The secret moon.　　　Ryōta

The point of the poem is in *hisoka ni*, secretly, stealthily. The moon is seen suddenly, after many days, when least expected, as something new. We see Nature proceeding on its way like the river in *Sohrab and Rustum*, with a tranquillity that is not ours to mar, as it is not ours to make. And this is seen in an instant, when the mind is empty of thought, empty of feeling. There, in the pine-tree hangs the moon, its brightness sliding unawares into our hearts.

五月雨やながう預る紙包　　　杉風
Samidare ya　nagō azukaru　kami zutsumi

> The rains of May;
> Here is a paper-parcel,
> Entrusted to me long ago.　　　Sampū

The May rains continue day after day; the sky is leaden in hue, all the colour and life taken from the earth; everything is tasteless and meaningless. By accident, the poet comes upon a parcel that has been kept by him unopened. As he looks at the parcel, in the quietness of thought, the unceasing rain sounds loudly in his ears. The parcel, with its unknown or long forgotten contents, has a curious consonance, a meaningful correspondence with the monotony, the *taedium vitae* of the outside world.

日 の 道 や 葵 か た む く 五 月 雨   芭 蕉
Hi no michi ya   aoi katamuku   satsukiame

In the rains of May,
Does the hollyhock turn
    To the path of the sun?   Bashō

It is raining, and the hollyhock turns perhaps in the direction of the unseen sun. We feel the secret life and faithfulness of things, the bond that unites them.

五 月 雨 に 鶴 の 足 み じ か な れ り   芭 蕉
Samidare ni   tsuru no ashi   mijika nareri

    The legs of the crane
Have become short
    In the summer rains.   Bashō

Bashō is not saying anything so absurdly obvious as that with the rise of the water the crane's legs appear shorter, but that this particular crane, as it stands (quite accidentally) deep in the water, only the upper part of the legs showing, has an indescribable relation to the deepening of water everywhere.

ち か 道 や 水 ふ み わ た る 五 月 雨   蕪 村
Chikamichi ya   mizu fumi wataru   satsukiame

A short cut;
Splashing through the water
    Of the summer rains.   Buson

Buson takes a short cut across the rice fields, but finds to his dismay that he must tuck up his skirts, take off his *geta* and hold them in one hand, the umbrella in the other, and wade along the narrow path between the fields, whose rice shows green above the surface of the water. The thought, "I ought to have gone the longer way; shall I retrace my steps?" the feeling of water on his bare legs, and the muddy, slippery path underfoot, the sound of the rain on the umbrella, all come to make this an experience,— of what? Of a short cut.

髪剃や一夜に錆て五月雨   凡 兆
Kamisori ya ichiya ni sabite   satsukiame

> A razor,
> Rusted in a single night,—
> The summer rains!   Bonchō

If this is taken as a simple statement of cause and effect, there is no poetry here. The razor is used every day, and carefully wiped before it is put away. The next morning it is found to be rusted with the extreme dampness of the air. The poetry of this verse is in the perception of the omnipresence, one might almost say the omnipotence of the rain, of nature everywhere. There is also a feeling of the secret faithfulness of nature, present when we least suspect it, working while we sleep, remembering though we forget.

紙燭して廊下通るや五月雨   蕪 村
Shishoku shite rōka tōru ya   satsukiame

> The rainy season;
> A paper lantern in hand,
> I walk along the verandah.   Buson

It is deep night, and the rain sounds louder now than in the day-time. The dripping does not cease. Along the dark verandah walks the poet, with slow and silent steps, holding a paper lantern in one cold hand. There is in this verse something of what Keats expressed with more effort and wordiness in *The Eve of St. Agnes:*

And the long carpets rose along the gusty floor.

But Keats is almost entirely objective, whereas in Buson, who is among the most objective of haiku poets, there is something subjective. Even when the poet has passed through it, the corridor remains palpitatingly dark, alive in its length; the wind and rain are still heard though there is no one to hear them.

蓑蟲の運の強さよ五月雨   一 茶
Minomushi no   un no tsuyosa yo   satsukiame

The *mino-mushi,*
Darling of fortune,
    In the summer rain.   Issa

The bagworm is connected with autumn rather than summer. "The voice of the bagworm" is one of the indispensable signs of autumn, though in actual fact the insect does not cry at all. But Issa has broken through the convention, and looking at the bagworm sees in it the relation between the creature and the summer rains. All other insects, all other animals and men themselves are drenched with the continuous downpour, but the "straw-raincoat insect" sits snug and dry within, as if in a world where storms cannot assail, a windless abode.

水がめに蛙うくなり五月雨   子 規
Mizugame ni   kawazu uku nari   satsukiame

A frog floating
In the water-jar:
    Rains of summer.   Shiki

The point here is the feeling of the ubiquity of the rain. It seems to be not only outside but inside the house; and where water goes, frogs go too. We find them in all kinds of unexpected places. There are similar verses by Sampū:

さみだれに蛙のおよぐ戸口かな
Samidare ni   kawazu no oyogu   toguchi kana

> Summer rains;
> Frogs swim
> At my very door.

五月雨や蟹の這ひ出る手水鉢
Samidare ya   kani no haideru   chōzu-bachi

> Summer rain;
> A crab crawling
> Out of the stone wash-basin.

年寄の袖としらでやとらの雨　　　　一、茶
Toshiyori no   sode to shirade ya   tora no ame

> Rain of the Tiger;
> Know you not
> They are an old man's sleeves?　　Issa

Soga Sukenari[1], 曾我祐成, the elder of the two Soga brothers, parted from Ōiso no Tora Gozen, 大磯の虎御前, on the twenty eighth day of the Fifth Month, and her tears were such that ever afterwards rain fell upon that day. It was known therefore as the Rain of the Tiger, 虎が雨.

Issa says, "This rain is the tears of the young lovers in the anguish of their eternal separation. What meaning can it have for me, an old man, these romantic griefs of past ages?" Further, in the spirit of King Lear, he feels that in addition to the burden of old age, he must bear the falling of the pitiless rain, tears not shed for him or his like, adding the insults of the elements to the injuries of time.

雨の降る日はあはれなり良寛坊　　　良 寛
Ame no furu   hi wa aware nari   ryōkanbō

> On rainy days
> The monk Ryōkan
> Feels sorry for himself.　　Ryōkan

[1] 1172–1193.

Ryōkan, 1758–1831, a Zen priest of the Sōtō school, was an eccentric but sweet-tempered man, very fond of children and flowers, and a great calligrapher. His waka are very good and his Chinese poems also, but in haiku he is not so strong. In the above verse we see him as he really is. He lives alone, and on rainy days he cannot go out and pluck violets or play with the village children. He must pass the harmless day alone, and looking at himself he feels somewhat sorry for his monotonous hours. But in this self-pity we feel more resignation, more fortitude than in the vociferations of Henley's *Invictus*.

一人居る編輯局や五月雨   子 規
Hitori iru   henshūkyoku ya   satsukiame

Alone
In the editorial department;
Summer rain falling.   Shiki

A newspaper-office, when everyone has gone home, is more lonely than a desert or a grave-yard. It is the *positive* absence of things which affects us most, and the rain falling ceaselessly, without variation of tone or timbre, the silence inside felt against the watery sounds outside intensify each other in a contrast that is a unity of separateness.

夕立や草葉をつかむ村雀   蕪 村
Yūdachi ya   kusaba wo tsukamu   murasuzume

A sudden summer shower;
The village sparrows
Hang on to the grasses.   Buson

The humour and the pathos of this bring out the power of nature and the insignificance of its parts, in a way that greater phenomena, such as whirlwinds and earthquakes, could not. This peculiar virtue of the smallness of things is yet another example of "strength made perfect in weakness." The sparrows are hanging on to anything and everything with their claws, with their beaks, their wings, while the warm rain pours down about them and upon them, pulling them down and away.

This verse illustrates the double function of haiku. The shower is so sudden and heavy that the sparrows, like soldiers ambushed, are forced to hold on for dear life, and we have a picture of animation and humour. From the point of view of the seasonal subject, this verse expresses the violence and abruptness of the shower. But there is not felt to be any division of the subject, the shower—the sparrows. It is a unity, and the sparrows are felt to have their place (albeit a wet and uncomfortable one) in the larger movements of nature.

旅中

夕立や雨戸くり出す下女の數　　　　　　　子規

Yūdachi ya   amado kuridasu   gejo no kazu

On a Journey

A summer shower!
What a number of servants
Closing the shutters!　　　　　Shiki

This has a kind of fairy-tale atmosphere. The way in which the servants appear from nowhere, the wind blowing, the rush of the rain, the patter of footsteps, the clatter and sliding of the shutters look and sound like the work of some genii.

夕だちや家をめぐりて啼く家鴨　　　　　　其角

Yūdachi ya   ie wo megurite   naku ahiru

A sudden summer shower;
The ducks run round the house,
Quacking.　　　　　Kikaku

The disproportion of the fright of the ducks and its cause, the sudden shower, is exactly paralleled by that of the poetical thrill and the mediocre matter of the poem.

夕立やはだかで乗りしはだか馬　　　　一　茶
Yūdachi ya　hadaka de norishi hadaka-uma

> Naked,
> On a naked horse
> 　　Through the pouring rain.　　　　Issa

This is a verse of sensation, of touch, that Keats would have
enjoyed. The summer shower endues both horse and rider
with beauty.

撫子を打つ夕立やさもあらき　　　　杉　風
Nadeshiko wo　utsu yūdachi ya　samo araki

> The summer shower
> Falls on the pinks,
> 　　So roughly.　　　　Sampū

This is a pianissimo variation on the theme of

> Nature red in tooth and claw.

The pinks bow their heads as each heavy drop falls on them.
Though we know it to be inevitable, we feel grief at its very
necessity.

夕立にうたる〻鯉のあたまかな　　　　子　規
Yūdachi ni　utaruru koi no　atama kana

> A summer shower;
> The rain beats
> 　　On the heads of the carp.　　　　Shiki

Just as the sun shines on the just and on the unjust, so the
rain falls on the dry land and the wet heads of the fish. But
besides this pleasant humour, there is in this verse some dim
realization of the life of the carp. What are their vague feel-
ings as the yellow sunlight pales, the water darkens, and, as
they rise slowly to the surface, the drops patter on their broad
snouts?

夕立にひとり外見る女かな   其　角
Yūdachi ni   hitori soto miru   onna kana

A summer shower;
A woman sits alone,
　　Gazing outside.   Kikaku

What the woman is thinking, dreaming, does not come within
the purview of the poem, which requires us to be as thought-
less as the rain, as the picture of a woman gazing out at it.

夕立や智慧さまざまのかぶり物   乙　由
Yūdachi ya   chie samazama no   kaburimono

A summer shower,—
According to their wisdom,
　　The various head-coverings.   Otsuyū

The shower suddenly falls with quite alarming violence, and
in his reaction to this, each shows his character; some running
to shelter; some hurrying slowly, trying not to lose too much
dignity; some seizing hold of anything that will keep them dry
for a few moments; others gnashing their teeth as they think
of their clothes or their complexions. The poet looks particu-
larly at the assortment of things that are being held over the
heads, fans, bowls, handkerchiefs, sleeves, straw mats, and
oddest of all, a sieve.

音計りでも夕立の夕かな   一　茶
Oto bakari demo   yūdachi no   yūbe kana

Just the sound of it,—
But it was an evening
　　With a summer shower.   Issa

In life, in Zen, the less the better:

多言多慮、轉不相應。

The more talking and thinking.
The farther from the truth.   (*Shinjinmei*)

If we only hear the rain, the impression is deeper than if we
see it and touch it. There is a similar delight in what is small
and apparently insignificant, a pleasure which is in no way
perverse, in the following, also by Issa:

一尺の瀧も音して夕納涼
Isshaku no   taki mo oto shite   yū suzumi

Only a one-foot waterfall,
But in the sounds it makes,—
Cooling in the evening.

稲妻や森の隙間に水を見たり　　　　　　　　子　規
Inazuma ya   mori no sukima ni   mizu wo mitari

A flash of lightning;
Between the trees of the forest,
Water appears.   Shiki

Shiki has here restricted the subject to its own domain, that
of physical sight. When the lightning flashes, pools of water
left from the rain and the streams and rivulets suddenly flash
white and blinding before us. The world become a place of
black and white, with no other colours.

稲妻にこぼるゝ音や竹の露　　　　　　　　　蕪　村
Inazuma ni   koboruru oto ya   take no tsuyu

A flash of lightning!
The sound of the dew
Dripping down the bamboos.   Buson

As Buson stands in the bamboo forest in the early morning,
there is a flash of lightning; the whole of nature seems in a
state of tension, the mind of the listener with it. At this
moment of suspense, the drip-drip of dew falling through the
bamboo grove is felt so deeply, it can hardly be called hearing.

稲妻に大佛拝む野中かな   荷 兮
Inazuma ni   daibutsu ogamu   nonaka kana

Amid lightning flashes
I worshipped before a Great Buddha,
On the moor.   Kakei

Man with his little hour of breath, man that makes the
angels weep, man is the measure of all things. But he must
not know this. Kakei, a pupil of Bashō, stands before a large
statue of Buddha, not of Kamakura or Nara, but one standing
alone on a solitary moor. There is thunder and lightning, and
the poet feels the power of Nature, and the power of that which
symbolizes the power of both man and nature. He himself is
a nothing before this mighty manifestation. There is a rather
similar verse by Shiki:

提灯で大佛見るや時鳥
Chōchin de   daibutsu miru ya   hototogisu

With a lantern,
I looked at the Great Buddha:
A *hototogisu* sang!

Compare the following by Tōsha, 桐舎, a modern poet:

評定もしばし止みけり雷神
Hyōjō mo   shibashi yamikeri   raijin

The Supreme Court also,
Paused for a while,
During the thunder claps.

"The Supreme Court" is that of the Shogunate. This ad-
visory council first received its name in 1225. It was held at
Kamakura, at the so-called Mandokoro, the central admini-
stration, founded towards the end of the 12th century. The
greatest dignitaries of the land (excluding the Emperor) sit in
their stiff, ceremonial robes, deliberating on affairs of state,
and as one of them is speaking in haughty, measured tones,
there is a flash, and thunder begins to roll. The speaker is
silent, with whatever dignity he can muster. Each nobleman
sits there, thinking his thoughts mixed with the rumbling of
thunder.

稲妻やきのふは東今日は西　　其　角
Inazuma ya   kinō wa higashi   kyō wa nishi

Summer lightning!
Yesterday in the East,
Today in the West.　　Kikaku

The original does not say "Summer" lightning, but actually in Japan summer is the season for lightning and storms generally.

There is a feeling of vastness in this verse, in which east and west take their proper place. But it is the causelessness which gives the verse its depth of meaning. It is not that we do not know the meaning, the reason why the lighting flashes are today in the west, yesterday in thè east. It is that we are in a realm which is not reasonful nor reasonless, but something which includes and transcends both and yet is not itself anything at all, so that in the final result we are left simply with lightning in the east and lightning in the west.

Contrast this verse with the following, by Otsuyū:

萍や今日はあちらの岸に咲く
Ukigusa ya   kyō wa achira no   kishi ni saku

Floating duckweed:
Today blooming
By the farther shore.

This verse implies the uncertainty and changeability of nature, but Kikaku's verse has a feeling of *free inevitability*.

稲妻にさとらぬ人の貴さよ　　芭　蕉
Inazuma ni   satoranu hito no   tōtosa yo

How admirable,
He who thinks not, "Life is fleeting,"
When he sees the lightning flash!　　Bashō

Whitman says,
And I say to any man or woman,
Let your soul stand cool and composed before a million universes.

炎天に菊を養ふあるじかな   子 規
Enten ni   kiku wo yashinau   aruji kana

In the burning sunshine,
The master cherishes
His chrysanthemums.   Shiki

Enten is extreme, windless heat under the direct rays of the
sun. The old man waters the plants, loosens the soil, adds earth
to the pots, does the hundred and one little things that make
all the difference to the growth of the flowers. He treats them
as tenderly as if they were his own children, and though the
contrast is hardly even implicit, let alone explicit, there is some
faint feeling of the inflexibility of nature in the burning heat,
and the tenderness of man in the way he cares for living
things.

地 理 FIELDS AND MOUNTAINS

大木を見てもどりけり夏の山   蘭 更
Taiboku wo   mite modorikeri   natsu no yama

I came back,
Having seen a gigantic tree:
The summer mountains.   Rankō

In the very simplicity of this bald statement lies the pro-
fundity of the experience of the power of life. The summer
mountains are not a mere background for the memorable tree,
that now grows, in all its vast bulk, in his mind. They are
in some way the general of which the single tree is the parti-
cular. The giant tree is like Masefield's lily, which may

Spring in my heart agen,

but without any afterthought,

That I may flower to men.

Compare Rankō's poem with Kyoroku's even simpler verse:

大木を眺めてゐたり下すずみ
Taiboku wo   nagamete itari   shita-suzumi

I sit cooling beneath it,
Looking up
At the great tree.

Meisetsu's verse is very good:

夏山の大木倒すこだまかな
Natsuyama no   taiboku taosu   kodama kana

A giant tree felled,
Echoes and re-echoes
Among the summer mountains.

A tree is cut down, and in its fall, with the sense of space,
of size, of heat and weight, summer is expressed in its entirety.
Issa does the same thing, expressing the nature of the summer
mountain through multitudinous sounds:

Summer Mountains by Kōzenki, 高然暉

夏山や鶯雉子時鳥
Natsuyama ya   uguisu kigisu   hototogisu

> In the summer mountains,
> The cries of uguisu, pheasants,
> Hototogisu.

馬ほくほく我を繪に見る夏野哉   芭蕉
Uma hoku hoku   ware wo e ni miru   natsuno kana

> I find myself in a picture;
> The cob ambles slowly
>   Across the summer moor.   Bashō

It is interesting to compare this with the original version:

馬ほくほくわれを繪に見る心かな
Uma hoku hoku   ware wo e ni miru   kokoro kana

> The cob ambles along;
> I feel as if
> In a picture.

The emphasis here is on Bashō's state of mind. In the revised form all is objective, Bashō as well; nature alone remains. There is very similar verse in the *Zenrinkushu.*

看盡瀟湘景、和舟入畫圖。

I gazed to my heart's content at the scenery of Shosho,
Painting even my own boat into the picture.

巡禮の棒ばかり行く夏野かな   維舟
Junrei no   bō bakari yuku   natsuno kana

> Only the staves
> Of the pilgrims pass
>   Across the summer moor.   Ishū

The grass is rank and high, the country roads are deep. As they pass by, only the tips of the long staves are seen moving along in procession. The pilgrims may be chanting or not. They are swallowed up in nature and we feel them to be undifferentiated from nature in its "natural piety." Again, in this "only the staves" there is something that reminds us of the stones that would have cried out had the people been silent. The staves themselves would rise up and walk were there no pilgrims to go to holy places. A more subtle example of the same thing, by Issa, is the following:

陽炎や寺へ行かれし杖の穴
Kagerō ya   tera e yukareshi   tsue no ana

> Heat waves;
> The holes of the stick
> That went to the temple.

The season of this is spring.

秣負ふ人を枝折の夏野かな　　　芭蕉
Magusa ou   hito wo shiori no   natsuno kana

> A man carrying fodder on his back,
> As if our guide
> Over the summer moor.　　Bashō

Bashō and Sora had lost their way on the vast Musashi Plain. Seeing a man with a load of grass in the distance, they followed him. The poetic point is in the unconsciousness of the man. We are accustomed to it in things but it is equally common, though unnoticed, with human beings. There is also here a feeling of the blind, the unknown destinies to which life leads us.

絶えず人憩ふ夏野の石一つ　　　子規
Taezu hito   ikou natsuno no   ishi hitotsu

> One after another,
> People rest on this stone
> On the summer moor.　　Shiki

The stone is under a tree, in the shade, and it is just the right height and shape, so that it seems to invite everyone to sit on it. Without exception everybody who passes across the moor in the heat rests for a few minutes here. The stone seems not an ordinary stone. Speaking more profoundly, there is a relation between men and things, between men and stones, which comes out with a strange clearness in the case of this particular stone.

野を横に馬牽きむけよほととぎす   芭 蕉
No wo yoko ni   uma hikimuke yo   hototogisu

Riding over the summer moor,—
"Ah! lead the horse that way!"
Where the *hototogisu* is singing.   Bashō

This verse occurs in *Oku no Hosomichi*. The context is:

是より殺生石にゆく。館代より馬にて送らる。
此の口付のをのこ短冊得させよと乞ふ。やさし
きことを望み侍るものかなと。

From here, I went to see the Death Stone. The
Deputy sent me there on horseback, and the man
who led the horse asked me for a *tanzaku*.[1] I was
moved with admiration at his request, [and composed
the verse above].

The pleasant thing about this is the way in which Bashō shows indifference to where he is going, and to everything in fact but the cry of the bird. This is the artist and the poet, far above time and place, enduring all things for that moment when the song of the bird breaks out again.

水ふんで草で足ふく夏野かな   來 山
Mizu funde   kusa de ashi fuku   natsuno kana

Splashing across the water,
Wiping my feet on the grass,—
The summer moor!   Raizan

The touch of the cold water, the sound of it; the feel of the grass, both soft and rough; the other, unmarked sensations, the myriad, faint, evanescent emotions that lack a local habitation and a name,—all these are the summer moor, not its symbol or part, but the whole truth and reality of it.

[1] A strip of thin cardboard, on which a verse is to be written.

おろし置く笈に地震る夏野哉　　蕪　村
Oroshioku oi ni nae furu   natsuno kana

The *oi* just set down,
Swayed with an earthquake,
On the summer moor.　　　　　Buson

Out in the fields, an ordinary earthquake is hardly noticeable, but the *oi*, a portable altar that a travelling priest carries on his back, is light, and will register a shock by the swaying of the shoulder straps that hang down when it is stood on the ground.

The fact, the thing of value that Buson perceived, was the *faithfulness* of things, the love that makes the world go round, the love that makes it shrink and crack and engulf myriads of lives in a moment. The most terrible thing that could happen in this world is however that, for example, a stone should not fall when thrown into the air. When a very slight earthquake occurs, nothing in Nature's aspect shows it. But God counts the hairs of our heads; not a sparrow can fall to the ground but he knows it. THAT IS TO SAY, not an earthquake can occur but the strings of the portable altar show it. In this verse, the sounds of *o* and *na* are repeated:

oroshioku oi ni nae furu   natsuno kana

行々てここに行々夏野かな　　蕪　村
Yukiyukite   koko ni yuki yuku   natsuno kana

On and on,
And here, in this place, on and on,
Over the summer moor.　　　　　Buson

What the poet has grasped, but not quite expressed, is the sensation of static movement, of moving immobility. On the far horizon behind the blue hills, white clouds are piling. The traveller moves onwards, yet there is a sameness about the trickle of water, the chirping of the cicadas, the burning sun glittering on the leaves. The now is an eternal now; the here is everywhere.

曠野行く身に近づくや雲の峰   蕪　村

Kōya yuku　mi ni chikazuku ya　kumo no mine

Walking over the vast, empty moor,
The towering clouds
　　　Draw near me.   Buson

The wide plain over which the poet is walking seems small
because of its lack of objects above the horizon; he himself
feels correspondingly insignificant and puny. In the sky above
him, huge masses of billowing clouds threaten to crumble and
fall upon him.

あつき日を海に入れたり最上川   芭　蕉

Atsuki hi wo　umi ni iretari　mogami-gawa

The Mogami River
Has swept the burning Sun
　　Down into the Ocean.   Bashō

Is this true, that is, poetical? or is it only fancy, that is,
false? May a thing be poetical, yet untrue in fact? We need
to consider the meaning of "fact," without being jesuitical or
sophistic, and without depriving words of all meaning. It is
clear, first of all, that the "fact" which is asserted in this poem
is not that the sun is actually extinguished in the waters of the
sea down to which the river has washed it. Then what is the
truth stated here? It is not the decoration of a lie, nor a trick
of words; it is not the invention of a poetical wonderland in
which we escape from reality. Above all, it is not an intel-
lectual association of incompatibles by the choosing of some
identical characteristics and rejection of all other differences.
What is it then? They of old time said unto you, "The river
flows on ceaselessly, and day by day the sun sinks below the
horizon, but I say unto you,

　　　The Mogami River
　　Has swept the burning Sun
　　Down into the Ocean."

低き木に馬つなぎたる夏野かな　　　子　規
Hikuki ki ni   uma tsunagitaru   natsuno kana

　　A horse tied
To a low tree,
　　In the summer moor.　　　Shiki

If one can see the poetry of this at a glance, he may be said
to have some understanding of haiku. This verse reminds one
a little of those pictures in which one has to find what is wrong
with the objects drawn in it. Where we should have a tall
tree we have a bush,—that is all there is, and yet one smacks
one's lips as at a poetical feast.

夏川を越す嬉しさよ手に草履　　　蕉　村
Natsukawa wo   kosu ureshisa yo   te ni zōri

　　What happiness,
Crossing this summer river,
　　Sandals in hand!　　　Buson

When we do this kind of thing, we feel what Wordsworth
calls "the primal sympathies," our common nature with water
and stones and sand. And the touch of cold water on the feet
has something in it that defies all explanation, and even ex-
pression. Simply isolated and simply stated, such things find
us young and keep us so. In the *Saikontan*, we read:

真味只是淡。
Only plain things have real taste.

Like the voices of birds and the songs of insects, the touch of
cold water

　feeds the mind with pure joy, and is free from all sadness.

夏川や馬つなぎたる橋柱　　　子　規
Natsukawa ya   uma tsunagitaru   hashibashira

　　The summer river;
A horse tied
　　To the post of the bridge.　　　Shiki

The stream is not a broad one, but the water is high. It reaches to the horse's knees, and his tail dips in the water. His head is drooping, but not with weariness; rather, he feels a quiet pleasure in the cold feeling in his summer-swollen legs, round which the water swirls gurgling past the posts that hold up the bridge. Another verse that expresses more explicitly the feelings of the horse:

夏川や橋あれど馬水を行く
Natsukawa ya   hashi aredo uma   mizu wo yuku

> The summer river;
> There is a bridge,
> But the horse goes through the water.

Another expresses the feelings of the rider:

馬上より手綱ゆるめる清水哉
Bajō yori   tazuna yurumeru   shimizu kana

> On horseback,
> I loosened the reins,—
> The clear water!

夏川や中流にしてかへり見る   子 規
Natsukawa ya   chūryū ni shite   kaerimiru

> The summer river;
> In mid-stream,
> Looking back.   Shiki

We may compare and contrast this verse with one by Bonchō:

渡りかけて藻の花のぞく流れかな
Watarikakete   mo no hana nozoku   nagare kana

> Half way across the stream,
> Gazing
> At the duckweed flowers.

In the verse of the earlier poet (d. 1714) the world becomes small and intense. The mind contracts to the span of a few small water flowers, their white petals and the green leaves. In Shiki's verse, the world becomes larger as, for some odd

reason, we look back when we reach the middle of the river.
The mind expands, time is added to space, as we see the shore
from which we came, and to which we can never return.

あとざまに小魚ながるる清水哉 　　　　　　几董
Atozama ni　kouo nagaruru　shimizu kana

The little fish
Carried backwards,
　　In the clear water. 　　　　　　Kitō

The power and the weakness of nature are seen here, the
weakness of the struggling little creatures and the power of
the invisible element.

底の石動いて見ゆる清水かな 　　　　　　漱石
Soko no ishi　ugoite miyuru　shimizu kana

The stones at the bottom
Seem to be moving;
　　Clear water. 　　　　　　Sōseki

This poem is a failure, for the poet has allowed his intellect
to interfere with his imagination. Movement, simple movement,
is perhaps the greatest mystery of the universe. This is the
meaning of our deep interest in earthquakes, the stormy sea,
horse-races, the clouds, streams and rivers, tobacco smoking.
In the above verse, the stones of the bottom of the brook are
moving. The water is so clear that the movement can be
exactly and vividly seen. The intellect qualifies this with
"*seems* to be moving" but the imagination takes no notice of
this. It loves movement for its own sake; whether the move-
ment is in the mind or outside it, does not matter. Rogetsu
says:

野分吹けど動かざる雲高し
Nowaki fukedo　ugokazaru　kumo takashi

The autumn tempest rages,
But high in the sky
　　The clouds are motionless.

The mind desires change, motion, as such. But it desires
also rest, as such. Somehow, somewhere, beyond this life of
agitation and movement there are windless abodes, a world of
serenity,—such is the faith of our heart. What the mind really
desires, that exists.[1] And this instinctive belief is not so
absurd, not so ill-founded as it seems, to superficial criticism, if,

> Nothing is but thinking makes it so.

This is Heaven, Paradise, the New Jerusalem, Utopia, that is,
nowhere. We say

> The land of dreams is better far.
> Above the light of the morning star,

and see far, far above us the clouds set in motionless serenity.
But this that we suppose to be the desire of our inmost heart
is not really so. Deeper than this, the deepest thing in the
universe, is man's *love of destiny*, the Buddha nature.

> The Kingdom of Heaven is within you.

菩提只向心覓、何勞向外求玄。(六祖壇経,三)

> Bodhi is to be sought for within our own mind;
> You seek in vain for a solution of the mystery
>   in the outside world.

Motionless activity, active rest, both in the microcosmos and
the macrocosmos, is what our Buddha nature requires us to
attain; our whole life is simply one long, continuous, un-
conscious search for it.

清瀧や浪にちりこむ青松葉　　　　芭蕉
Kiyo-taki ya　nami ni chirikomu　aomatsuba

> A clear waterfall;
> Into the ripples
>   Fall green pine-needles.　　Bashō

[1] Lawrence says something very similar to this:
You say, "it is life, life is like it." But this is mere sophistry.
Life is what one wants in one's soul.

This verse has a clarity and simplicity corresponding to that of the scene and the mind of the poet. The combination of simplicity and subtlety, clarity and profundity is what we admire so much in Goethe.

さざれ蟹足はひ上る清水かな   芭 蕉
Sazare-kani   ashi hainoboru   shimizu kana

A tiny crablet
Climbs up my legs
In the clear water.   Bashō

A spring bubbles out of the gravel and runs away as clear water. Standing in the rivulet, something seems to be tickling one's legs, and looking down, a small, a very small crab is seen to be climbing up. It gives one an added feeling of freshness together with a touch of the crab's nature that makes all the world kin.

錢龜や青砥もしらぬ山清水   蕪 村
Zenigame ya   aoto mo shiranu   yama-shimizu

Not knowing Aoto,
Only the clear water from the hill,
A spotted turtle.   Buson

This may be taken as an example of Buson's excessively difficult style of haiku, and also as one more evidence of the early haiku poets' deep interest in Taoism in general and Sōshi in particular. In a prescript, we are told that Buson was asked to write a verse on the painting of a small turtle by Maruyama Ōkyo (1733-95) a famous painter of the Kano school. His own originality consisted in exact reproduction of nature. Buson writes:

仕官懸命の地に榮利をもとめんよりは、しかじ
尾を泥中に曳んには、

Rather than seek glory and profit in the ranks of
the officials,

I would prefer to wag my tail in the mud.

This is taken from Sōshi, who says:

荘子釣於濮水、楚王使士大夫往先焉、曰願以境
内累矣、荘子持竿不顧曰、吾聞楚有神龜死己三
千歳矣。王巾笥而藏之廟堂之上。此龜者寧共死
爲留骨而貴乎。寧其生而曳尾於塗中乎。二大夫
曰寧生而曳尾塗中、荘子曰、往矣、吾将曳尾於
塗中。

    Sōshi was fishing in the River Bokusui. The Prince
of So sent two messengers to him beforehand, asking
for help as the internal affairs of his country were
troubled. Sōshi, holding his rod, and without looking
round, said, "I have heard that there was a sacred
tortoise in the land of So; it died three thousand
years ago. The then Prince put it in a fine box and
had it placed in the Mausoleum. Which is better
off, this tortoise, a dead one, with its bones preserved
and honoured, or a living one wagging its tail in the
mud?" The two messengers replied that the latter
was better off. "Be off with you!" cried Sōshi, "I
wish to wag my tail in the mud!"

Aoto Fujitsuna was a minister under Tokiyori and Tokimune,
in the 13th century, famous for his thrift and uprightness. He
is associated in this verse with the turtle because of the word
zeni-game, which means literally "smallcash turtle." Once
when he dropped a small coin in the darkness, he bought a
torch worth five times as much to look for it, saying that if
the coin were lost, something irreplaceable would have dis-
appeared. The verse then means that this turtle does not
know even such a famous man as Aoto Fujitsuna, and is all
the happier for it, like Sōshi's turtle, because it can live freely
in the mountain water.

    This verse requires a prodigious amount of explanation, and
is hardly worth it, but when such classical and historical
matters can be taken in one's stride, haiku becomes literature,
though not necessarily poetry.

金持も熊も來てのむ清水哉　　　　　子 規

Kanemochi mo   kuma mo kite nomu   shimizu kana

Millionaires,
Come and drink of this clear water,
And bears.　　　　　Shiki

Nature is at one and the same time just and unjust, imperious and democratic. She makes one rich, another poor, one a man, another a bear, but clear water for all. Some are born to luxury, others to semi-starvation, but as the comic song says, there's nothing to eat but food, nothing to wear but clothes. Shiki's haiku is not supposed, of course, to arouse such thoughts as these, but they are the aura, the background, the "ground" of the verse. The haiku is composed in praise of the clear water, that flows for all without distinction, that flows merely,—and this is enough.

石工の飛火流るゝ清水かな　　　　　蕪 村

Sekkō no   tobihi nagaruru   shimizu kana

The mason's sparks
Flow away
In the clear water.　　　　　Buson

There are two kinds of poetry, that is, two kinds of experience, corresponding to the paradoxical nature of things. A thing both is and is not, or, it neither is nor is not. Intellectually speaking, only one of these pairs of contraries is true at any given time, in any given place. (Or it may be that it is true for all times and all places,—in this rationally conceived universe). In Zen, however, in poetry, in haiku, either of these pairs may be asserted. Descriptions of nature, affirmations of ordinary life are of the first kind. Sparks fall in the water, and are extinguished. Sometimes, however, we flatly deny facts; "all men are equal" we say with poetico-political fervour. "Sparks flow away in the clear water." To preserve a proper proportion between these two, means mental and emotional health. It means that we know what God and what man is. Then, when we wish it to be so, sparks from the mason's chisel are seen to be flowing away on the clear water of the stream that runs by him.

Another verse, by the same author, an "affirmation of ordinary life":

石工の鑿冷したる清水かな
Sekkō no   nomi hiyashitaru   shimizu kana

> The clear water;
> The mason
> Cools his chisel in it.

In the sweltering sun, and with the repeated blows of the hammer, the chisel becomes unpleasantly hot. The mason plunges it in a small stream that runs swiftly by. The water takes the heat from the tool, so willingly, so thoughtlessly. The iron gives up the heat so freely, without regret. The water gurgles round the hand of the mason, the sun shines down on all things.

A quite different verse of Buson's, with the same surroundings, is the following:

石工の指やぶりたるつゝじかな
Sekkō no   yubi yaburitaru   tsutsuji kana

> The mason's
> Injured finger,—
> And the azaleas.

The bleeding hand of the mason caught up by the red azaleas blooming nearby make a colour scheme that belongs to another world, yet is an essential element of this one.

山門や青田の中の並木松　　　　　　子 規
Sanmon ya   aota no naka no   namiki-matsu

> The Great Gate of the temple;
> Through the midst of the rice field,
> An avenue of pine-trees.　　　　Shiki

This has the simplicity of an ukiyoe, and in it is contained nature, man's path through it, and the "something evermore about to be," the hope that springs eternal in the human breast, without which life is only existence. However, this verse is not a parable, a symbol of anything,—but neither is it a mere picture, art for art's sake. The temple gate has a meaning which is not that of the gate of a brothel. The green rice has "the sentiment of being" spread over it. The double row of ancient pine-trees that winds through the field gives us a feeling of time, and human beings coming and going in space and in eternity. All this is perceived in one moment of unification; all the various elements become pure and translucent, like white flowers in the snow.

神　佛　GODS AND BUDDHAS

すずしさの野山にみつる念佛かな　　　　去　來
Suzushisa no　noyama ni mitsuru　nembutsu kana

Chanting the Nembutsu,
Coolness fills
Fields and mountains.　　　　Kyorai

The poet did not suppose that the air actually became cooler.
On the other hand, he did not make the common mistake of
supposing that the coolness was a purely scientific, objective
matter; scientists think like men just as they feel and act as
men.　For Kyorai, mountains and fields were filled with cool
air as a result of the tranquillizing of his mind by repeating
Namuamidabutsu.

錦着て牛の汗かく祭かな　　　　子　規
Nishiki kite　ushi no ase-kaku　matsuri kana

Wearing brocade,
The bull is sweating
At the festival.　　　　Shiki

This reminds us of the poem of Hakurakuten, *The Govern-
ment Bull*, 官牛.　The Government bull is pulling the Govern-
ment cart backwards and forwards from the river to the road
so that the hooves of the horse of the High Official may not
be dirtied:

踢沙雖淨潔、牛領牽車欲流血。

It is true that it is clean to tread on,
But pulling the cart, the bull's neck is running
blood.

Hakurakuten here falls into, or rises into something other than
poetry.　He is thinking of the bull with grief and indignation,
and this is good, provided that we think so at the same mo-
ment of all other things.　Poetry never forgets the all even
when it is dealing exclusively with one thing.　But righteous

indignation has departed somewhat from the serenity of painful joy which is to be ever in the mind of the poet. Shiki's verse simply gives us the picture and lets it go at that. The bull is covered with brocade, and people are playing and dancing and beating drums, but for him there is dust and noise and heat, and a heavy wagon pulling at his neck.

松島観瀾亭にて豐臣、伊達兩公を憶ふ。

ふわふわと亡き霊ここに來て涼め   子 規
Fuwa-fuwa to   naki rei koko ni   kite suzume

Come here and cool yourselves,
Wavering, wavering
   Spirits of the dead.   Shiki

There is a mansion in Matsushima dating from the end of the 16th century, a gift from Hideyoshi to Date Masamune. This verse was composed by Shiki while at this Kanrantei, or "Wave-viewing house." He asks the departed shades of the two famous warriors to join him in cooling at night on the rocky cliff where the house stands. This verse is an example of haiku which cannot stand alone, but needs a prescript to elucidate the meaning. It illustrates further the way in which, to the Japanese mind, gods and spirits as well as animals and plants are nearer to human beings than in Western thought-feeling.

人 事　HUMAN AFFAIRS

大風の俄に起るのぼり哉　　　　　　　　子 規
Ōkaze no　niwaka ni okoru　nobori kana

A great wind
Suddenly arose,—
The banner!　　　　　　　　　　　　Shiki

This "banner" is a long, rectangular, hanging flag or
standard. When it is calm, it hangs perpendicular; when the
wind blows, it stands away from the pole. In the present
verse, there is a violent gust of wind, and the banner thrashes
about, making visible the invisible. The living, animate nature
ascribed to the banner is seen again in the following, also by
Shiki:

雨雲をさそう嵐の幟かな
Amagumo wo　sasou arashi no　nobori kana

Drawing on the rain-clouds,—
The banner
Of the storm!

Yet another by Shiki, in which the relation between the banner
and clouds is shown to be a direct one:

山里に雲打ち拂ふ幟かな
Yamazato ni　kumo uchiharau　nobori kana

In the mountain village,
Sweeping away the clouds,—
Paper carps.

Paper carps (also of cloth) are floated in the air for the Boys'
Festival on the fifth of May. The verses refer to these. The
following is also by Shiki:

幟たてゝ嵐のほしき日なりけり
Nobori tatete　arashi no hoshiki　hi narikeri

Hoisting the banner,
It was a day when we wanted
A gusty wind.

Inability to control the elements is the origin of such modesty

Summer Landscape　by Sesshū, 雪舟, 1420–1506

and humility as we have, and when not a breath of wind stirs
the banner, we can only sigh with impotence.   This haiku is
somewhat senryū-like.

幟立てる人家は遠し大伽藍   子　規
Nobori tateru   jinka wa tōshi   dai-garan

> The banners raised above the dwellings
> Are distant;
> The great abbey.   Shiki

This is a verse of the poetry of height and mass and distance.
The banners float out above the far-off farm houses, relatively
high, absolutely low.   Here the dark building rises up and
looms into the sky in great contrast to the floating, brightly-
coloured *nobori* that rise and fall in the summer sunshine.

出がはりや幼心に物あはれ   嵐　雪
Degawari ya   osanagokoro ni   monoaware

> The change of servants;
> The pathos
> Of her childish heart.   Ransetsu

In olden times, on the fifth day of the third month, there
was a general change of servants, old servants being replaced
by young ones, young ones going away to new positions.
Especially the young boys and girls were full of excitement
and anticipation about their prospective places, touched with
gratitude for past benefits of their old masters.   The pathos
of this moment is that of Conrad's *Youth*.   In the very hope-
fulness itself there is something pitiful:

> It was because you did not weep,
> I wept for you.[1]

There is a similar kind of experience expressed in:

> Alas! The gratitude of men
> Hath oftener left me mourning.

[1] *Hidden Sorrow*, Cecil French.

Besides the pathos of the probabilities of failure and disappoint-
ment, besides the regret that older people feel for their past
youth, there is the poet's momentary realization of the insepara-
bility of youth and old age, of joy and sorrow, of life and death.
Kyoroku, has a verse with a similar feeling, but more pictur-
esque:

出代りや 傘提げて夕ながめ
Degawari ya   karakasa sagete   yūnagame

> The departing servant;
> Umbrella in hand,
>   She gazes out at the twilight.

出代やかはる箒のかけどころ　　　也 有
Degawari ya   kawaru hōki no   kakedokoro

> The change of servants;
> The broom is hung
>   In a different place.　　　Yayū

Everything is the same, yet everything is different. The
broom is still there, there is no profit or loss, addition or sub-
traction; but the new servant has hung the same broom on a
different nail, and the poetic mind sees freedom and life, where
the intellect recognises only cause and effect. The place where
the broom used to be, the place where it now is, are both
charged with human feeling. Invisible things are seen, and the
visible is almost palpable.

出代や疊へ落す涙かな　　　太 祇
Degawari ya   tatami e otosu   namida kana

> The change of servants;
> Her tears
>   Splash on the tatami.　　　Taigi

There is something inherently pathetic about a servant, not
a superficial pathos, but something deeply tragic, something
that endues Christ's words,

He that would be master, let him be the servant
of you all,

with a whole world of emotion.   In the *Hōjōki* we are told to
do things ourselves as far as possible, since we know our own
pains and weariness of mind and body:

人 を 苦 し め 人 を 悩 ま す は ま た 罪 業 な り。

To harass and afflict others is a sin.

To be the servant is to be Master of all, but to *have* a servant
is to fly in the face of nature, the Buddha nature.   When the
poet sees the young servant's tears fall at the prospect of
leaving, a feeling of impotence and dismay comes over him.
It is so little we can do for one another.   Gratitude is indeed
hard to bear.

紙 屑 や 出 代 の あ と の 物 淋 し　　　　千　那
Kamikuzu ya   degawari no ato no   mono-sabishi

Some scraps of paper,
After the servant has gone;
A feeling of lonesomeness.   Senna

Personal relics, the paraphernalia of life, sensational objects,
funeral ceremonies,—these do not move us, though we pretend
they do.   A few scraps of paper left in the corner of the room
or the cupboard, and we have a painful feeling of the transi-
toriness and meaninglessness of all things, which goes to the
very roots of life.   As the most primitive form of Buddhism
taught, life is suffering; living equals suffering.

出 代 や い づ く も お な じ 梅 の 花　　　一　茶
Degawari ya   izuku mo onaji   ume no hana

The change of servants;
Wherever it is,
The same flowers of the plum.   Issa

This is Issa's version of

> Men may come and men may go,
>   But I go on for ever.

It lacks, perhaps to its advantage, Tennyson's "for ever." The flowers have rather a timeless, placeless quality, a universality of existence that brings out the temporary nature of human life.

長持に春ぞくれ行く更衣　　　西鶴
Nagamochi ni   haru zo kureyuku   koromogae

> The change of clothes;
> Spring, alas, has disappeared
> Into the long chest.　　　Saikaku

On the first Day of the Fourth Month, according to the Lunar Calendar, wadded clothes were changed for lined garments. In this verse we have a so-called "figure of speech"; it is, was once, and may be again, a form of the creative imagination.

戀のない身にも嬉しや更衣　　　鬼貫
Koi no nai   mi ni mo ureshi ya   koromogae

> Though I have no lover,
> I too rejoice;
>   The change of clothes.　　　Onitsura

We may compare this to lines from Landor's *To Robert Browning:*

> There is delight in singing tho' none hear
> Beside the singer; and there is delight
> In praising tho' the praiser sit alone
> And see the praised far off him, far above.

としとへば片手出す子や更衣   一 茶
Toshi toeba   katate dasu ko ya   koromogae

Asked how old she is,
She holds up the fingers of one hand;
The change of clothes.   Issa

The little girl has changed into her new clothes. She becomes excited, clothes-conscious, and even self-conscious; her black eyes sparkle. The visitor asks, "How old are you?" and instantly she takes her tiny hands out of her sleeves and holds out one, showing she is five years old. Where is the poetry here? It is in the "life more abundantly" of the child who feels her personality expanded into her clothes.

更衣憂しと見し世も忘れ顔   蕪 村
Koromogae   ushi to mishi yo mo   wasuregao

The change of clothes;
What seemed a world of grief and woe,—
You look as if you had forgotten it all.   Buson

The poet is looking in the mirror and speaking of himself. Man is a strange creature. On the one hand, we must say with Hamlet.

What a piece of work is man!
How noble in reason!
How infinite in faculty!
In form and moving, how express and admirable!
In action how like an angel!
In apprehension, how like a god!
The beauty of the world!
The paragon of animals!

On the other hand there is nothing more petty, lacking in dignity, unreasonable and awkward than a human being. A trifle will raise him to the seventh heaven of bliss, and a trifle will make him commit suicide from despair. Life is suffering. We have no hours of unalloyed happiness, hardly an instant's freedom from care for the morrow. Our friends are dying round us, our own death approaching,—but a new dress, a new hat, and we have for the moment utterly forgotten the tragedy of life.

This is all true enough, even trite and hackneyed. The poetical point is here: may there not be perhaps some deep meaning in these moments? From what region of the soul do they come, transcending as they do, reason and our deeper experience?

その門にあたま用心更衣　　　　　一　茶
Sono mon ni　atama-yōjin　koromogae

The change of clothes;
Be careful of your head
　　With that door!　　　　　　Issa

When people put on their new clothes they feel rather pleased with themselves, and this is a dangerous time. The small door (about four feet high) at the side of the main gate always needs a little care, or one will bump one's head, and at this time it is particularly easy to be violently reminded of the lowness of the lintel. This verse is not a senryu, in so far as it portrays the feeling of elation at the time of the change of clothes; and to go much deeper, in its expression of a relation between two things which seem to have but little connection, the putting on of summer clothes, and the height of a doorway.

更衣へ坐つて見てもひとりかな　　　　　一　茶
Koromogae　suwatte mite mo　hitori kana

The change of clothes;
And sitting down,—
　　But I am alone.　　　　　　Issa

The desire to be well-dressed is a deep-seated instinct. Darwin accounted for all the myriad forms of ornamentation among birds and beasts and insects by the appreciation of form and colour in the other sex. This may have been a misapprehension or an exaggeration, but there is little doubt that it plays an important part in the life even of a spiritual Robinson Crusoe.

The change of clothes is a kind of moulting, quicker than
that of animals and birds, and comparatively painless. Issa
was never very well dressed or clean, and would have said,
like Dr. Johnson, with regard to clean linen,

> I have no passion for it.

He puts on his washed and ironed summer clothes, holds out
his arms and looks at himself, sits down rather awkwardly
and looks at himself again,—but there is no one to say any-
thing about it, even adversely. It seems as if all the meaning
of the change of clothes vanishes in this isolation and lone-
liness.

越後屋に絹さく音や更衣   其　角
Echigoya ni   kinu saku oto ya   koromogae

> The time of changing clothes;
> In Echigo-ya,
>   The sound of tearing silk.   Kikaku

Echigo-ya was the largest shop in Edo, a draper's. At the
beginning of summer, a busy street full of sunshine, people
coming and going in all their important unimportance, the
inevitable luxury of an old civilization, and in it, something
pathetic, something to pull the heartstrings,— all in the sound
of silk being torn across.

下谷一番の貌して更衣   一　茶
Shitaya ichi-ban no   kao shite   koromogae

> The change of clothes;
> Now he looks like number one man
>   Of Shitaya Ward!   Issa

This refers of course to Issa himself, who has just changed
into his not very new summer clothes, but who looks as if he
thinks he is the boss of the district. Issa notes the human
weakness, the false elation and self-importance we feel at such
trifles as a new hat or a new tie.

一つ脱いでせなに負けり衣更　　　　　芭　蕉
Hitotsu nuide　sena ni oikeri　koromogae

Taking one off,
And carrying it on my back,—
The change of clothes.　　　　　　　Bashō

This verse is found in the *Yoshino Kikō*, 芳野紀行, and was composed on the way to Nara from Waka no Ura. Being on a journey, Bashō does not change any clothes, but simply takes off one of his kimono and carries it in the bundle on his back. We see here the simple, unaffected character of the poet, his embrace of poverty, and yet his realization of its humorous side. This verse is hardly poetry, yet it is a small portion of the poetical life, and in this slight circumstance we see the whole duty of man as man fulfilled, void of greediness, pride, luxury, sloth, malice. And is this so far from poetry after all?

乞食かな天地を著たる夏衣　　　　　其　角
Kojiki kana　tenchi wo kitaru　natsugoromo

The beggar!
He has Heaven and Earth,
For his summer clothes.　　　　　　Kikaku

Many people look upon Kikaku as the obverse, or complement of Bashō, and there is good reason for this. He is the non-religious, non-moral poet. He and Bashō correspond to Ritaihaku and Hakurakuten in Chinese poetry and to Byron and Wordsworth in English poetry. In the above verse of Kikaku, haiku is doing something which it was never intended, perhaps, to do. There is a similar passage at the end of Sōshi; there may be some relation between the two:

荘子将死弟子欲厚葬之。荘子曰、吾以天地爲
棺槨、日月爲連壁、星辰爲珠璣、萬物爲齎送。
吾葬具豈不備邪。何以加此。

When Sōshi was about to die, his disciples wished to bury him in a grand style, but Sōshi said, "My coffin will be Heaven and Earth; for the funeral ornaments of jade, there are the sun and moon;

for my pearls and jewels I shall have the stars and
constellations; all things will be my mourners. Is
not everything ready for my burial? What should
be added to this?"

衣がへや鳥は黒く鷺白し   樗 良
Koromogae ya   karasu wa kuroku   sagi shiroshi

> The change of clothes;
> The crow is black,
> The heron white.   Chora

Human beings are a feeble tribe, always changing. The
crow remains as it is, the heron also. This haiku is somewhat
epigrammatic; it is of intellectual content, but its meaning is
expressed with such directness, simplicity, and concreteness
that we welcome it as a lower but interesting use of the haiku
form.

晝寢して手の動きやむ團扇かな   太 祇
Hirune shite   te no ugokiyamu   uchiwa kana

> A nap in the day-time;
> The hand stops moving
> The fan.   Taigi

The fan gently rises and falls, remains motionless for a time,
begins again, then finally stops. In this cessation there is a
deep feeling of inevitability, finality, of something ended that
can never be again.

二階から屋根船まねく團扇かな   子 規
Nikai kara   yanebune maneku   uchiwa kana

> Beckoning from upstairs,
> To a house-boat,—
> The fan.   Shiki

This fan beckoning from an unknown to an unknown, from
the upper to the lower, has something unforgettable about it. Its

meaning comes from our lack of understanding of its significance.
It may be beckoning someone to love and life, or to death, to
pleasure or intrigue. It is like the song of the Solitary Reaper,
which would lose all its poetical significance if someone had
told Wordsworth what she was singing. And if we say it is
the mystery of life that is here seized and manifested, this also
is somewhat shallow, because the meaning of this verse is not
in the mere negative unundarstandability and lack of intellectual
knowledge, but in the universality and omnipotence of each
thing; in particular, of this beckoning fan. Of each thing as
of each man and of ourselves we may say, "For thine is the
kingdom, the power and the glory, Amen!"

目に嬉し戀君の扇ましろなる   蕪 村
Me ni ureshi   koigimi no sen   mashiro naru

So happy to the eye,
The pure white fan
Of you whom I dearly love.   Buson

When we are in love, when we are happy, when we accept
things as they are, some simple thing has a sweet or bitter
or fearful meaning. The "meaning" and its depth is common
to every such experience. In the verse above, the mere white-
ness of the girl's fan, the fact that it is this colour and no
other, is full of grateful significance to the lover, who does not
however realize that the meaning of the colour of the fan is
partly in his own feelings. At the moment, his emotion is
white, and he sees, rightly enough, what a white fan is, what
its whiteness means, why it is white.

山水に米をつかせて晝寢かな   一 茶
Yamamizu ni   kome wo tsukasete   hirune kana

I take a nap,
Making the mountain water
Pound the rice.   Issa

"Here we have the identification of Man with Nature; Man=
Nature. Issa-in-the-water turns the mill-wheel that pounds the

rice, while Issa-by-the-water slumbers,—yet there is only one
Issa. Thoreau tells us that it is Nature that does the best part
of the work of a carpenter, Nature that does the best part of
the work of an arist, a poet. This is the identification of Nature
with Man; Nature=Man. That is to say, Nature-in-the-water
drives the water-wheel; Nature-in-Issa sleeps,—yet there is only
one Nature. Combining the two, Issa pounds the rice while
asleep; Nature sleeps while pounding the rice." [1]

Mozeley says, in *University Sermons* (Sermon on Nature),

> Nature, all the time that it is working as a
> machine, is also sleeping as a picture.

Compare also the following, by Kikaku:

傾　郭

時鳥あかつき傘を買はせけり
Hototogisu akatsuki kasa wo kawasekeri

A Courtezan Enclosure

> A hototogisu sings;
In the dawn
> I am made to buy an umbrella.   (p. 770)

ひやひやと壁をふまへて畫寢かな   芭　蕉
Hiya-hiyato kabe wo fumaete hirune kana

A midday nap;
Putting the feet against the wall,
> It feels cool.   Bashō

Even on the hottest day, if we put our bare feet against the
wall when we are lying down, it feels cool. If you ask where
the poetry is in this verse, we can only answer, that there is
a contact with *things* here that is of the essence of poetry. It
needs, however, a great effort to work up in the mind this
experience of physical coolness into one's own poetical life.
Bashō is doing too little, according to the standards of the poetry
of all other nations, to assist the reader. Nevertheless, he has

---

[1] *Zen in English Literature.* (p. 104)

done one all-important and *unique* thing, in isolating the fact, the simple experience. He then expects us to take it and make it our own. Onitsura (1666–1738), the contemporary of Bashō said,

まことの外に俳諧なし

Without Reality [sincerity, fidelity to nature, truth] there is no haikai.

But we do not like reality just thrown in our faces, and this verse of Bashō is only the seed of which poetry is the flower.

もたいなや畫寝して聞田植唄   一 茶
Motaina ya   hirune shite kiku   taue-uta

In my mid-day nap,
I hear the song of the rice-planters,
And feel somehow ashamed of myself.   Issa

All those who work with the head only must have had this kind of uneasy feeling, an unreasonable thought of the inferiority of mental labour compared with that of the engine-driver or carpenter. There is the Buddhist story of the farmer who accused Buddha of idleness and was told, "I scatter the seeds of faith" and so on, but we cannot help thinking that the farmer was talked into silence but was not convinced. Issa's feeling is a just one. Every man must do a certain amount of physical labour every day, or suffer the spiritual consequences.

信濃路や上の上にも田うえ唄   一 茶
Shinanoji ya   ue no ue ni mo   taue-uta

The road to Shinano;
Higher and yet still higher,
The song of the rice-planters.   Issa

As the poet goes up the hill he hears the voices of the rice-planters. What are they singing,

some more humble lay,
Familiar matter of today?
Some natural sorrow, loss, or pain,
That has been, and may be again?

Whatever it may be, he climbs on, and their voices grow faint and are lost in the distance below him, but again from another terraced field above him the voice of the planters is heard. And so it goes on as he rises, fresh voices, voices above voices in a Dantean paradise of light and sound.

さゞなみにうしろ吹かる〻田植かな   太 祇
Sazanami ni   ushiro fukaruru   taue kana

Rice planting;
Ripples,
The wind blowing up behind.   Taigi

The rice-planters are planting the rice, gradually moving backwards across the expanse of water. From behind and towards them comes a wind blowing the surface of the water into ripples. The wind and the planters are in some relation which is one of opposition, of indifference, and yet of some secret harmony which strikes the poet so that he cannot help recording the scene. It is also a pictorial verse, the tufts of planted rice dotting a part of the field, while the remainder is ruffled into wavelets by the breeze. The planters form the boundary of the two areas.

我笠や田植の笠にまじりゆく   支 考
Waga kasa ya   taue no kasa ni   majiriyuku

As I move by,
My *kasa* and the *kasa* of the rice-planters
Mingle together.   Shikō

The *kasa*[1] has its own separate existence; it has nothing whatever to do with any human being. It may be placed on

[1] A plaited, umbrella-like hat.

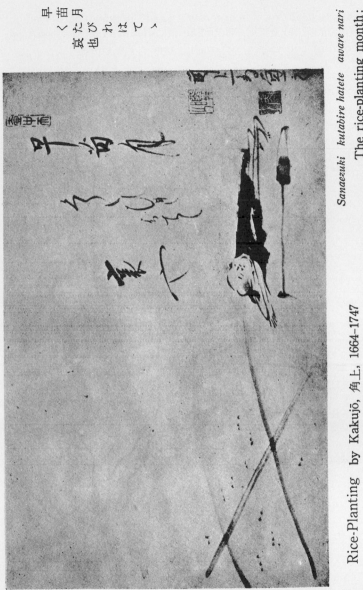

早苗月
くたびれはてゝ
哀れ也

Sanaezuki kutabire hatete aware nari

The rice-planting month;
Weary and exhausted,
He is pitiful.

Rice-Planting by Kakujō, 角上, 1664-1747

someone's head, on a scarecrow's head; it may float on a pond
or rot on a dunghill.   But like all other things, it is entirely
purposeless and exists for itself alone.   Yet since

> Now *kasa* liveth unto itself and no *kasa* dieth
> unto itself,

there is some profound, never-to-be-explained relation between
these *kasa* of the unconscious rice-planters and that of the
traveller as he passes by them forever.   It is the mind of the
poet that creates by perceiving, that perceives by creating, the
deep affinity between his own *kasa* and theirs.

風流のはじめや奥の田植唄   芭 蕉
Fūryū no   hajime ya oku no   taue-uta

The beginning of poetry:
The song of the rice-planters,
In the province of Ōshū.

Bashō

This verse is found in *Oku no Hosomichi;* it was composed
at the request of Tōkyu, 等躬, at whose house he was resting
after passing the barrier at Shirakawa.

Like Wordsworth, who thought of man as the main region
of his song, Bashō felt that without man nature was empty,
meaningless, barren, in a word, unpoetical.   It is the song
which gives life to the world.   Bashō has the same feeling,
that has not yet expressed itself in articulate thought, in *Oi
no Nikki;*

送られつ送りつ果は木曾の秋
Okurare-tsu   okuri-tsu hate wa   kiso no aki

Seeing people off,
Being seen off,—
Autumn in Kiso.

This verse, which comes in *Oi no Nikki*, is saying good-bye
to friends at Gifu.

It is the partings and separations that give meaning to
autumn.   Again at the beginning of *Oku no Hosomichi*, another
verse of farewell:

行く春や鳥啼き魚の目は涙

Yuku haru ya   tori naki uo no   me wa namida

> Departing spring;
>   Birds crying,
>   Tears in the fishes' eyes.

Here the melancholy of the traveller is ascribed to the birds
and fishes, and when we go beyond this we get Milton's words
in the Nativity Ode:

> Nature in awe to Him
>   Had doff'd her gaudy trim,
> With her great Master so to sympathize.

藪陰やたつた一人の田植唄   一 茶

Yabu-kage ya   tatta hitori no   taue-uta

> In the shade of the thicket,
> A woman by herself,
>   Singing the planting-song.   Issa

When we compare this to Wordsworth's *The Solitary Reaper*,
we feel a difference which is perhaps due partly to the dis-
similar financial condition of the two poets:

> Behold her, single in the field,
>   You solitary Highland Lass!
> Reaping and singing by herself;
>   Stop here or gently pass!
> Alone she cuts and binds the grain,
> And sings a melancholy strain;
> O listen! for the vale profound
> Is overflowing with the sound.

To Wordsworth this scene has the romantic meaning of another
world. The strange tongue, the unconsciousness of the woman,
the echoing valley intensify this feeling of mystery. For Issa,
in this rather dark paddy-field under the shade of the over-
hanging bamboos, the woman singing, though by herself, the
song that the planters all sing in unison, has a meaning that
could not be elaborated, even though he were to use Words-

worth's thirty two lines. It is not in the least romantic. It is humanity going on with its job of living, whatever happens, something that we feel in *Robinson Crusoe*. There is a selection of incidents or accompanying circumstances, but no "colouring of the imagination" thrown over them, or additions of the wayward fancy.

藪むらや貧乏馴れて夕すゞみ   一 茶
Yabumura ya   bimbō narete   yūsuzumi

An out-of-the-way hamlet;
Used to their poverty,
    They sit in the evening cool.   Issa

This has the profound compassion of Buddha in it. It is not simple pity, for Issa himself is poor. It is the realization that things are so, with the inward feeling of pathos that is pity without superiority or self-pity. The villagers sit there in their unselfconsciousness, and Issa is conscious for them, conscious, without undue emotion or intellection, of life being lived.

身の上の鐘とも知らで夕涼み   一 茶
Mi no ue no   kane to mo shirade   yūsuzumi

The evening cool,
Not knowing the bell
    Is tolling our life away.   Issa

身の上の鐘と知りつゝ夕涼み   一 茶
Mi no ue no   kane to shiritsutsu   yūsuzumi

The evening cool,
Knowing the bell
    Is tolling our life away.   Issa

These two verses express the difference between the ordinary man and the enlightened man. Both know, if they think of it, that the evening bell from the temple sounds the passing of one more day of their life. But only the enlightened man *knows*, as part of his hearing the bell, as part of every breath he draws, as part of the coolness, that all is fleeting and evanescent. Only the enlightened man enjoys this whole truth of the temporary nature of the coolness. For the unenlightened man, the coolness, the sense of well-being has for its enemy the *thought* of the transitoriness of everything. We may compare the reply of Ryūtan Sōshin 龍潭崇信, to Tennō Dōgo: 天皇道語:

見 則 直 下 便 見 、 擬 思 即 差。

Seeing is direct seeing. Hesitate and think about it, and you have gone astray.

皿鉢もほのかにやみの宵すゞみ   芭 蕉
Sara hachi mo   honokani yami no   yoisuzumi

Plates and bowls,
Faintly through the twilight,
In the evening cool.   Bashō

The vessels used at the evening meal are seen glimmering in the dusky air. But the coolness plays an important part here. Only when the mind and body are perfectly at rest can we see the infinite meanings of trivial and everyday occurrences. Bashō would have appreciated deeply Katherine Mansfield's description in *Bliss*, though this was a perception of the same thing in a moment of physical and mental excitement. Bertha was arranging the fruit, tangerines and apples, pears, and white and purple grapes:

When she had finished with them and had made two pyramids of these bright round shapes, she stood away from the table to get the effect... and it really was most curious. For the dark table seemed to melt into the dusky light, and the glass dish and the blue bowl to float in the air.

夕涼みあぶなき石にのぼりけり　　　　野坡

Yūsuzumi　abunaki ishi ni　noborikeri

> Evening coolness;
> Climbing onto
> A dangerous rock.　　　　Yaha

This kind of verse is very simple, almost too shallow and psychological to be called poetry. The poet climbs on to a high and dangerous rock, perhaps near the sea-shore, in order to sit there on the top to be cool in the hot summer evening. The danger of it causes him to shudder a little, and this feeling of danger and the feeling of coolness unite in him and are not to be distinguished. If we push the matter far enough we can say that there is here also a kind of harmony perceived, but it is too vague to be of great significance.

月と我ばかり殘りぬ橋涼み　　　　菊舍尼

Tsuki to ware　bakari nokorinu　hashisuzumi

> The cool on the bridge;
> The moon and I
> Alone remain.　　　　Kikusha-ni

Hashisuzumi, means literally, "cooling on the bridge," standing or sitting on the bridge on a hot summer evening to catch the breeze, if any, that comes up the river. If a man can take the moon for his friend, the sun for his children, what more can he want?

The above verse is reminiscent of a Chinese poem by Ōi, 王維, entitled *The Bamboo Arbour:*

竹里館

獨坐幽篁裏、　彈琴復長嘯、
深林人不知、　明月來相照。

Sitting alone in the depths of the bamboo thicket,
At times I play the lute, at times hum a melody.
None know of these far-off woods;
Together with me, the moon comes and shines.

夕涼みよくぞ男に生れたる   其 角
Yūsuzumi   yoku zo otoko ni   umaretaru

> The evening cool;
> How glad I am
> I was born a man!   Kikaku

What Kikaku meant was that being born a man enabled him
to sit practically naked and cool himself in the evening breeze.
But in addition, there is the fact that to be born a man instead
of a woman is as much a matter of congratulation as being
born a man instead of a giraffe.

湯上りや乳房吹かるゝ端涼み   子 規
Yuagari ya   chibusa fukaruru   hashisuzumi

> Coming out of the bath,
> The wind blows on the nipples;[1]
> Cooling on the verandah.   Shiki

Though this is not poetry, it shows vividly the sensitivity
of the haiku poets, both to the physical sensations, and (what
is the same thing at bottom) the possibility of poetical meaning
in them.

星の名をよく知る人や門涼   子 規
Hoshi no na wo   yoku shiru hito ya   kadosuzumi

> Cooling at the gate,
> There was a man who knew well
> The names of the stars.   Shiki

The poetical point of this is not easy to put into words. The
poet is sitting outside his gate in the summer dusk, together
with several neighbours and other people. One of them tells
the names of the stars, of which everyone else is almost entirely
ignorant. As they sit there in the starlight listening to the
man speaking, the poet gets a sensation very similar to that

[1] Literally "breasts."

of Wordsworth when he was listening to the old leech-gatherer.
A similar verse by the same author is:

或る人の平家びいきや夕涼み
Aru hito no   heike-biiki ya   yūsuzumi

> Cooling in the evening,
> A certain man
> Favouring the Heike.

Most people sympathize with the Genji, but this man was a
partizan of the Heike and this gave a spice of novelty to his
talk.

夏痩と答へてあとは涙かな   季　吟
Natsuyase to   kotaete ato wa   namida kana

> "It is summer thinness," she replied,—
> And then
>   The tears fell.   Kigin

The young girl, deeply in love, is asked by her friend why
she is so pale and thin. She answers that it is merely the heat,
but the tears start from her eyes, revealing the truth.

What a medley of emotions here! The tears spring from the
shamefulness of telling a lie, tears of unrequited love, even of
a subconscious feeling that it is all

> An expense of spirit in a waste of shame.

And in all this apparent lack of Zen, there is something living,
something alive, something that will not submit to be named,
that hides when we question it, that, like the girl, denies when
it is accused.

The concluding verse of Edna St. Vincent Millay's *Departure*
is very similar to Kigin's verse, but more restrained:

> "Is there something the matter dear," she said,
> "That you sit at your work so silently?"
> "No, mother, no, 'twas but a knot in my thread.
> There goes the kettle, I'll make the tea."

There is a verse by Issa in which the poet has found in nature

also what he experiences, and the pleasure of this recognition
we call humour, but how much deeper it goes than any mysti-
cism or transcendentalism.

我庵は草の夏痩したりけり
Waga io wa   kusa no natsuyase   shitarikeri

    The grass round my hut also,
Has suffered
    From summer thinness.

和歌に痩せ俳句にやせぬ夏男   子 規
Waka ni yase   haiku ni yaseru   natsu otoko

    One man this summer
Getting thin over waka,
    And over haiku.   Shiki

Shiki is here speaking of himself. He was one of the greatest
writers of haiku, but his waka are not nearly so good; it was
with considerable effort that he composed either. Another verse
by Shiki concerning getting thin in summer is the following:

夏痩の骨にとゞまる命かな
Natsu yase no   hone ni todomaru   inochi kana

    Summer thinness;
My life saved
    At my bones.

This was composed on getting up after a long bout of illness.
He means that he got thinner and thinner, until all his flesh
was gone, and because only bones were left, he could not get
any thinner, and could hardly therefore die.

雨乞や天に響けと打つ太皷   子 規
Amagoi ya   ten ni hibike to   utsu taiko

    Prayers for rain:
Rise up to heaven
    O beating drums!   Shiki

In times of drought, special clothes were worn, drums were

beaten, and prayers offered, especially at mountain shrines. Customs vary in different parts of the country. In some places fires are lit on the tops of hills and various ceremonies are performed there. The drums are beaten and there is a feeling that the reverberation will be communicated to the clouds, and they will break and pour forth the rain. Such a verse as this belongs to a very primitive world of feeling, a life that is lost to us, and for which we have no substitute.

山も庭もうごき入るゝや夏座敷　　芭蕉

Yama mo niwa mo　ugoki-iruru ya　natsuzashiki

Included
In the summer drawing-room.
The mountains and the garden also move.

Bashō

Bashō composed this verse in admiration of the beautiful scenery from the house of Shūa, 秋鴉, about whom practically nothing is known. When Bashō says that the mountains and the garden "move," he means that they are full of life, of aesthetic as well as natural life. "The summer drawing-room includes them," means that the room puts the mountains and the garden into itself, in this living, palpitating state. The verse is a fine expression of the ideal of Japanese gardens, which are to be walked in though we never leave the house.

There are verses by both earlier and later poets for example, Sōin and Tōrin, more or less on the same subject, but none of them have the power and particularity of Bashō's.

芝というものの候夏座敷

Shiba to iu　mono no sōro　natsu-zashiki

The grass,—
How wonderful it is!
The summer drawing-room.

樹も石も有の儘たり夏座敷

Ki mo ishi mo　ari no mama tari　natsu-zashiki

Trees and stones,
Just as they are,—
The summer drawing-room.

とも綱に蟹の子並ぶ遊泳かな　　　　子 規
Tomozuna ni　kani no ko　narabu　oyogi kana

Swimming about,
Little crabs aligned
On the hawser.　　　　　　　　Shiki

As a poetic composition, we may admire the brevity, the justness, the objectivity of this verse. As a poetic experience, what is noteworthy is the way in which the ego suddenly dissolves into the larger life through, it may be, small and insignificant creatures with a life much poorer than our own. The sweetness and light of their existence is suddenly apparent to us, but the suddenness has nothing shocking in it. In fact, it is only the poet who notices the poetic experience which everyone has. This is what distinguishes not only the poet but the Buddha from the ordinary man, the simple but far-reaching fact that the Buddha, the poet, knows that the activity within and around him is the Buddha activity, the poetic life. He knows this, not in the purely intellectual sense, but in the way that a man in love knows that he is in love; and this knowledge is not something outside the feeling, but leavens, deepens, and universalizes it.

がさがさに粽をかぢる美人かな　　　一 茶
Gasa-gasa ni　chimaki wo kajiru　bijin kana

The beautiful girl,
Munching and rustling
The wrapped-up rice-cake.　　　　Issa

A *chimaki* is a rice-dumpling wrapped in the sheaths of the bamboo shoot. This is an example of what Aldous Huxley calls "the whole truth," not a romantic abstraction, the truth which he finds in Homer, and in none of the moderns. Yet it is not an example of "debunking." The girl is no less pretty than she always is. Another example, by Buson:

さくら狩美人の腹や滅却す
Sakuragari   bijin no hara ya   mekkyaku su

> Going to see the cherry blossoms,
> The beautiful girl
> Looks hungry.

旅寝して香わるき草の蚊遣かな　　　　　　　去　來
Tabine shite   ka waruki kusa no   kayari kana

> A lodging for the night;
> Mosquito smudge
> From rank weeds.   Kyorai

This is an example of the fact that pain is more profitable, that is, has more meaning, than pleasure. Just as

> There is more joy in heaven over one sinner that
>   repenteth,

so the strong smell of weeds is more signicant than the sweetest perfumes of Arabia.

一日のけふも蚊遣のけむりかな　　　　　　　蕪　村
Ichinichi no   kyō mo kayari no   kemuri kana

> Today, another day also,
> In the smoke
> Of the mosquito smudge.   Buson

In some districts, mosquitoes are busy with their victims not only at night but all day long. The mosquito smudge may have to be lit at any time in the day. Evening is falling and the poet has lit some dried leaves to make the smudge. It rises slowly, in wreaths of its own making, up into the purple sky, clouding the first faint stars of night. A few insects twitter and tweet. A frog chuckles in the distance. One more day, that was called today, disappears like smoke in the air, never to return.

The poet sits watching the smoke, how it eddies and then rises upwards. To say that human life is only a dream and vanishes like this smoke, is to say too much; is to say something that the poet is not experiencing. It is today, and all the things of today, that is passing. The smoke is only a part, a visible part of everything that is changing every moment.

蚊いぶしも慰になるひとり哉　　　　　一　茶
Ka-ibushi mo　nagusame ni naru　hitori kana

The mosquito smudge
Is also a consolation,
　　Being alone.　　　　　　　　　　Issa

Fire, and smoke, are mysterious things. Like the flowing of water, their movement and noise gives them an appearance of life, of will and purpose, which many living creatures lack. Issa sits watching the evening fall. The stillness and silence become almost unbearable, and he collects some leaves and sticks and weeds to make a mosquito smudge. A yellow flame appears and disappears, twigs sizzle and crack, smoke seeps through the rubbish and rises into the air, disappearing above the house. Issa feels not entirely alone. Through all the quietness and monotony there is the comfort of change in the flame that flickers, and the smoke that wreathes and sways.

蚊遣火の煙の末に鳴く蚊かな　　　　白　雄
Kayaribi no　kemuri no sue ni　naku ka kana

Just outside the smoke
Of the smudge,
　　Mosquitoes are humming.　　　　Shirao

This is a pleasantly objective verse, in which however we feel the power of nature that is held in feeble and temporary check.

大津繪の赤鬼いぶる蚊遣哉   子 規
Otsu-e no   aka-oni iburu   kayari kana

The red demon in the Otsu Picture[1]
Is being smoked out
By the mosquito smudge.   Shiki

There is only an accidental relation between the smoke of
the mosquito smudge and the picture of the red demon hung
on the wall, around which it is rising. However, nothing is
accidental, but thinking makes it so. What is purposeful and
what is accidental, even in purely human affairs,— who can
decide? The lurid picture of the ferocious demon gives life
and meaning to the swirling smoke. The smoke makes real and
tangible the devil that gnashes his teeth in the picture. The
humour of the verse is in thinking of the demon as being
smoked out like a mosquito.

手をすりて蚊帳の小隅を借りにけり   一 茶
Te wo surite   kaya no kosumi wo   kari ni keri

Rubbing my hands together beseechingly,
They let me have a small corner
Of the mosquito net.   Issa

Issa has something very Shakespearean about him sometimes.
This verse, in which his own struggles are portayed so vividly,
speaks for all humanity. Poor and rich, tyrant and slave, we
all have to rub our hands and bow and scrape to something or
somebody. During his thirty six years of wandering after he
left home, Issa tasted humble pie on many a day.

This verse is an example of most haiku, whose authors we
must know, in the deep sense of the word, before we can pro-
perly appreciate their work.

[1] A certain kind of very cheap and rather crude picture produced
in Otsu, from about 250 years ago, the commonest subject being that
of demons.

人もなし子一人寝たる蚊帳の中   子 規
Hito mo nashi   ko hitori netaru   kaya no naka

> Nobody there;
> A child asleep
> In the mosquito-net.   Shiki

Strangely enough, the mosquito-net, like a road, where people also associate, is a symbol of loneliness and grief.   Another verse by Shiki with this same significance:

君を送りて思ふ事あり蚊帳に泣く
Kimi wo okurite   omou koto ari   kaya ni naku

> Seeing you off,
> I had thoughts of grief,
> And wept in the mosquito net.

尼寺やよき蚊帳たるる宵月夜   蕪 村
Amadera ya   yoki kaya taruru   yoizukiyo

> A nunnery:
> A fine mosquito net hanging;
> An early evening moon.   Buson

Near Kyōto there are or used to be many Buddhist "nun-temples," and here the widows of great warriors would spend their remaining years.   One summer evening Buson passes through one of these temples.   The moon is shining brightly into a room where a beautiful mosquito net is already hung for the night.   It is made of some silky material, quite different from the common hemp ones.   The nun asleep within, her shaven head white in the moonlight, a calm, noble face,—these things may be imagined, though not seen.   The evening, the moon, the nun, the mosquito net are all in quiet harmony.

逃るなり紙魚が中にも親と子よ   一 茶
Nigeru nari   shimi ga naka ni mo   oya to ko yo

> The silver-fish
> Are running away, among them,
> Parents and children.   Issa

Silver-fish are small white insects that "infest" clothes, books and pictures, paper screens and papered cupboards. They are rather charming-looking creatures, and as Issa carries out clothes and boxes from the cupboards to dry in the sun (this is the season of 虫干, summer airing), he sees them, large and small, running hither and thither to save their lives. They are like people during an earthquake, running out of danger into danger, mother and child looking for each other and finding only death. Issa does not suppose the insects are actually parents and children, nor does he wish us to do so. He only strives to stir our sluggish feelings into compassion with these living creatures, and does it by stirring our maternal, paternal, filial sentiments so that they may overflow to these little animals also. Such thoughts and feelings are the beginnings of religion and poetry; they are equally the end and consummation, the flower of religion and poetry. Another example by Issa, also of animal life, is the following:

鵜も親子鵜飼も親子二人かな
U mo oyako   ukai mo oyako   futari kana

Cormorants,
And cormorant fishers, too,
Parent and child.

Issa carries this human feeling into the plant world, as shown in the verse quoted before:

我庵は草も夏痩したりけり
Waga io wa   kusa mo natsuyase   shitarikeri

The grass round my hut also,
Has suffered
From summer thinness.

鵜と共に心は水をくぐりゆく　　　鬼貫
U to tomo ni   kokoro wa mizu wo   kuguriyuku

My soul
Dived in and out of the water
With the cormorant.　　Onitsura

This rather talks *about* the thing than shows us the thing

itself. The real subject of the poem is the mind of the poet. It agrees with the anecdote of the Sixth Patriarch in the *Rokusodangyō*:

值印宗法師講涅槃經、 時有風吹旛動、
一僧曰風動、 一僧曰旛動、 議論不已、
慧能進曰、 不是風動、 不是旛動、
仁者心動。

In those days, Inju was preaching on the *Nehan-gyō*. At a certain time a flag was waving in the breeze. One monk said, "The wind is moving," another said, "The flag is moving," and the argument was endless. Enō said, "The wind is not moving, the flag is not moving; what is moving is your minds."

面白うてやがて悲しき鵜船哉　　　　　芭 蕉
Omoshirōte　yagate kanashiki　ubune kana

How exciting, the cormorant fishing-boat!
But after a time,
　　I felt saddened.[1]　　　　　　　　　Bashō

"Bashō does not tell us what made him sad. Was it pity for the fish? for the cormorants forced to regurgitate what they had swallowed? for the men engaged in such a labour of preying on the greediness of the birds? or for humanity in its endless desire and craving? The simplest and best answer is that Bashō himself did not know. It was

"Tears, idle tears, I know not what they mean." [2]

Some critics, however, take the above kind of "sympathetic" interpretation as explanatory, as meaningless and vulgar. They say that Bashō is recording the reaction he felt after the boats

---

[1] There is an apparently earlier version,
　　面白うてやがてなかるゝ鵜ぶねかな
where we have "weeping" instead of "sad."
[2] *Zen in English Literature.* (p. 409)

had passed by, and all the excitement was over. This inter-
pretation might be called trivial and psychological. The truth
is that the verse, though undoubtedly interesting, is not great
poetry at all. However, there can be no doubt, I think, that
Bashō's humanitarian feelings were stirred. As indirect evi-
dence of this we may quote the following haiku of Bashō:

振賣の雁あはれなりえびす講
Furiuri no   kari aware nari   ebisukō

> The hawker's geese
> Are pitiful:
> Fēte of Ebisu.

初時雨猿も小みのをほしげなり
Hatsushigure   saru mo komino wo   hoshige nari

> The first rain of winter:
> The monkey also seems to want
> A straw coat.

草枕犬もしぐるゝか夜の聲
Kusa-makura   inu mo shigururu ka   yoru no koe

> A poor lodging;
> The whimpering of the dog
> In the rain at night.

毛衣につゝみてぬくし鴨の足
Kekoromo ni   tsutsumite nukushi   kamo no ashi

> The legs of the wild ducks
> Are snug and warm
> In wooly clothes.

よき家や雀よろこぶ背戸の粟
Yoki ie ya   suzume yorokobu   sedo no awa

> A nice house:
> The sparrows are happy at the millet
> In the field at the back.

鷹の目もいまや暮れぬと啼く鶉
Taka no me mo   ima ya kurenu to   naku uzura

> Now that the eyes of the hawks
> Are darkened,
> The quails are chirping.

稲雀茶の木ばたけや逃げ處
Inasuzume   chanokibatake ya   nigedokoro

> The tea plantation
> Is a haven of refuge
> For the harvest sparrows.

We may quote the two following passage from the Nō play
Cormorant Fishing, 鵜飼, and suggest that they may have been
in Bashō's mind when composing the above verse:

隈なく魚を食ふ時は罪も報も後の世も
わすれはてゝ面白や

> O how pleasant, when the cormorants vigilantly
> swallow the fish, forgetting completely the sin and
> punishment in the world to come!

鵜舟に燈す篝火の消えて闇こそかなしけれ

> The fire on the fishing-boat goes out; how sad
> is the darkness!

鵜の面に川波かゝる火影かな   楢良
U no tsura ni   kawa-nami kakaru   hokage kana

> On the faces of the cormorants
> Splash waves,
> > Glittering with light.   Chora

We may compare this picture with the verse of an earlier
poet, Kakei:

鵜のつらに篝こぼれて哀也
U no tsura ni   kagari koborete   aware nari

> How pitiful!
> The torches drip
> On the faces of the cormorants.

The latter verse is too painful. It is like the blinding of
Edgar. It is one of those things that poetry sees and is silent
about, not because it lacks courage, or because it wishes to
whitewash the universe, but because,—well, for some other
reason.

暁や鵜籠に眠る鵜の疲れ   子 規
Akatsuki ya   u-kago ni nemuru   u no tsukare

Morning twilight;
In their basket, the cormorants
Asleep, exhausted.   Shiki

This is indeed a scene to touch a tender heart, but how many there will be to pass by, like the Levite, on the other side, without a second glance. What can be done to soften the heart, to enable them to reap

The harvest of a quiet eye,

to feel the Buddhist compassion? Nothing, perhaps. For other reasons, more indirect, mankind grows more sensitive, more subtle, more conscious of other living creatures. It may be that the best way to communicate our tender feelings to others is by more vigorous, aggressive methods, such as De la Mare employs in the following verse:

Hi! handsome hunting man,
Fire your little gun.
Bang! Now the animal
Is dead and dumb and gone.
Never more to peep again, creep again, leap again,
Eat or sleep or drink again, oh, what fun!

But poetry but rarely uses this means. It usually understates, changes the subject, reveals its most painful feelings by its silence.

老なりし鵜飼ことしは見えぬかな   蕪 村
Oinarishi   ukai kotoshi wa   mienu kana

The cormorant keeper,
Grown old,
Is not to be seen this year.   Buson

We all, without exception, have an illusion of the permanence of things. It stays with us all our life, because things change so imperceptibly that there seems to be a general stable state of things. The world consists of babies, young people, adults, old men, dead men, and this never changes, but we forget that one is replacing the other incessantly. Every year the same festival takes place, every year there is the same cormorant fishing at the same place. Only sometimes, as here, we notice with a shock that someone has gone, never to return. That old man, who last year was so skilful at controlling the birds, who for many years was admired by the spectators, — this year is absent. The illusion is swept away for a moment and we see things as they really are, of no self-existence.

しのゝめや鵜をのがれたる魚淺し   蕪 村
Shinonome ya   u wo nogaretaru   uo asashi

The dawn of day;
The fish that have escaped the cormorants
Are shallow.   Buson

The last line may mean "the fish are in the shallows," but more probably, "the fish are near the surface of the water." The meaning of this verse is not in the sympathy with the fishes that have escaped the horrible beaks of the voracious cormorants. Or rather, it is this emotion recollected, that is, transformed and recreated in tranquillity, *into* a kind of tranquillity, which surveys these things *sub specie aeternitatis*, and yet also *sub specie temporis*.

雨にもゆる鵜飼が宿の蚊遺哉   蕪 村
Ame ni moyuru   ukai ga yado no   kayari kana

Burning in the rain,
The mosquito smudge
Of the cormorant fisher.   Buson

As it is raining the cormorant fisher cannot ply his trade, and he has lit a mosquito smudge to drive away the mosquitoes. It burns, or rather smoulders, in spite of the rain. The life of the cormorant fisher is made of fire and water, the torches burning so that he can see what he is doing, and to attract the fish. Even when he is not at work, rain and smoke are his portion.

鵜 の 眞 似 を 鵜 よ り 巧 者 な 子 供 哉　　　一 茶
U no mane wo　u yori kōsha na　kodomo kana

The child's imitation
Is more wonderful
Then the real cormorant.　　　Issa

This can hardly be called a poem, but it contains a real intuition of great interest and value. It is not in itself poetical, because it stands quite apart from child and bird, and compares the two dispassionately. That is to say, it is simply the statement of the result of the comparison of the intuitions, one of the bird itself and one of the child's imitation of it. Either would be or might be poetry when expressed, but Issa has simply declared that, to his surprise, the imitation had a deeper meaning for him than the real thing. And notice why this is. The life of the bird is worked up in the mind and body of the child so that its real nature, the nature of the cormorant is made visible and tangible. Beside this, the cormorant nature of the child is also apparent. In other words, the common nature, the Buddha nature of things is manifested in an easily apprehensible way. This is what poetry *is*. Man in the likeness of God, God in the likeness of man, of a cormorant, of a child imitating a cormorant,—this is the meaning and value of things; they have no other.

鮓 壓 し て 暫 く 淋 し き 心 か な　　　蕪 村
Sushi oshite　shibaraku sabishiki　kokoro kana

Pressing *sushi*;
After a while,
A feeling of loneliness.　　　Buson

It is astounding what subjects the haiku poets choose, how they feel the quiver of poetic life in the most unlikely places. *Sushi* is salted fish pressed for some time and eaten with rice.

Boat in a Creek by Kakei, 夏珪, a Chinese painter of the Southern Sung.

From whence does this feeling of loneliness come? It comes, and that is enough, whether it is by silent sympathy with the heavy stones pressing it down, or the suggestion of time passing, or the thought of the person for whom it is being prepared. Buson has written quite a number of verses on this subject, all rather difficult to understand. One of the less obscure is:

なれ過た鮓を主の恨哉
Naresugita   sushi wo aruji no   urami kana

At the over-matured *sushi*,
The master
Is full of regret.

The seasoning and maturing of *sushi* is a very delicate operation, and after specially inviting a guest, the master of the house finds to his chagrin that the *sushi* has been left too long. His feeling is no different from that which he would have if he found that the flowers in the vase had wilted.

麥刈つて遠山見せよ窓の前   蕪 村
Mugi katte   tōyama mise yo   mado no mae

Cut the oats in front of the window!
Let me see
The distant mountains!   Buson

Buson remembered perhaps the poem of Hakurakuten:

截　樹

種樹當前軒、　樹高柯葉繁。
惜哉遠山色、　隱此蒙籠間。
一朝持斧斤、　手自截其端。
萬葉落頭上、　千峰來面前。
忽似決雲霧、　豁達覩青天。
又如所念人、　久別一欵顏。
始有清風至﹑　稍見飛鳥還。
開懷東南望、　目遠心遼然。
人各有偏好、　物莫能兩全。
豈不愛柔條、　不如見青山。

CUTTING DOWN TREES

The trees that were planted have reached the eaves
  in the front.
As they grew taller, the branches and leaves were
  luxuriant.
I missed the forms of the distant hills,
Hidden under this thick screen of leaves.
One morning, I took an axe
And cut them down in one place.
A myriad leaves fell about my head,
But a thousand peaks appeared before my eyes.
It was like the clouds and mists suddenly opening,
And seeing the expanse of blue heaven,
Like being confronted with the friend we have
  yearned for
After long years of separation.
First a cool breeze flows in;
Now at last I see the birds fly back to their nests.
My soul is enlarged; I gaze southward and east-
  ward;
My eyes look into the distance; my heart is calmed.
Every man has his own peculiar bent;
We cannot have our cake and eat it too.
It is not that I do not love the tender branches,—
But ah, the blue hills!

夕にも朝にもつかず瓜の花   芭 蕉
Yūbe ni mo   asa ni mo tsukazu   uri no hana

It belongs
Neither to morning nor to evening
The flower of the melon.   Bashō

The morning glory belongs to the morning, and the evening
glory to the evening, but the flower of the melon does not
come into either category, and thus has something pathetic
about it; it seems to have nothing to depend on. This verse
is an example of Bashō's extraordinary sensitiveness to the
most trivial-seeming aspects of nature. But it is poetry, it is

the poetical world. This we can easily verify by comparing it
with a verse by Yayu that has no poetical, but only a hard,
intellectual life:

昼顔やどちらの露も間にあはず
Hirugao ya　dochira no tsuyu mo　maniawazu

　　The midday glory,
Not in time
　　For either dew.

朝露によごれて涼し瓜の泥　　　　　　　芭蕉
Asatsuyu ni　yogorete suzushi　uri no doro

　　The melons look cool,
Flecked with mud
　　From the morning dew.[1]　　　Bashō

Such poems as these baffle the commentator. All he might
say is legs to the snake, horns to the rabbit, for these lines
bring us as close to the thing-in-itself as possible. Immediately
we explain it, the wave recedes, leaving us with dry prose.

西瓜ひとり野分を知らぬあしたかな　　　素堂
Suika hitori　nowaki wo shiranu　ashita kana

　　The morning after the storm;
The melons alone
　　Know nothing of it.　　　Sodō

The melons, from their heaviness, are not blown about by
the autumn whirlwind, and the next morning, in their round
smoothness, they look complacent and unaware of the violent
tempest which was raging the night before. This verse express
the nature of two things, by contrast.

---

[1] Another, earlier version has 瓜ノ土, "earth," instead of "mud."

盗人の見るともしらで冷し瓜   一 茶

Nusubito no   miru to mo shirade   hiyashi uri

Oblivious
Of the gaze of the thief,—
Melons in cool.   Issa

The essential immobility, imperturbability of the melons being cooled in cold water is here grasped and expressed through the contrast with the greediness of the would-be thief, probably Issa himself. Man, and the world of things he is in, are brought before the single eye of the mind.

人來たら蛙となれよ冷し瓜   一 茶

Hito kitara   kawazu to nare yo   hiyashi uri

If anyone comes,
Turn into frogs,
O cooling melons!   Issa

Issa has just put some melons into a tub of water outside the house, to cool them. As they float on the surface of the water, their green bellies remind him of frogs, just at the moment that he has a feeling of hesitation, of uneasiness, at leaving them unguarded. This momentary see-sawing of the mind makes the notion of melons turning into frogs more than merely fanciful. The humour also, joins where it seems to separate.

去年まで叱つた瓜を手向けり   大江丸

Kyonen made   shikatta uri wo   tamuke keri

The melons
I scolded him about last year,
I now offer to his spirit.   Ōemaru

Only last year he scolded his son for eating the melons. This year he offers them at the family altar for the repose of his soul. Everything is usable in every way. Good or bad, holy or unholy, profitable or unprofitable—these qualities do not even in the slightest degree inhere in the things themselves:

The stone of stumbling is made the chief of the corner.

草いきれ人死居ると札の立   蕪　村
Kusa ikire   hito shini oruto   fuda no tatsu

Hot, rank grasses;
A notice-board standing there:
Someone has died.   Buson

Some person has fallen ill and died by the wayside. His name and a description are written on a roughly-made notice-board stuck up by the side of the road. The body itself is not visible, but all around the summer grasses are growing rank and lush as though in a churchyard.

青梅に眉集めたる美人哉   蕪　村
Aoume ni   mayu atsumetaru   bijin kana

Green plums;
The eyebrows of the beauty
Are gathered together.   Buson

This verse has several explanations. The translation given above adopts the view that it is the picture of some beautiful woman or women eating a kind of pickle made from plums, salted. These are new and especially sour and sharp, and the black, clearly marked (because shaven at the edges) eyebrows of the beautiful creatures are drawn together as if in pain. In this case "atsumetaru" is used in a figurative or at least unusual sense. Another, more romantic explanation of the original, which the translation also can bear, with "beauty" as "beauties," is that several beautiful young women are met together under a plum tree in summer. In this case "gathered eyebrows" is an example of synechdoche. Both are interesting, both are poetical. If we wish to support the first, we may quote, rather convincingly, another of Buson's:

青梅に打鳴す歯や貝のおと
Aoume ni   uchinarasu ha ya   kai no oto

> The tooth grating
> On the green plum,—
> It sounds like a shell.

To support the second view, we may quote, not so convincingly:

梨の花月に書よむ女あり
Nashi no hana   tsukini fumi yomu   onna ari

> A pear-tree in bloom;
> In the moonlight,
> A woman reading a letter.

Kimura, 木村架空, in his 蕪村夢物語, makes the suggestion, and a very good one, that the girl does not actually eat or taste the pickled plum but only looks at it, and frowns at the mere thought of the sourness. He quotes, or rather refers to the 32nd case of the *Mumonkan*, where at the end, the Buddha says of the quick understanding of truth by a non-Buddhist:

如世良馬見鞭影而行。

> He is like a splendid horse that, seeing the shadow
> of the whip, starts off.

He then applies this to the former verse, "The tooth grating," but this is quite inappropriate here. In regard to the original verse, the first explanation is undoubtedly better.

動　物　BIRDS AND BEASTS

時鳥啼くや有磯の波がしら　　　　　　　　暁　臺
Hototogisu　naku ya ariso no　nami-gashira

A *hototogisu* cries:
On the wild shore,
　　Foamy wave-crests.　　　　　　　　Gyōdai

Ariso, 有磯, means rough beach, 荒磯. This haiku is unusual
in combining the *hototogisu* with the wilder aspects of nature.
It reminds us of Keats' nightingale, and

　　Magic casements opening on the foam
　　Of perilous seas, in faery lands forlorn.

A somewhat similar verse by Shirao, 1735–1792, Gyōdai's con-
temporary:

時鳥啼くや夜明けの海が鳴る
Hototogisu　naku ya yoake no　umi ga naru

　　A *hototogisu* cries;
　　The sea roars
　　　In the dawn.

But this is much inferior to the former; it has no point of rest
in the commotion.

ほとゝぎす大竹藪をもる月夜　　　　　　　芭　蕉
Hototogisu　ōtake yabu wo　moru tsukiyo

Moonlight slants through
The vast bamboo grove:
　　A *hototogisu* cries.　　　　　　　　Bashō

　It is said that even now there are great bamboo groves
around the place where once Kyorai's villa stood at Saga.
Bashō spent two weeks here in April, in the fourth year of
Genroku (1692).
　The *hototogisu* corresponds more or less to the English cuckoo.
The breast of the male is blackish, with white blotches.　The

breast of the female is white, the inside of the mouth red; it
has a crest of hair on the head. The legs are greenish. It
does not make a nest of its own, but borrows that of the *uguisu*.
From early summer, it sings day and night, and ceases in
autumn. It is said to vomit blood and die after it has sung
eight thousand and eight times.

月 の 出 の 草 に 風 吹 く 時 鳥　　　　　　子 規
Tsuki no de no　kusa ni kaze fuku　hototogisu

> The moon arising,
> There is wind in the grass;
> A *hototogisu* sings.　　　　Shiki

Over the mountains the moon appears; a gust of wind moves
the summer grasses, the sound already a little dry and melan-
choly. In the distance, a *hototogisu* suddenly breaks into song.
The combination of sight and touch and sound is perfect, is
complete; nothing more is required. In the succeeding still-
ness, the moon climbs higher and higher into the sky.

これ は さ て 寝 耳 に 水 の 時 鳥　　　　一 茶
Kore wa sate　nemimi ni mizu no　hototogisu

> Struck all of a heap,—
> Bless my soul!
> The voice of the *hototogisu*.　　　　Issa

It is interesting to compare the Zen of Issa (a fervent believer
of the Shin sect) with the "poetry" of Shiki in the following
verse:

提 灯 で 大 佛 見 る や 時 鳥
Chōchin de　daibutsu miru ya　hototogisu

> Gazing at the Great Buddha
> In the light of the lantern,—
> The voice of the *hototogisu!*

Issa's verse is apparently subjective, but where is the *hototogisu*
if not within Issa himself. In Shiki's poem, the feeling is more

diffused, in the lantern he holds up, in the majestic figure of the Buddha with all its lineaments changed by the underneath lighting.

郭公いかに鬼神もたしかにきけ　　　　宗因
Hototogisu　ika ni kijin mo　tashika ni kike

A *hototogisu!*
Gods though ye be,
O listen!　　　　　　　　　Sōin

"Kijin" means literally "demon gods." Sōin has taken the last two lines bodily from the Nō play *Tamura*. Sakanoue Tamuramaro, 坂上田村麿, 758–811, was ordered to suppress the Ebisu in an expedition against them in 801 A.D. It was to them he uttered the words of the verse. The song of the *hototogisu* has this strong and martial sound, and though the verse is humorous, like most early haiku (Sōin lived 1604–82), there is also some expression of the nature of the song of the bird, and a eulogy of it.

時鳥なきなきとぶぞ忙しき　　　　芭蕉
Hototogisu　naki naki tobu zo　isogashiki

The *hototogisu*,
Singing, flying, singing,—
What a busy life!　　　　　Bashō

The difference between the *hototogisu* and us is that the bird is always busy being a bird, and we are so seldom busy being human beings. The table is completely occupied in being a table for twenty four hours a day. It never feels bored, dissatisfied or undecided. Issa has a subjective verse on it:

せはしさを我にうつすな時鳥
Sewashisa wo　ware ni utsusu na　hototogisu

Hototogisu!
Do not let me catch
Your busyness!

But Issa also is expressing the energy and vitality of the bird through his pretended warning.

時鳥啼くや五尺のあやめ草　　　　　　芭　蕉
Hototogisu　naku ya goshaku no　ayamegusa

The voice of the *hototogisu*,
And the five-foot
Irises.　　　　　　　　　　　　　　　　Bashō

The sharp spears of the irises and the shrill voice of the *hototogisu* are in harmony.　Form and timbre say the same thing.

這渡る橋の下よりほとゝぎす　　　　　一　茶
Haiwataru　hashi no shita yori　hototogisu

Creeping over the hanging bridge;
From beneath it
The voice of the *hototogisu*.　　　　Issa

Deep in the mountains, the ravine is crossed by a hanging bridge of ropes and chains.　The poet creeps carefully over it, and as he reaches the middle where it sways most, from far below a *hototogisu* suddenly breaks into song, emphasizing the depth of the abyss and filling his heart with terror and joy.

ほとゝぎす消行く方へ島一つ　　　　　芭　蕉
Hototogisu　kieyuku kata e　shima hitotsu

The cry of a *hototogisu*,
Vanishing towards
A solitary island.　　　　　　　　　　Bashō

There is a unity here of the sound of the bird's cry, its movement through space, and the distant scene, a unity so perfect that it can be said that we hear the far-off island, we see the voice of the *hototogisu*.　There is an ancient waka by Sanesada, 實定, 1139-91, of similar import:

ほとゝぎす鳴きつる方をながむれば
たゞ有明の　　　月ぞ殘れる

        Gazing where
    A *hototogisu*
        Had cried,
        Only there remained
        The moon of early dawn.

ほとゝぎす平安城を筋違に　　　　　　　蕪　村
Hototogisu　heianjō wo　sujikai ni

    Ah! the *hototogisu*
Has flown athwart
    Heian Castle!　　　　　　　　　　　Buson

"Heian Castle" means Kyōto, the ancient capital of Japan. This poem is therefore a wonderful example of hyperbole. In addition, Kyōto was built almost exactly four square, and we get a geometrical picture of the bird flying over a diagonal of it. The *hototogisu* of course cries as it flies across the city.

時鳥あかつき傘を買はせけり　　　　　　其　角
Hototogisu　akatsuki kasa wo　kawasekeri

    A *hototogisu* cries;
The dawn makes me buy
    An umbrella.　　　　　　　　　　　Kikaku

Kikaku is about to come back from the Yoshiwara in the early morning. As he stands at the door, a nightingale in a nearby thicket suddenly sings, and at the same time drops of rain begin to fall, and he is compelled to buy an umbrella. The expression, in the second and third lines, of the overlapping of the dawn and the shower, and of the omnipotence of nature in regard to mankind, reminds us of Lyly, *Spring's Welcome:*

    Brave prick-song! Who is't now we hear?
    None but the lark so shrill and clear;

Now at heaven's gates she claps her wings,
The morn not waking till she sings.

Kikaku's verse is rather too *recherché*; it smacks of the wit of
the place he is just leaving.

ほとゝぎす聲横たふや水の上   芭蕉
Hototogisu   koe yokotau ya   mizu no ue

> The cry of a *hototogisu*
> Goes slanting—ah!
> Across the water.   Bashō

What power is it that can eternalize a moment, make infinite
the one single line of flight of the cuckoo "that singeth as she
flies"? When Keats says in the *Grecian Urn*, to the bold lover
who cannot snatch a kiss from the sidelong maid,

> She cannot fade, though thou hast not thy bliss,
> For ever wilt thou love, and she be fair,

he is speaking of the world of art, the world of poetry.
Bashō's poem is concerned with the real world of stone and
dust, blood and feathers, and its eternity and infinity is not an
invention but a discovery of something present here and now.

さてはあの月が鳴いたか時鳥   梅室
Sate wa ano   tsuki ga naita ka   hototogisu

> What! Was it the moon
> That cried?
> A *hototogisu*!   Baishitsu

This needs no explanation, but it is necessary to realize the
instantaneousness of the experience. There was no time to
think "It is as if the moon cried," or, "There is nothing else
in sight which could have uttered a cry." The voice of the
hototogisu and the sight of the moon were synchronous. In
this fact lies the poetry of this verse. However, such percep-
tions are so uncommon as to make even the one who experi-

ences them doubtful of their validity. Better a plain picture
with a touch that lifts it above the blankly lifeless catalogue
of objects.

提灯の次第に遠し時鳥   子　規
Chōchin no   shidai ni tōshi   hototogisu

Farther and farther away it goes,—
The lantern:
    The voice of the *hototogisu*.   Shiki

The lantern moves away into the surrounding darkness. It
grows fainter and fainter and fainter. The voice of the *hototo-
gisu* sounds nearer and nearer by contrast, but the idea of
contrast is not presented to the mind at all. The receding
light, the increasing insistence of the voice of the bird are the
ebb and flow of life, the one sea of being.

山寺や晝寢のいびき時鳥   子　規
Yamadera ya   hirune no ibiki   hototogisu

From the mountain temple,
Midday snores,—
    And the voice of the *hototogisu*.   Shiki

In this remote mountain retreat there is no need to keep up
an appearance of piety or zeal in the middle of the hot summer
day. The priest lies down and unashamedly snores away. This
double-bass is countered by the fluty voice of the *hototogisu*
with it.

魚はねて水靜也ほとゝぎす   言　水
Uo hanete   mizu shizuka nari   hototogisu

A carp leaped out;
The water became smooth;
    The voice of the *hototogisu*.   Gonsui

The function of the imagination is to perceive the connection, or rather, the common element in apparently unrelated things, their unity in diversity, without losing their diversity in unity. Here, we have the sight and sound of the leaping carp; the mirror-like serenity of the lake after the disturbance; then the voice of the *hototogisu*. However much we explain their relation, physically, psychologically, or philosophically, we are no nearer the truth, that is, the poetry of the matter. It is there, it is so, and that is all.

郭公顔の出されぬ格子かな　　　　　　　野坡
Hototogisu   kao no dasarenu   kōshi kana

A *hototogisu!*
I tried to see,—
But the lattice....　　　　　　　　　　Yaha

The original says, "I could not put my face out of the lattice." A *hototogisu* is a little-seen bird, and upon hearing one the poet tried to put his head out, but the lattice of the window, pieces of wood nailed across at distances of an inch or so, prevented him from doing so. The point of the poem is in the lattice, not in the bird. At such a moment the poet has an insight into the nature of a lattice, what it is, into the nature of brute matter, in all its pliancy and obstinacy, its service and yet separate existence, the fact that it is both master and servant to man. There is a very similar verse by Issa:

歩きながら傘干せばほとゝぎす
Aruki nagara   karakasa hoseba   hototogisu

Walking along with the umbrella up,
Drying it,—
The voice of the *hototogisu*.

The summer rain stops. In the heat, Issa walks along though the rain has stopped, drying the drenched umbrella. Suddenly, he hears the cry of the *hototogisu*. Furling the umbrella, he gazes round, but it is too late. The sound of this verse is rather interesting.

是でこそ御時鳥松に月　　　　　　　一 茶
Kore de koso　on hototogisu　matsu ni tsuki

The moon in the pine-tree;
And with the *hototogisu*,
　　Ah, how glorious!　　　　　　　Issa

　The beauty of the moon and the beauty of the pine-tree,
their combined beauty, is perfect.　But when the *hototogisu*
suddenly sings, their beauty is overwhelming, and this ecstasy
is entirely due to the *hototogisu*.

ほとゝぎす柩をつかむ雲間より　　　蕪 村
Hototogisu　hitsugi wo tsukamu　kumoma yori

A *hototogisu*,
Snatching at the coffin,
　　From between the clouds.　　　　Buson

　The *hototogisu* often flies in the dark night, when the bravest
man must be on his guard.　Devils and demons stretch forth
their hands from the low-lying clouds that seem almost to
touch the heads of those in the funeral procession.　Here the
bird and the demons and the clouds are mingled as they
threaten to snatch away the corpse so that the spirit will be
left without a body.

我汝を待事久し郭公　　　　　　　　一 茶
Ware nare wo　matsu koto hisashi　hototogisu

How long
Have I waited for you,
　　O *hototogisu*!　　　　　　　　Issa

　This has a postscript:―老翁岩に腰かけて一軸をさづく
る圖に, "On a picture of an old man sitting on rock and
bestowing a scroll [on Chōrō]" The anecdote referred to is the
following.　One day in his youth Chōrō, 張良, was on a bridge
when he met an old man, Kōsekikō, 黄石公.　The old man
took off a shoe, threw it over the side of the bridge and told
young Chōrō to dive in and get it for him.　Chōrō did so

without hesitation. Perceiving him to be a man of promise, he arranged to meet him at sunrise on a certain day in order to teach him the Art of War. On the appointed day Chōrō arrived on the bridge to find the old man there before him. He was severely scolded and told to come on another day. The next time Chōrō was very early and was from that time initiated in the Art of War.

The waiting for the *hototogisu* is the waiting of the old man for Chōrō, in the same atmosphere of impatience. This association of two entirely different things by the similarity of emotion has its origin in humour. It is the function of humour to show the underlying identity of disparate things, and the wider the distance between them the greater pleasure of the recognition of their oneness.

鴉賊賣の聲まぎらはし時鳥　　　　　　芭蕉

Ika-uri no koe magirawashi hototogisu

The call of the cuttle-fish vendor,
Mingles with the voice
Of the *hototogisu*.　　　　　　Bashō

This does not mean that Bashō thought that the sound of the cry of the cuttle-fish seller resembled the singing of the bird, but that both came at the same time, with something perhaps common between them.

はしたなき女嬬の嚏や杜鵑　　　　　蕪村

Hashitanaki nyōju no kusame ya hototogisu

The vulgar sneeze
Of a palace maid-servant,—
The *hototogisu* cried.　　　　　Buson

With this we may compare the following, also by Buson:

時鳥歌よむ遊女聞ゆなり

Hototogisu uta yomu yūjo kikoyu nari

While a courtezan
Was making a waka,
The *hototogisu*!

In the first, the contrast is very great; there is a sudden, unexpected sneeze, and then immediately after, as if in answer, the cry of the bird. In the second, the bird is heard crying while a girl is singing some song to the accompaniment of the samisen.

郭公鳴くや湖水のさゝ濁り   丈 草
Hototogisu   naku ya kosui no   sasa nigori

A *hototogisu* cries;
The waters of the lake
Are slightly muddy.   Jōsō

In spring, the waters of rivers and lakes become muddied, but we do not notice this mark of life and overflowing richness until the *hototogisu* cries. The word "slightly" suggests the possible relation between bird and water.

時鳥けふに限りて誰もなし   尚 白
Hototogisu   kyō ni kagirite   dare mo nashi

A *hototogisu* is calling,
But today, just today,
No one is here.   Shōhaku

From one point of view we may say with Stevenson,

> One thing calls for another; there is a fitness in events and places.[1]

On the other hand, everything is fortuitous. Nothing, in fact, in real life, fits in as art and romance would have us believe. Whole cities are engulfed, whole nations swept away; the *hototogisu* sings just when there is no one to enjoy it with.

---

[1] *A Gossip on Romance.*

京にても京なつかしや時鳥　　　　芭蕉
Kyō nite mo　kyō natsukashi ya　hototogisu

I am in Kyōto,
Yet at the voice of the *hototogisu,*
Longing for Kyōto.　　　　　　　Bashō

Bashō is at this moment living in Kyōto, but at the sound
of the voice of the *hototogisu* a wave of yearning flows over
him for the past, the Kyōto of dead and gone poets of old.
Even in life we are in death; the past is ever-present with us.

そのあとは冥途できかん郭公　　　　無名氏
Sono ato wa　meido de kikan　hototogisu

Ah, *hototogisu!*
I will hear the rest of the song
In the land of the dead.　　　　　Anon

This is said to have been composed by a prisoner just before
his execution.

兄弟が顔見合はすや時鳥　　　　去來
Kyōdai ga　kao miawasu ya　hototogisu

A *hototogisu* called;
The brothers turned
And looked at each other.　　　　Kyorai

These two brothers are Soga Sukenari, 1172–1193, and Soga
Tokimune. 1174–1193.　Their father Sukeyasu was murdered
by a relative, Kudo Suketsune, in 1177, and their revenge is
the subject of many stories, poems and dramas. It is the
subject of two Nō plays, *Kosode Soga* and *Youchi Soga.* Here
Kyorai imagines the two brothers as they approach the tent of
Suketsune. A *hototogisu* suddenly cries, as if in omen of the
coming death, and the two brothers instinctively turn their
faces to each other in the darkness.

時鳥蠅虫めらもよっく聞け   一 茶
Hototogisu   hae mushimera mo   yokku kike

Hark! ah, the *hototogisu*!
Lend ear, you too, O wretched flies,
And other creeping things!   Issa

This is a kind of parody of Sōin's verse on page 768. It is
deep enough to correspond to Arnold's definition of poetry as
"a criticism of life."

郭公なくや雲雀と十文字   去 來
Hototogisu   naku ya hibari to   jūmonji

The skylark and the *hototogisu*
Make a cross
With their singing.   Kyorai

The skylark flies straight up; the *hototogisu* flies slanting
and horizontal. To say that their respective flights make a
cross is not poetry at all, but their *singing* making a cross is
quite a different matter.

仙人は人閑古鳥は鳥なりけり   蕪 村
Sennin wa hito   kankodori wa   tori nari keri

Hermits are human beings;
The *kankodori*
Is a bird.   Buson

This is called "a Himalayan cuckoo." It lives in the depths
of the forests, and from olden times its form was unknown.
Its voice is something like that of the pigeon, but much louder,
being heard for a mile or two distant. It is said to herald
both the approach of rain and of returning fine weather by its
cry; wood-cutters listen for it to decide when to enter and leave
the mountains. There are other verses by Buson which refer
to its unknown home and habits, and the superstitions that
gathered round it:

羯鼓鳥木のまたより生れけん
Kankodori ki no mata yori umareken

The *kankodori*
Is born, I suppose,
From the crotch of a tree.

なに食ふて居るかも知らず閑古鳥
Nani kūte iru ka mo shirazu kankodori

The *kankodori*:
What it lives on,
I know not.

むづかしき鳩の禮儀や閑古鳥
Muzukashiki hato no reigi ya kankodori

All the proprieties
For the pigeon,
But the *kankodori?*

食次の底たゝく音や閑古鳥
Meshitsugi no soko tataku oto ya kankodori

The sound of scraping
The bottom of the rice-tub,—
The *kankodori*.

ごつごつと僧都の咳や閑古鳥
Gotsugotsu to sōzu no seki ya kankodori

The hacking cough
Of the abbot,
And the voice of the *kankodori*.

我が捨しふくべが啼くか閑古鳥
Waga suteshi fukube ga naku ka kankodori

The gourd I threw away,—
Is it singing?
The voice of the *kankodori*.

親もなく子もなき聲や閑古鳥
Oya mo naku ko mo naki koe ya kankodori

The voice of the *kankodori*:
Without parents,
Without children!

よい聲を鼻にかけてや閑古鳥　　　　一 茶
Yoi koe wo　hana ni kakete ya　kankodori

The *kankodori:*
A fine voice,—
　　　And proud of it!　　　　　　Issa

By speaking in a rather belittling way of the note of the bird,
Issa manages to stimulate us to perceive something of the
humanity of the *kankodori*.　There is here a kind of "debun-
king", but Issa's purpose is serious, though, like Bernard Shaw,
he enjoys his own versatility.　A similar verse by Issa is the
following:

閑古鳥泣坊相違なく候
Kankodori　nakibō sōi　naku sōro

　There is no mistake,
The *kankodori*
　　Is a cry-baby.

しんしんと泉湧きけり閑古鳥　　　　子 規
Shin-shin to　izumi wakikeri　kankodori

　　The spring
Gushes out:
　　The *kankodori* sings.　　　　Shiki

The water flows out of the ground; the voice of the bird
flows out of its body.　Both have something in common.　What
a pleasure there is in such discords of distant harmony!　The
multifarious world is a unity, with its variety unclouded.

うき我をさびしがらせよ閑古鳥　　　　芭 蕉
Uki ware wo　sabishigarase yo　kankodori

　　Ah, *kankodori!*
In my sadness,
　　　Deepen thou my solitude.　　　Bashō

Literally translated, this is, "Kankodori, make lonely melan-
choly me!"　This verse expresses Bashō's aim in life, which

was to get into the deepest possible contact with the greatest possible number of things. "Solitude," "loneliness," *sabishisa* is the name given to this state of contact, and the *kankodori* has the peculiar quality of voice, of timbre and pitch and volume, to intensify our minds, to increase their depth and receptivity. "*Sabishisa* must be Lord of all."

風ふかぬ森のしづくやかんこ鳥   其角
Kaze fukanu   mori no shizuku ya   kankodori

The wind ceases;
Water drips in the forest;
A *kankodori* sings.   Kikaku

This verse has a perfection of description and restraint that Kikaku did not often attain to. It was composed near Kannō Temple, in Ueno. There the forest is deep, and dark even at midday, and when the wind drops and only the dripping from leaf to leaf is heard, then from the farther deeps of the forest the voice of the *kankodori* has an intimate yet occult sound.

先住のつけわたりなり閑古鳥   一茶
Senjū no   tsukewatari nari   kankodori

Left behind
By the previous tenant;
The voice of the *kankodori*.   Issa

Elemental things, the voice of birds, the rising of the sun, the winds of evening,—these things cannot be gained or lost.

The day in his hotness,
    The strife with the palm;
The night in her silence,
    The stars in their calm.[1]

They can neither be bestowed nor taken away; they can be accepted when we are there, and when death comes as it must, as it will, be left behind.

[1] Arnold, *Empedocles on Etna*.

死んだならおれが日を鳴け閑古鳥   一 茶
Shinda nara   ore ga hi wo nake   kankodori

When I die,
Sing my death song,[1]
O *kankodori!*

Issa

Listening to the melancholy notes of the *kankodori*, Issa
wishes it to chant his requiem when he dies, and on those days
when his death is to be remembered. There is a kind of pun
on "sing" and "weep," but singing or crying, for Issa or not
for Issa, these distinctions are not felt by the poet when he
listens to the voice of the unseen bird.

水鶏なく拍子に雲が急ぐぞよ   一 茶
Kuina naku   hyōshi ni kumo ga   isogu zoyo

The clouds hasten
To the rhythm
Of the moor-hen's cry.

Issa

Issa listens to the moor-hen's insistent cry, and for some
reason or other his eyes lift up to the grey heavens. The
clouds which until this moment seemed to be hardly moving
at all, are seen to be rushing along as though in sympathetic
motion with the bird's cry. In a sense, this may be called a
subjective interpretation, but in the true sense of the word this
is an objective poem, in that the mind of the poet is used not
to colour or distort for artistic purposes, but to reflect with a
faithfulness that is not mechanical but moves as a mirror might
move together with a moving object, or as the untouched string
of a harp vibrates to the voice of the singer.

翡翠や水すんで池の魚深し   子 規
Kawasemi ya   mizu sunde ike no   uo fukashi

The kingfisher;
In the clear water of the pond,
Fishes are deep.

Shiki

[1] Literally, "my day," the anniversary of my death.

In this simple verse, the silence, the fearful silence of nature
is felt because not expressed or implied. It is of the essence
of the kingfisher that it loves a quiet place, a willow tree over
it, and a long, lonely expanse of stream in either direction.
But when this silent loneliness is stated or hinted at, we feel
a faint kind of disillusion, as in the following verses by the
same author:

かわせみや柳静に池深し
Kawasemi ya   yanagi shizuka ni   ike fukashi

> The kingfisher;
> The willow is still,
> The pool is deep.

しんとしてかわせみ飛ぶや山の池
Shin to shite   kawasemi tobu ya   yama no ike

> The stillness:
> A kingfisher flies
> Over the mountain lake.

In this last verse, the kingfisher flies straight as an arrow over
the water.

翡翠やぬれ羽にうつる夕日影   桃 李
Kawasemi ya   nureha ni utsuru   yūhikage

> The kingfisher;
> On its wet feathers
> Shines the evening sun.   Tōri

This has something a little too beautiful for haiku. Signi-
ficance and beauty often coincide, sometimes overlap, but have
some distinct and separate life of their own. On the bright
blue feathers of the kingfisher the yellow light of the evening
sun glitters with a brightness that comes from the water that
is half the element of the bird. It is the *wetness* of the feathers
in which the poetical significance is to be found.

Heron and Lotuses by Sesson, 雪村, 1504-1589

夕風や水青鷺の脛をうつ   蕪 村
Yūkaze ya   mizu aosagi no   hagi wo utsu

With the evening breeze,
The water laps against
The heron's legs.   Buson

Buson's intuitions are strong and clear and *quick* enough to
avoid the colouring of his mind by emotion, or its distortion
by intellection.

日盛りや葦切に川の音もなき   一 茶
Hizakari ya   yoshikiri ni kawa no   oto mo naki

It is the noon;
Orioles are crying;
The river flows in silence.   Issa

The sunshine floods everything, the river is brimming.
Contrasted with this full, silent life there are the twittering
and jerky movements of the reed-sparrows among the rushes
on the bank.   These long-tailed uguisu-like birds cry loudly
kukushi! kukushi!

蝙蝠や鳥なき里の飯時分   一 茶
Kōmori ya   tori naki sato no   meshijibun

Bats are flying
In a village without birds,
At the evening meal-time.   Issa

Though bats seem to be a likely subject for haiku, they are
neither popular nor successful in verse.   In the present poem,
what Issa is expressing is the strangeness that he feels in
seeing a bird-like creature flitting about in the dusk, when in
the daytime no bird is to be seen or heard in that district.
The fact that it is meal-time gives the bat a kind of domestic,
familiar meaning.   There is the same pleasant familiarity in
the following, also by Issa:

烟して蝙蝠の世もよかりけり
Kemuri shite   kōmori no yo mo   yokarikeri

> With smoke rising,
> The world of a bat
> Is good too.

Another verse by the same author in which he brings out the more sinister and malefic aspect of the bat:

蝙蝠や仁王の腕にぶら下る
Kōmori ya   niō no ude ni   burasagaru

> Bats
> Hanging on the arm
> Of the Niō.[1]

かわほりや向ひの女房こちを見る   蕪　村
Kawahori ya   mukai no nyōbō   kochi wo miru

> Bats flit to and fro;
> The woman of the house over there
> Is looking this way.   Buson

It is growing dark, but only here and there in the distance lights are being lit. Bats swerve down and flit off, and the eye of the poet involuntarily falls on the figure of a woman who also, for some unknown reason, looks towards him, her face pallid in the gloom.

蝙蝠の飛ぶ音くらし藪の中   子　規
Kōmori no   tobu oto kurashi   yabu no naka

> The sound of the bat
> Flying in the thicket
> Is dark.   Shiki

The leathery wings of the bat have a peculiar sound, different form that of birds, even of owls, which are soft and half-silent in their movement through the air. Darkness has a kind of

[1] One of the two huge, ferocious-looking images of Deva Kings that guard the entrance to large temples.

ponderability, a tangibility that if struck might emit a sound. These two elements of sound and sight are confused in the mind, or rather, they are perceived as one by a faculty in which the two are not yet differentiated.

庭鳥に踏まれて育つ鹿の子かな　　　　一 茶
Niwatori ni fumarete sodatsu kanoko kana

> The fawn
> Was brought up,
> Trodden on by the fowls.　　　Issa

This verse reminds one of the Berlin Zoo, where monkeys and bears used to be kept in the same large cage. The deer has been reared from a tiny, harmless thing that even the chickens of the yard took no notice of and walked over as if it were an old basket. This point is brought out by contrast with the fawn's timid and sensitive nature. We have the strange sight spoken of by Wordsworth, where we oppose to nature a deeper nature.

What is this deeper nature which allows monkeys and bears, men and dogs, cats and mice to live together, where the lion lies down with the lamb, and the little child plays on the cockatrice' den?

馬の子が口つん出すや杜若　　　　一 茶
Uma no ko ga kuchi tsundasu ya kakitsubata

> The foal
> Sticks out his nose
> Over the irises.　　　Issa

Compare this verse, in which we have the young horse in its relation to nature, with the following, also by Issa, where some human feeling seems to creep in:

母馬が番して呑ます清水哉
Haha-uma ga ban shite nomasu shimizu kana

> The mother-horse on guard,
> The foal drinks
> The clear water.

The former verse has the lightness and freshness of youth; the latter is intense and emotional.

大猫のどさりと寝たる團扇かな   一 茶
Ōneko no   dosari to netaru   uchiwa kana

Flopped on the fan,
The big cat,
Asleep.
                                                    Issa

Cats will sit or lie on anything rather than the floor. The cause of the picture of the cat and the representation of its character is the feeling of irritation at the fact that the creature will always sit on what is wanted.

飛下手の蚤のかはいさまさりけり   一 茶
Tobibeta no   nomi no kawaisa   masarikeri

The flea
That is poor at jumping,
All the more charming.
                                                    Issa

The tenderness and humour of Issa are all his own, though the gentleness may be found long before in Bashō, for example:

うき人の旅にも習へ木曾の蠅
Ukibito no   tabi ni mo narae   kiso no hae

Flies of Kiso,
Learn from the journey
Of this grief-laden wanderer.

This is too sad and serious; it is making a mountain out of a mole-hill. Bashō is asking the flies to live as he does without interfering with the lives of others. Issa is not thinking of anything but the charm and pathos of the flea. He does not preach to it, even humorously, but brings out the latent absurdity of the flea itself.

蚤 の 迹 か ぞ へ な が ら に 添 乳 か な   一 茶
Nomi no ato   kazoe nagara ni   soeji kana

> Giving the child the breast in bed,
> The mother counts
> The flea-bites.   Issa

> Can a mother's tender care
> Cease toward the child she bare?

No pains and no discomforts, no "woes that infants bear",—
and what should a mother's love be for? The child is bone of
her bone and flesh of her flesh, it is on her own body that she
counts the flea-bites, she is drinking her own milk. In just the
same way Issa watches her, drinks the milk, is bitten by the
fleas, counts his flea-bites. In just the same way, the whole
universe is bone of our bone, flesh of our flesh, all created
by us.

三 界 唯 心、 万 法 唯 識。   （禪林句集）

> The three worlds are only mind;
> All things are simply perception.

And this fact, which seems irrelevant to Issa's verse, is that
which makes it possible for Issa to write it, to see the poetry
of the mother's half-humorous concern.

蚤 の 迹 そ れ も 若 き は 美 し き   一 茶
Nomi no ato   sore mo wakaki wa   utsukushiki

> A flea-bite also,
> When she is young,
> Is beautiful.   Issa

It is not clear whether it is Issa's wife or child who has been
bitten. The flea-bite also is pink and round, young and beautiful
like the person bitten. This beauty of a flea-bite is something
very elementary in the scale of things, but it is the same eye
which supplies something without which the greatest art is only
mud in a frame.

とぶな蚤それそれそこは隅田川   一　茶
Tobu na nomi   sore sore soko wa   sumidagawa

O flea!
Don't jump whatever you do;
That way is the River Sumida.   Issa

This was composed on the bank of the river, and the interest
is in the spontaneity, the instinctive feeling of protection that
Issa has, that we all have deep down in us towards all things,
even inanimate things.   There is in us a profoundly protective
and a profoundly destructive character.   Which of these two is
the deeper, the course of human history will perhaps show.

蚤どもに松島見せて逃すぞよ   一　茶
Nomidomo ni   matsushima misete   nogasu zoyo

Now you fleas!
You shall see Matsushima,—
Then off you go!   Issa

Matsushima is one of the three most beautiful places in Japan.
What is difficult in reading this haiku is to hit the right mean
between whimsicality and seriousness.   It is a joke, — and yet
Issa is in earnest.   Issa loves all living things as God does, yet
he is only a flea-incubator himself.

狭くともいざ飛習へ庵の蚤   一　茶
Semaku tomo   iza tobinarae   io no nomi

My hut is so small,
But please do practice your jumping,
Fleas of mine!   Issa

The tenderness of Issa's heart is not something separate from
the humour which reveals in hiding it.   And Issa could forget
his own troubles, thinking of the imaginary woes of the flea:

蚤どもも夜永だらうぞ淋しかろ
Nomidomo mo   yonaga darō zo   sabishikaro

> For you fleas too,
> The night must be long,
> It must be lonely.

庵の蚤不便やいつか痩る也　　　　一 茶
Io no nomi   fubin ya itsu ka   yaseru nari

> Fleas of my hut,—
> I'm sorry for them;
> They become emaciated soon enough.　Issa

We must not be misled into supposing that Issa is here using
the fleas to point to his own indigence. The poet's own poverty
is certainly included in the poem, but the emphasis is on the
fleas, the humour, the poetry is with them, in our sharing a
common life with so many other creatures whose happiness
depends directly (or conversely) on ours. Compare Pope's lines,
which Issa himself could have written:

> In the worst inn's worst room, with mat half-hung,
> The floor of plaister, and the walls of dung,
> On once a flock-bed, but repaired with straw,
> With tape-tied curtains, never meant to draw,
> The George and Garter dangling from that bed,
> Where tawdry yellow strove with dirty red,
> Great Villiers lies.

Where is the emphasis, on the Minister of State, or on the bed?

あばれ蚤我手にかゝつて成佛せよ　　一 茶
Abare-nomi   waga te ni kakatte   jōbutsu seyo

> Spirited, restive flea,
> Become a Buddha
> By my hand!　　　Issa

Issa means, of course, that he killed it. This is humorous,
yet Issa is also in earnest. Love of the flea, pity for its death,

belief in its life and destiny, relentless will to destroy it, acceptance of all that happens through him and to him, all this fused into one emotion and one "pop" of the flea.

蚤嚙んだ口でなむあみ陀佛哉　　　　一 茶
Nomi kanda　kuchi de namuamidabutsu kana

The mouth
That cracked a flea
Said, "Namuamidabutsu."　　　　Issa

It is the same mouth that blesses and curses, the same sword that kills and makes alive, the same universe that brings us into being and takes everything from us.

蚤虱馬の尿する枕元　　　　　　芭 蕉
Nomi shirami　uma no shito suru　makuramoto

Fleas, lice,
The horse pissing
Near my pillow.　　　　Bashō

This verse comes from Bashō's *Oku no Hosomichi*; the preceding passage is:

此道旅人稀なる所なれば、關守にあやしめら
れて、漸にして、關をこす、大山にのぼつて
日既に暮ければ、封人の家を見かけて舎をも
とむ。三日風雨あれて、よしなき山中に逗留
す。

Since travellers on this road were few, the barrier-guards were suspicious of us and would not let us through for some time. It was dark by the time we had passed over Great Mountain. Seeing the house of a frontier guard, we asked for lodging there and had to stop in this unatractive mountain for three days during a rain-storm.

Yaichiro Isobe, in his translation of *Oku no Hosomichi*, *The*

Poetical Journey in Old Japan, translates the above verse as follows:

> Harassed by vermin and to hear the staling of a
> horse at the pillar,—oh, how disgusting it is!

Bashō's verse is to be read with the utmost composure of mind. If there is any feeling of disgust and repugnance as a predominating element of the mind, Bashō's intention is misunderstood. Fleas are irritating, lice are nasty things, a horse pissing close to where one is lying gives one all kinds of disagreeable feelings. But in and through all this, there is to be a feeling of the whole, in which urine and champagne, lice and butterflies take their appointed and necessary place.

This of course is not Bashō's meaning; this was certainly his experience, but we are concerned with his *poetical* experience, which is a different thing and yet somehow the same thing. Sometimes, not by any means always, the simple, elemental experiences of things, whether of lice or of butterflies, the pissing of horses or the flight of eagles, have a deep significance, not of something beyond themselves, but of their own essential nature. But we must lodge with these things for a night, for a day, for three days. We must be cold and hungry, flea-ridden and lonely, companions of sorrow and acquainted with grief. Bashō's verse is not an expression of complaint or disgust, though he certainly felt irritation and discomfort. It is not an expression of philosophic indifference nor an impossible love of lice and dirt and sleeplessness. What is it an expression of? It is the feeling "These things too..." But anyone who tries to finish this sentence does not understand what Bashō meant.

我味の柘榴へ這す虱かな　　　　　　　　　一　茶
Waga aji no　zakuro e hawasu　shirami kana

> Poor louse!
> I made it creep upon the pomegranate,
> That tastes of my flesh.　　　　　　　Issa

This has the following prescript:

虱を捻りつぶさんことのいたはしく、又門に
捨て断食きすを見るに忍ばざる折から、御佛
の鬼の母にあてがひ給ふものをふと思ひだし
て。

While thinking that crushing lice is a pitiful
thing, and throwing them outside and starving
them to death makes a melancholy sight, I sud-
denly called to mind Buddha's instructions con-
cerning a mother-devil.

The tradition referred to is this. A certain Mother-devil
went about the country devouring, à la Grendel, the children
of human beings. Hearing of this, Buddha said, "Get her son
away from her by making him a Buddhist disciple, and she
will realise the anguish of losing children. If further she still
retains a taste for human flesh, let her eat pomegranates,
which have the same taste as human flesh." Thinking of this
anecdote, Issa compassionately puts the louse onto a pome-
granate.

This again is fanciful, but a fancifulness that is imbued with
deeper feelings. What shall we do with lice, with tigers, with
madmen, with this violent and uncontrollable universe?

夏衣いまだ虱をとりつくさず   芭 蕉
Natsugoromo   imada shirami wo   toritsukusazu

In my summer clothes,
There are still
Some uncaught lice.   Bashō

In his poverty, Bashō goes deeper than Issa; it has more
volition, more willingness in it. In love of life, of living, of
living things, Issa is more profound than Bashō.

やれうつな蠅が手をすり足をする   一 茶
Yare utsu na   hae ga te wo suri   ashi wo suru

Do not kill the fly!
See how it wrings its hands,
Its feet!   Issa

Issa was of course perfectly well aware that the fly was not rubbing its hands together in supplication for its life. But this is not fancy, as opposed to that imagination which sees into the life of things. It is humorous pretence, and under this cloak of pretence Issa hides and thus reveals his insight into the living nature of the fly. Blake's

> Am not I
> A fly like thee?
> Or art not thou
> A man like me?

comes near it, but lacks the poetry of Issa's humour. A verse of similar meaning but grimmer, less compassionate:

> 椽の蠅手を摺るところ打れけり
> *En no hae te wo suru tokoro utarekeri*
>
> A fly on the verandah,
> Killed,
> While rubbing its hands.

Hardy has this in a short poem, *An August Midnight*:

> there idly stands
> A sleepy fly that rubs its hands.

The feeling of this is quite different from Issa's poem. Hardy's grim stoicism is partly due to his deep modesty, shown in the last two lines. In this at least he is near to Issa:

> "God's humblest, they!" I muse. Yet why?
> They know Earth-secrets that know not I.

There is one more well-known passage in English literature which we may bring up; *Titus Andronicus*, Act III Scene II:

MARCUS STRIKES THE DISH WITH A KNIFE.

> What dost thou strike at, Marcus, with thy
> knife?
> *Marc.* At that that I have killed, my lord, a fly.
> *Tit.* Out on thee, murderer! thou kill'st my heart;
> Mine eyes are cloy'd with view of tyranny:

A deed of death, done on the innocent,
Becomes not Titus' brother. Get thee gone;
I see thou art not for my company.

Marc.   Alas my lord, I have but kill'd a fly.

Tit.   But how if that fly had a father and mother?
How would he hang his slender gilded wings,
And buzz lamenting doings in the air!
Poor harmless fly,
That, with his pretty buzzing melody,
Came here to make us merry! and thou hast
kill'd him.

One must admire the brilliant insincerity of this, exactly contrary to the attitude of Issa, who is pretending to be insincere, pretending to be humorous when he is deeply compassionate. He feels that the fly is living. The same feeling animated the breast of Chiyo when she said:

拾ふもの皆生きて居る汐干かな
Hirou mono   mina ikite iru   shiohi kana

All I pick up
At the ebb-tide
Is alive!

Another such verse by Kinya:

野の石の皆生きてをり冬の雨
No no ishi no   mina ikite ori   fuyu no ame

All the stones on the moor
Come alive
In the winter rain.

Another verse by Issa on the same subject:

世がよくばも一つとまれ飯の蠅
Yo ga yokuba   mo hitotsu tomare   meshi no hae

Everything is going well in the world;
Let another fly
Come on the rice.

蠅を打つ音も嚴しや關の人   太　祇
Hae wo utsu   oto mo kibishi ya   seki no hito

Even the sound of fly-swatting,
By the officers of the barrier,
Is strict and rigorous.   Taigi

There is a kind of painful humour in this. Those who are
waiting to pass through the barrier sit there bearing the heat
and burden of the day. The guards, quite indifferent to their
feelings, strike at the flies; and the sharp, vicious *smack*, so
well in keeping with their professional character, has a sinister
sound to the travellers and pilgrims, who give a jump every
time.

蠅打つてつくさんと思う心かな   成　美
Hae utte   tsukusan to omou   kokoro kana

Killing flies,
I begin to wish
To annihilate them all.   Seibi

This is a common experience. We begin to kill flies, and in
our hearts arises a kind of lust, that makes us wish for more
and more flies to kill. In this case we may call it a blood-lust,
but there is the same thing in painting a fence or watering a
garden. There is a tendency in human nature to go to ex-
tremes. This instinct, that Confucius spent his life in fighting
against, is so deep, so original that it is not to be repressed,
not to be overlooked in its most casual forms.

病中

生きた眼を突きに來るか蠅の飛ぶ   子　規
Ikita me wo   tsutsuki ni kuru ka   hae no tobu

On a Sick-bed

Have you come to vex
My still-living eyes,
Criss-crossing fly?   Shiki

Arnold says, in *Empedocles on Etna:*

Yet even when man forsakes
All sin,—is just, is pure,
Abandons all which makes
His welfare insecure,—
Other existences there are, that clash with ours.

What are we to do with them? Do what Shiki did, make
poetry of them; not written poetry necessarily. See them as
life, and live in them, not willy-nilly, but move down the
stream of time together with pain, weakness, irritations, not
in vainly attempted separation from them. This is what Shiki
does to these "other existences," the flies, at the moment the
poem is creating itself in his mind.

蠅打に花さく草も打れけり   一 茶
Hae utsu ni   hana saku kusa mo   utarekeri

Striking the fly,
I hit also
A flowering plant.   Issa

This is what makes action so difficult to the tender-minded.
Goodness and badness, profit and loss are mingled in a way
that cannot be said in analogy, for one is continually changing
into the other. Life is so unpredictable, cause and effect so
continuous, all we can say is what Issa has said, that hitting
at a fly means striking a flower. For something to live, some-
thing else must live; for something to die, something else
must die. And the contrary is equally true, that for something
to die, another thing must live; for a thing to live, something
else must die. But living means striking.

人一人蠅も一つや大座敷   一 茶
Hito hitori   hae mo hitotsu ya   ōzashiki

One human being,
One fly,
In the spacious chamber.   Issa

This human being is Issa himself; the fly is one that roves backwards and forwards in the strong afternoon sunlight. The solitary fly and the yet more solitary man, (because he is aware of his solitude) in the large room with all its windows and doors open, exist without self-consciousness, like the earth in space, or roots in the ground. The repetition of "one," not the word, but the idea, introduces an element of personality, of choice and arrangement, of harmony, of value, of poetry, of Zen. And if of Zen, then the activity is both complete and all-including, and has no element of self in it.

蠅憎し打つ氣になればよりつかず　　　　子規
Hae nikushi　utsu ki ni nareba　yoritsukazu

The hateful flies;
When I wanted to kill the things,
They wouldn't come near me.　　Shiki

Shiki's attitude to flies and the killing of them is quite different from that of Issa. When idealistic, we are in danger of falling beyond the place we have risen from. Issa, in his compassion for living things, is in danger of sentimentality and insincerity. Shiki is here the normal, unenlightened, unpoetic man, who nevertheless in his dispassionate regard for what seems to him fact, gives us a solid satisfaction of a homely kind that if not poetry is at least the basis of it. Shiki has another verse which is a kind of sequel to this:

蠅打つてしばらく安し四疊半
Hae utte　shibaraku yasushi　yojōhan

Killing the fly,
For some time, the small room
Is peaceful.

A perfectly natural state of irritation and desperation is followed by a sense of peace and calm, both these states being illusory, but the portrayal of illusory states may itself be poetry, for

Every error is an image of truth.

眠らんとす汝靜かに蠅を打て   子 規
Nemuran to su   nanji shizuka ni   hae wo ute

> I want to sleep;
> Swat the flies
> Softly, please.   Shiki

This is an expression of the physical and mental weariness
of the invalid of long standing. The nerves are on edge, and
we feel as if the fly-swat were striking us. There is a similar
expression of extreme sensitivity in the following, from *Summer
Rain*, by Herbert Read:

> Against the window pane
> against the temple of my brain
> beat the muffled taps of rain.

晝 の 蚊 を 後 に か く す 佛 か な   一 茶
Hiru no ka wo   ushiro ni kakusu   hotoke kana

> Mosquitoes in the day-time;
> Buddha hides them
> Behind him.   Issa

We have here the curious mixture of fancy and deep truth
that is a characteristic of Issa's poetry. The *fact* is that
during the day, mosquitoes hide in the darkness behind the
image or hanging picture of Buddha in the shrine. The *fancy*
is that Buddha is actually hiding the mosquitoes behind himself.
The *truth* is that there is nothing which is not the Buddha,
and the mosquitoes are hidden by him wherever they hide.
And somewhere in this compound of fancy, fact, and truth,
what we call poetry is to be found, that which makes life
worth living, that which gives things their meaning, but is not
itself a thing.

古井戸や蚊に飛ぶ魚の音闇し   蕪 村
Furuido ya   ka ni tobu uo no   oto kurashi

> In the old well,
> A fish leaps up at a gnat:
> The sound of the water is dark.   Buson

Not merely the water sounds cold and dark, but the life of the fish also is a shadowy one, dark and unknown.

わが宿は蚊のちいさきを馳走かな　　　芭蕉
Waga yado wa　ka no chiisaki wo　chisō kana

At my hut,
All that I have to offer you,
　　Is that the mosquitoes are small.　　Bashō

This was addressed to a Buddhist priest of Kanazawa, Aki no Bō, 秋の坊, asking him to call on his hermitage Genju-An, near Lake Biwa. Issa has a verse which expresses the extreme viciousness and number of the mosquitoes:

我宿は口で吹いても出る蚊かな
Waga yado wa　kuchi de fuite mo　deru ka kana

In my hut,
I have only to whistle,
　　And out the mosquitoes come!

目出度さは今年の蚊にも喰れけり　　　一　茶
Medetasa wa　kotoshi no ka ni mo　kuwarekeri

A matter for congratulation!
I have been bit
　　By this year's mosquitoes too.　　Issa

This was written when Issa was fifty four, and he means, of course, that he is glad to have lived so long. To some people it may seem absurd to quote here Milton's

But who would lose, though full of pain,
This intellectual being,

but Issa's value is precisely this, that he is expressing a profound thought and feeling in the lightest and most assimilable manner. Issa was one of those few who

by mere playing go to heaven.

蚊 の 聲 す 忍 冬 の 花 散 る た び に   蕪 村
Ka no koe su   nindō no hana   chiru tabi ni

The voices of mosquitoes,
Whenever the flower of the honeysuckle
Falls.

Buson

This is one of the most interesting examples of the extra-
ordinary sensitiveness of the haiku poets; or rather, of the
way in which they bend their loving eyes and ears upon the
slightest of things. The *nindō* is not a very striking flower,
white, and afterwards becoming yellowish. It does not fade in
winter, and from this comes its name, "enduring winter."

When a flower falls, mosquitoes that have been hiding in
the undergrowth rise up, and their humming is heard. The
voice of the mosquito also is very small indeed, not to be
heard far away from the ear. We have in this verse two
hardly noticeable things, yet they and their chance relation are
clearly perceived and expressed.

蚊 が ち ら り ほ ら り こ れ か ら 老 が 世 ぞ   一 茶
Ka ga chirari   horari kore kara   oi ga yo zo

A glimpse of a mosquito;
From now on,
And old man's world.

Issa

Issa describes his native place Kurohimeyama in Shinano,
信濃黒姫山, as a place where "snow melts in summer, frost
falls in autumn." For this reason summer is the best and most
looked-forward-to season of the year, especially, of course, by
old people. When therefore mosquitoes appear, people feel that
the summer has really begun, and the ideal world of aged
people is attained. There is a similar verse also by Issa:

ひ ま 人 や 蚊 が 出 た 出 た と ふ れ 歩 く
Himabito ya   ka ga deta deta to   fure aruku

People of leisure
Noise abroad the news
That mosquitoes *are here!*

蚊も居らず出水のあとの淋しさよ   子 規
Ka mo orazu   demizu no ato no   sabishisa yo

There are no mosquitoes even,
After the flood:
Ah, the loneliness!   Shiki

The loneliness of human beings is perhaps the deepest subject
for contemplation. But the thing itself, the feeling of loneliness,
comes and goes beyond our will or thought. So here, the scene
is one of desolation; crops spoiled, bridges broken down, paths
covered with rubbish, streams boiling by, everything we feel
wet and dripping. But all these things do not touch the quick
of life within him. As evening falls, in mist and gloom, there
is something missing, some accustomed, familiar sound. There
is no hum of mosquitoes, that annoying yet intimate sound,
and through this lack the sense of loneliness is aroused. The
smallest creatures are our companions, more faithful than our
dearest friends, always ready to bite and sting us, never failing
in their services.

Shiki has another verse similar in feeling but more inward,
more suppressed. The "loneliness" of this verse is far deeper
than that of the previous one.

野分して蟬の少なきあしたかな
Nowake shite   semi no sukunaki   ashita kana

After the storm,
Cicadas are few,
This morning of autumn.

閨の蚊のぶんとばかりに焼かれ鳧   一 茶
Neya no ka no   bun to bakari ni   yakarekeri

A mosquito in the bedroom;
Just a hum,—
And it was burnt!   Issa

This is interesting as being an experience that is not quite
"digested" by the poet. There is a little buzz and silence, as
the mosquito flies into the flame of the lamp. It has a meaning
that somehow escapes; Issa points to it from a distance. It is

like Tennyson's "Ode on the Death of the Duke of Wellington."
Wife and children sleep sprawled in ungainly attitudes. Nothing
in nature's aspect intimates that a mosquito is dead.

蚊柱に夢のうき橋かゝるなり   其 角
Kabashira ni   yume no ukibashi   kakaru nari

Across the mosquito columns
Hangs the floating bridge
    Of my dreams.   Kikaku

The columns of gnats that rise into the evening sky from
the dark masses of trees are called *ka-bashira*, "mosquito-
pillars." Kikaku sits gazing at

The green light that lingers in the west.

His dreamy thoughts float over the piles of gnats like a bridge
that reaches out into infinity.

This verse, in the style of Yeats, seems very far from the
concreteness and objectivity of Zen. But just as these is no
Buddha without the ordinary man, so even where there is no
Zen, Zen is working there; even the unpoetical, or what is
worse, the anti-poetical, the sentimental, the snobbish, the
un-compassionate, are aspects of Zen when perceived in the
enlightened mind. A similar verse by Shiki:

蚊柱や太しき立てゝ宮づくり
Kabashira ya   futoshiki tatete   miyazukuri

The mosquito columns,
    Big and thick
        As of a palace.

蚊柱の穴から見ゆる都かな   一 茶
Kabashira no   ana kara miyuru   miyako kana

The Capital
Is visible through a hole
    In the pillar of mosquitoes.   Issa

While barred clouds bloom the soft-dying day,
And touch the stubble-plains with rosy hue;
Then in a wailful choir the small gnats mourn
Among the river sallows, borne aloft
Or sinking, as the light wind lives or dies.

On such an evening as this, Issa sits watching the gnats like a
pillar of smoke rising from the willow trees. Between them
is the distant sky that looms over Edo. The small gnats rising
above the trees, and the bustling capital,— what have they in
common? This quiet evening scene is the unspoken and un-
speakable answer.

蚊柱やなつめの花の散るあたり   暁 臺
Kabashira ya   natsume no hana no   chiru atari

Pillars of mosquitoes
By the flowers of the jujube,
That fall and scatter.   Gyōdai

In the summer evening rise cloudy columns of mosquitoes,
and the pale blue flowers of the *natsume* flutter down in the
warm silence. We feel a kind of evanescent permanence, the
changeless change of life.

宵越の豆腐明りに藪蚊かな   一 茶
Yoigoshi no   tōfu akari ni   yabuka kana

The bean-curd of last night
Gleams whitely;
Striped mosquitoes hover.   Issa

Issa is the unromantic poet, reminding us of Heine.
"The moon gleams whitely," "flowers of the pear-tree gleam
whitely," this we know and approve. But the bean-curd put in
water in a bowl the night before is Issa's poetical food. In·the
early morning, before the sun has risen, Issa goes to the
kitchen and sees the milky-white bean-curd glimmering in the
twilight of the room with its blackened walls and ceiling. A
few *yabuka*, "thicket-mosquitoes," hover round the bowl, their

long striped bodies clearly outlined. This moment is the real
poetic life, the life of haiku.

初螢ついとそれたる手風哉   一 茶
Hatsuhotaru   tsui to soretaru   tekaze kana

> The first fire-fly!
> It was off, away,—
> The wind left in my hand.   Issa

Issa has made an instinctive snatch at the fire-fly coming
towards him; it darts aside and he has the faintly cool sen-
sation in his hand that is in some mysterious way the very
being of the fire-fly, its lightness and impalpability; it is like
a spiritual exhalation.

逃げて來て溜息つくか初螢   一 茶
Nigete kite   tameiki tsuku ka   hatsubotaru

> Escaping here,
> Did you breathe a sigh of relief,
> First fire-fly?   Issa

The tenderness of feeling is regulated by the humour; the
truth is expressed through the question form. As a statement,
this verse would be false and sentimental. As a question, the
problem of the presence or absence of a feeling of relief in the
fire-fly is swallowed up in the compassion we feel. All things
are pitiful. Thus, as with Mr. Pecksniff's forgiveness of John
Westcliff in *Martin Chuzzlewit*, our compassion is there whether
the object is pitiful or apparently not. There is a verse in
August Night, by Sara Teasdale, in which the tenderness of
feeling is indeed deep, but we miss the humour of Issa. It is
about the glow-worm:

> We watched while it brightened as though it were
>   breathed on and burning,
> This tiny creature moving over earth's floor,—
> "*L'amor che move il sole e l'altre stelle*," You said,
>   and no more.

草の葉を落つるより飛ぶ螢哉   芭 蕉
Kusa no ha wo   otsuru yori tobu   hotaru kana

The fire-fly,
As it dropped from the leaf,—
Away it flew!   Bashō

Before our eyes we can see the fire-fly falling from the leaf
of some bush that has been shaken, opening its wings and
flying off just before it reaches the ground.

追はれては月に隠るゝ螢かな   蓼 太
Owarete wa   tsuki ni kakururu   hotaru kana

Being chased,
The fire-fly
Hides in the moon.   Ryōta

Does this mean, "Being chased, the fire-fly flies out into the
bright moonlight, and thus becomes invisible?" It does not.
Does it mean that the fire-fly actually flies to the moon and is
hid there? It does not. What does it mean? It means,

            Being chased,
        The fire-fly
            Hides in the moon.

飛ぶ螢あれと言はんも獨りかな   太 祇
Tobu hotaru   are to iwan mo   hitori kana

A fire-fly flitted by:
"Look!" I almost said,—
But I was alone.   Taigi

The fire-fly is seen, for a moment, but it cannot be held in
the mind; the union of poet and insect, the realization of the
essential, original oneness of the apparently two existences, is
over. The object, the fire-fly, being lost, the emptiness of the
mind is felt as painful. The mind seeks to fill itself with some-
thing, a mediator, in whom the former object, the fire-fly, may

be regained. The fire-fly is grasped by the mind momentarily and lost, because the poet has not attained to the true "loneliness" in which the fire-fly is enough, for it is all God offers.

To wish for compassion, sympathy, understanding, is deathly weakness, natural enough,—but so are sloth, cruelty, pride, and sentimentality. Only in so far as our desire is to enter into the feelings of another, is it towards the religious, the poetical life, the life of Zen. But just as the humourless man is a cause of mirth, just as the ideal is manifested in non-attainment, so here, in the melancholy arising from the transitoriness of the moments of vision, we see into the life of poetry. This is the state where

> Ye are dead, and your life is hid with Christ (i.e.
> the firefly), in God.

追ふ人にあかりを見する螢かな　　　大江丸
Ou hito ni　akari wo misuru　hotaru kana

> The fire-fly
> Gives light
> To its pursuer. Ōemaru

When we read this verse we suffer from a kind of confusion of mind which is near to the poetic state. In this intellectual bewilderment, we almost see into the nature of the light of the fire-fly; our extremity is God's opportunity, and the light and the seeing eye are almost one. If it had no light, it would not be pursued,—but it would not be a fire-fly; it would not be it.

一つ來て庭の露けき螢かな　　　其禮
Hitotsu kite　niwa no tsuyukeki　hotaru kana

> A single fire-fly coming,
> The garden
> Is so dewy! Kirei

When even a single fire-fly comes, the light shows the dew on the leaf, and the whole garden is felt to be full of dew. More simple than this verse is the following by Hōjo:

此處彼處螢に靑し夜の草
Koko kashiko   hotaru ni aoshi   yoru no kusa

> Here and there,
> The night-grass is *green*,
> From the fire-flies.

Still more simple, by Banko:

手のひらを這ふ足見ゆる螢かな
Te no hira wo   hau ashi miyuru   hotaru kana

> The fire-fly;
> As it crawls on my palm,
> Its legs are visible.

畫見れば首筋赤き螢かな   芭 蕉
Hiru mireba   kubisuji akaki   hotaru kana

> By daylight,
> The fire-fly has
> A neck of red.   Bashō

This is not "a typical example of disillusionment".

春色無高下、花枝自短長。   (禪林句集)

In the scenery of spring, there is nothing better,
  nothing worse:
The flowering branches are by nature, some long,
  some short.

Which is better, the Long Body of Buddha, or the Short Body?
Which is better, the sweetly shining fire-fly of the night, or its
red neck by day? Or is it true that there are "vessels of
honour and vessels of dishonour," and that "one star differeth
from another in glory"?

There are later verses somewhat similar to Bashō's but
weaker, for example, by Onchō and Aon:

明けぬれば草の葉のみぞ螢籠
Akenureba   kusa no ha nomi zo   hotaru-kago

> When dawn comes,
> Only grass
> In the fire-fly cage.

夜が明けて虫になりたる螢かな
Yo ga akete   mushi ni naritaru   hotaru kana

>   When dawn breaks,
> The fire-fly
>   Becomes an insect.

もえ易く又消え易き螢かな   千子女
Moeyasuku   mata kieyasuki   hotaru kana

>   How easily it glows,
> How easily it goes out,
>   The fire-fly.

Chine-jo

All that nature does is effortless, whether the germination of
of a seed or a volcanic eruption. Arnold, in *Morality*, speaks
with the voice of Nature:

>   There is no effort on my brow,
>   I do not strive, I do not weep;
> I rush with the swift spheres and glow
>   In joy, and when I will, I sleep.

When we remember that the above poem was Chine-jo's death-
verse, the meaning sinks even deeper.

手の内に螢つめたき光りかな   子 規
Te no uchi ni   hotaru tsumetaki   hikari kana

>   The fire-fly,
> Its glow
>   Cold in the hand.

Shiki

This verse expresses the "shock of mild surprise" on realizing
that though the insect is glowing, it is with light, not with
heat; its body is cool. But if the verse does not go beyond
this, it is entomology, not poetry. Yet if it goes beyond what
is stated, we may fall into philosophy, into principles and gener-
alities. What is necessary is to perceive the "oddness" of
things not as apart from, abstracted from the things, but as

the essence of the things, just as simply as the sensation of light or coldness. Our own minds are to be at one and the same time shining and cool, or to put it more exactly, we are to experience our own coldly glowing nature in the fire-fly held in the hand.

寂しさやわづらふ児に螢籠   蓼 太
Sabishisa ya   wazurau ko ni   hotaru-kago

A cage of fire-flies
For the sick child:
Loneliness.   Ryōta

The poet's child was sick, and one summer evening he brought back a few fire-flies to hang in the dark room to console him. As he is about to do this (if he is of grosser mould, when he has done it) he has an overwhelming and yet intense feeling of what is called "loneliness," but what is nameless; for it is the sorrow that is in joy, the inevitableness in our free choice, the helplessness of the love that moves the sun and the other stars.

うつす手に光る螢や指のまた   太 祇
Utsusu te ni   hikaru hotaru ya   yubi no mata

Between the fingers
Of the hand that put it in,
A fire-fly glowed.   Taigi

The hand takes the fire-fly from the net and transfers it to the cage. This verse gives us a deep feeling of the softly-burning life of the insect. Vaughan says of the eye of the cock,

Father of lights! what sunnie seed,
What glance of day hast thou confined
Into this bird!

川ばかり暗は流れて螢かな   千　代
Kawa bakari   yami wa nagarete   hotaru kana

In the river alone
Darkness is flowing,—
The fire-flies!   Chiyo

The fire-flies fill the sky and all around, so that darkness is
to be seen only in the river flowing below.   Darkness is
drifting along, while above it all is luminous and bright.

さし柳螢飛ぶ夜となりにけり   一　茶
Sashiyanagi   hotaru tobu yo to   nari ni keri

The willow grown from a cutting;
It has become a night
With fire-flies.   Issa

The poetic point of this verse is a very elusive one.   There
is the harmony of the sweetness of the fire-flies and the gentle,
feminine nature of the small willow-tree, but besides this, there
is a feeling of the passage of time.   The day when the willow
was put into the wet ground has in some extraordinary way
become a night when fire-flies are fleeting to and fro.   The
past is the past and the present is the present, but they also,
in some way, grow from each other.

迷ひ子の泣く泣くつかむ螢かな   流　水
Mayoigo no   naku naku tsukamu   hotaru kana

The lost child,
Crying, crying, but still
Catching the fire-flies.   Ryūsui

To call this a symbolic or parabolic poem would be to deny
the very nature of haiku and the essence of poetry.   But what
actually happens is that the depth of our appreciation of the
tragic futility of human life that comforts its short span with
toys and trifles, is what moves and lives when we read the
above verse.   Once the comparison between the lost child and

erring humanity is made, poetry, the poetical life, is over.
What is necessary is that the poetic life should be uncrystallized,
unintellectualized, should not begin to compare and contrast and
divide into this and that. In other words, it should be like
water, undivided, the whole flowing into the verse without
remainder.

さびしさや一尺消えて行く螢　　　　北　枝
Sabishisa ya　isshaku kiete　yuku hotaru

For the space of a foot,
The fire-fly's light goes out:
Loneliness.

Hokushi

The poet watches the fire-fly gliding along, when suddenly,
for no apparent reason, the light is extinguished, and for the
distance of about a foot it is invisible. Then again, for no
apparent reason, the light of the fire-fly burns again. His
feeling he describes by the word "sabishisa," which means
loneliness, not in the sense that he feels detatched from the
insect, but that its life is something mysterious, unknowable.
The light goes out, reappears, and in this the secret life of
things is manifested.

白雨にはしり下るや竹の蟻　　　　丈　草
Yūdachi ni　hashirikudaru ya　take no ari

An evening shower:
The ants are running down
The bamboos.

Jōsō

The touch of Zen here is in the unexpressed and therefore
all the more poignant feeling of the unity of our life with that
of nature. This is felt in the ants' agitated running back down
the trunks of the bamboos, the same ants that seem to have
been climbing *up* the bamboos all day.

蟻流す程の大雨となりにけり   駒　村
Ari nagasu   hodo no ōame to   nari ni keri

It became a rain
Heavy enough
　　To wash the ants away.   Kuson

This is not so much an expression of pity for the ants as a
description of the summer rain.　We may say the same even
of the following, by Gyōdai:

行衛無き蟻の住居やさつき雨
Yukue naki   ari no sumika ya   satsukiame

Nowhere to go;
The dwellings of ants
　　In the summer rain.

羽蟻とぶや富士の裾野の小家より   蕪　村
Haari tobu ya   fuji no susono no   koie yori

Winged ants fly
From a small house
　　At the foot of Mount Fuji.   Buson

This may be reminiscent of the beginning of Sōshi.　Winged
ants, a small house, Mount Fuji,— here is a gradation of size,
a relativity which shows the meaningless of mere quantity.
There is a mystery in this verse which is like that of *Alice in
Wonderland*, but not so obvious.

青蛙鳴くや若葉の通り雨   魯　月
Aogaeru   naku ya wakaba no   tōriame

The green-frogs are crying
As the passing shower
　　Falls on the young leaves.   Rogetsu

The green-frogs, or tree-frogs, are excited by the falling rain
that suddenly refreshes everything, and they sing louder and
more cheerfully than usual.　The double sound and the triple
sight make a fivefold pleasure to the single poetic mind.

雨蛙芭蕉にのりて戦ぎけり　　　其角
Amagaeru bashō ni norite soyogikeri

The tree-frog
Riding the banana-leaf
Sways and quivers.　　　Kikaku

Walt Whitman says,

And the tree-toad is a chef-d'oeuvre for the highest. And a mouse is miracle enough to stagger sextillions of infidels.[1]

This is the modern form of Dante's words, that have the suavity and grandeur of centuries behind them:

Si muovono a diversi porti
Per lo gran mar dell essere, e ciascuna
Con istinto a lei dato che la porti.[2]

They move to ports diverse
Over the great sea of being, each one
With instinct given it bearing it on.

鍋みがく音にまぎるゝ雨蛙　　　良寛
Nabe migaku oto ni magiruru amagaeru

The sound of the scouring
Of the saucepan, blends
With the tree-frogs' voices.　　　Ryōkan

The tree-frog has a sweet voice, and as it sings, at the same time, the saucepans are being cleaned of soot by the river. The sand on the iron is not a pleasant sound, but the resonance in the round concavity of the saucepan has something musical in it which is brought out by the voice of the tree-frog.

[1] *Story of Myself.*　　[2] *Poradiso*, 1, 112–114.

ゆく水や竹に蟬鳴く相國寺   鬼 貫
Yuku mizu ya   take ni semi naku   sōkokuji

The water is flowing,
In the bamboos a cicada is crying;
Sōkokuji Temple.   Onitsura

The flowing of the water, the crying of the insect, the age-old temple,—these three entirely unrelated things; yet in this world it is all we have and all we need to have.

鳥まれに水また遠し蟬の聲   蕪 村
Tori mare ni   mizu mata tōshi   semi no koe

Birds were few,
And waters distant;
The voice of the cicada.   Buson

The cry of the cicada has a peculiarly dry, a peculiarly *songless* quality that is brought out in this place where there is heard but seldom the voice of birds or the sound of running waters. In this ascetic, austere landscape, there is more poetic life than in the tropical forests. A single cicada, and the absence of birds, the distance of streams and waters is felt more strongly than the presence of great and glorious things. In this place where birds are seldom seen and rarely heard, where streams do not run, and the voice of the waters is silent, a cicada is now chirping. Trees and rocks are loud with his cry, and the world overflows with his passion.

閑さや岩にしみ入る蟬の聲   芭 蕉
Shizukasa ya   iwa ni shimiiru   semi no koe

The silence;
The voice of the cicadas
Penetrates the rocks.   Bashō

See page 975. In the *Saikontan* we read:

萬籟寂寥中、忽間一鳥弄聲、便喚起許多幽趣。
萬卉摧剝後、忽見一枝擢秀、便觸動無限生機。

When all things are hushed, suddenly a bird's
song arouses a deep sense of stillness. When all
the flowers are departed, suddenly a single flower
is seen, and we feel the infinity of life.

Thoreau is less explanatory:

After each sound which near at hand broke the
stillness of the night, each crackling of the twigs
or rustling among the leaves, there was a sudden
pause, and deeper and more conscious silence.[1]

The quietness near the temple of Ryushakuji (立石寺, in Dewa
Province) is broken by the sudden *zzzzz* of an early cicada in
June. The timbre of the cicada's cry makes it seem as though
drilling into the boulders that lie round the temple. The silence
is not only intensified in retrospect, it is not different from the
sound of the cicada. This movement in repose, repose in
movement, silence in sound, sound in silence is what Sōshi
speaks of:

It (the Way) cannot be conveyed either by words
or silence. In that state which is neither speech
nor silence, its transcendental nature may be ap-
prehended.

Nevertheless, when we say all this, when we explain Bashō's
state of mind, we explain it away,

所以論道而非道也。(荘子、二十二。)
because talking about the Way makes it not the
Way,

as Sōshi himself says. In *Oku no Hosomichi*, Bashō speaks of
the conditions which led up to the composition of the verse.

佳景寂寞として心すみ行くのみおぼゆ。
The beautiful scene was silent and still; my heart
was at rest. I was conscious only of this.

In its general aspect, it was something very similar to Words-
worth's

[1] *A Week on the Concord and Merrimack Rivers.*

we are laid asleep
In body, and become a living soul.

The particular experience, however, is given by Shelley in *The Recollection*:

How calm it was!—the silence there
By such a chain was bound,
That even the busy woodpecker
Made stiller with her sound
The inviolable quietness.

This is a silence beyond silence, as in Shōhaku's verse:

靜かさは栗の葉沈む清水かな
Shizukasa wa   kuri no ha shizumu   shimizu kana

The quietness;
A chestnut leaf sinks
Through the clear water.

蟬鳴や我家も石に成るやうに　　　　　　　一　茶
Semi naku ya   wagaya mo ishi ni   naru yō ni

The cicadas are crying so,
My hut will become
A rock!

Issa

This verse, though undoubtedly a kind of continuation of Bashō's, is nevertheless at the opposite pole of feeling and mood. Issa is here expressing the insufferable noisiness of a large number of cicadas nearby, and suggests that they are boring into his own house, into his own cranium. Bashō's verse gives us the quietness revealed by a few cicadas in the distance. Contrasting these two haiku we get a clear idea of the religiousness of Bashō and the humanity of Issa. In Bashō we have a suggestion of *something beyond*, which belongs rather to Shin than to Zen. Issa is all Zen, except when he is speaking of religion itself.

雷晴れて一樹の夕日蟬の聲   子 規
Rai harete   ichiju no yūhi   semi no koe

The thunder-storm having cleared up,
The evening sun shines on a tree
Where a cicada is chirping.   Shiki

After the mutter of thunder has ceased, when the rain has passed over and gone, the evening sun shines forth, and from the shadows of the tree, at first hesitatingly, then with increasing passion, comes the thin shrill note of a cicada.

This is not only a picture of splendour: it is something more intimate, more "innig." The feeling is not so much loneliness as tranquillity, with movement in immobility. The same splendour in harmony with the loud voice of the cicada is given in the following by Buson:

大佛の彼方宮様蟬の聲
Daibutsu no   kanata miya-sama   semi no koe

Beyond the Great Buddha,
A Shintō Shrine,
Cicadas chirping.

Here we have the grandeur of religion and the solemnity of filial piety expressed also in the intense voice of Great Nature.

空家の門に蟬なく夕日かな   子 規
Akiie no   mon ni semi naku   yūhi kana

At the gate of a deserted house,
A cicada is crying in the rays
Of the evening sun.   Shiki

In this verse we have pathos and loneliness expressed in the light of declining sun, the melancholy cry of a solitary cicada, the sight of the dilapidated gate with its "to let" sign askew upon it. The truth is that any sound or sight may have any meaning. Each type has its own tendency towards a particular meaning, as for example, death of tragedy, a snore of humour, and so on, but according to circumstances, death may be comic and a snore pathetic. The crying of a cicada has a passionate intensity, a wringing of the hands of the mind, that lends itself to the expression of the loneliness of things, but also to the simple, the objective, the clear and transparent, silence. Then, when the cicada sings, the gate is an entrance to nothing; the voice of the cicada is heard by no one: the level sunshine flows in unseen. When the house is empty all these things are only

> The words of a dream
> Remembered on waking.

名もしらぬ大木多し蟬の聲　　　　　　子 規
Na mo shiranu　taiboku ōshi　semi no koe

Huge trees are many,
Their names unknown:
　　The voices of the cicadas.　　　　　Shiki

Through these towering trees, and the mystery and power given to them by the poet's inability to name them, the cicadas become a vast concourse of creatures whose voices rise up to the summer sky; their chanting fills the whole of nature.

The absence of the names increases the grandeur of the trees. The voice of the cicada, though penetrating, grating, "sizzling," is nevertheless associated somehow with something magnificent, the setting sun, deserted mansions, a thunderstorm, great trees, temples.

やがて死ぬけしきは見えず蟬の聲　　　　芭 蕉
Yagate shinu　keshiki wa miezu　semi no koe

Nothing intimates,
In the voice of the cicada,
　　How soon it will die.　　　　　　Bashō

This may be taken in two ways. First, there is nothing in the singing of the cicada which shows that it will not sing for ever. Its singing has the quality of "pure present", the eternal now. Second, the cicada sings oblivious of and indifferent to its approaching death. It sings without fear or hope, without rhyme or reason; it sings because it sings.

聲に皆鳴きしまうてや蟬の殻   芭 蕉
Koe ni mina   nakishimōte ya   semi no kara

> ### The shell of a cicada;
> ### It sang itself
> ### Utterly away.
>   Bashō

This is the cicada's Zen.   In actual fact, of course, the cicada
is not dead, it has cast its skin.   But Bashō, indifferent to the
scientific truth of the matter, and taking the empty shell of
the cicada as a symbol of its extinction, perceives that the
cicada sings with all its mind and heart and soul; no "looking
before and after" spoils the eternal present of its complete and
full existence.

There is a verse by Yayu similar to the above but more
fanciful, the cicada being by its cast-off skin:

われとわが殻やとむらふ蟬の聲
Ware to waga   kara ya tomurau   semi no koe

> ### Mourning over its dead body,
> ### And over itself,—
> ### The voice of the cicada.

松の蟬どこまで鳴いて畫になる   一 茶
Matsu no semi   doko made naite   hiru ni naru

> ### Pine-tree cicadas,
> ### How much must you cry
> ### For it to be noon?
>   Issa

Pine-trees suggest age, continuance, immovability, and the
cicadas that are singing there, with their interminable, intoler-
able buzzing, — how much, or as Issa actually says, "how far"
will they have sung by the time this long summer morning is
at its end?   This expresses the unbearable state of mind of Issa,
but also, in so doing, what is the same thing, the persistence
and blind insatiability of nature, of the cicada's nature.

There is another verse by Shiki in which the cry of the
cicada comes up as the noises of other creatures decline:

いろいろの賣聲たえて蟬の聲
Iroiro no   urigoe taete   semi no koe

    Various street-cries
Dying away,—
    The voice of the cicadas.

鳴やめて飛ぶ時蟬の見ゆるなり   子 規
Nakiyamete   tobu toki semi no   miyuru nari

    The cicada is seen
When it stops crying,
    And flies.   Shiki

There is a very deep simplicity in this verse. When the cicada is crying, loud and persistent as its voice may be, we can hardly find it however much we look. But as soon as it ceases to sing and flies off to another tree, its flight is so erratic and blundering that it is much more visible than a bird or insect much larger. We cannot, in this relative world, have our cake and eat it too; the cicada is either audible or visible; not both. But in the world of poetry we both see and hear it,—yet it sings invisible and flies when its song has finished.

蟬あつし松きらばやと思ふまで   也 有
Semi atsushi   matsu kiraba ya to   omou made

    The cicadas, with the heat,—
I wished even
    To cut down their pine-tree.   Yayū

Yayū, speaking of this verse, says:

三伏の日ざかりの暑さにたえがたくて蟬あ
つし云々と口ずさびし日數も程なく立かはり
てやゝ秋風に其聲のべり行ほどさすが哀にお
もひかへりて
    死にのこれ一つばかりは秋の蟬

    In the days of the greatest heat, it being un-
bearably hot, I made the above verse, but as the

days passed swiftly by, and the voices of the cicadas
in the autumn wind sounded weaker and weaker,
in spite of myself I changed my mind and felt
sorrow for them:

> May at least one
> Live on
> Cicadas of autumn!

蟬鳴くやつくづく赤い風車　　　　　　一 茶
Semi naku ya　tsukuzuku akai　kazaguruma

> A cicada is crying;
> It is precisely
> A red paper windmill.　　　　　　Issa

Issa expresses here his experience that the sound of the
cicada is the same as the sight of the toy windmill. If the
windmill could cry, it would have the voice of the cicada. If
the voice of the cicada could be expressed in form and colour-
ation, it would be a bright red windmill.

蜩や捨て置いても暮るゝ日を　　　　　　すて女
Higurashi ya　suteteoite mo　kururu hi wo

> Ah! higurashi,
> Though you leave it be,
> Day darkens.　　　　　　Sute-jo

The higurashi, which some translate as "a clear-toned cicada",
but which means "day-darkener", is the most poetic of all
Japanese insects, and one may include the birds in this state-
ment. As to the sound it makes, some write it *kana, kana,
kana, kana, kana,* but it does not seem like this to me, but
rather, *ti, ti, ti, ti, ti, ti, ti.* It sings at sunset, and sometimes
in the early dawn. Each insect sings at a slightly different
pitch, but all have the same intense, unsentimentally tragic,
inevitable sound.

The above verse adds human anguish to the melancholy cry of the insect in the summer evening. Day darkens, time passes; it is not necessary for you, higurashi, to hasten the advent of night with the penetrating and musical sadness of your cry.

There is a verse by Rikei which shows one of the many aspects of the cry of the higurashi, its effect upon the human mind:

蜩や今日の懈怠をおもふ時
Higurashi ya   kyō no ketai wo   omou toki

Ah, day-darkener!
When I think
Of today's wasted hours!

そこのいて竹植えさせよ蟇   樗良
Soko noite   takeuesase yo   hikigaeru

Kindly move out of the way,
And let me plant these bamboos,
O Toad!   Chora

To realize once again what the savage never doubts, that mind is universally diffused throughout the visible world, that the toad is a man on four legs, is a pleasure that diffuses itself just as universally. The toad moves unwillingly, like many other people, and we feel, rightly, an irritation towards him greater than we feel towards a stone.

罷り出でたるは此藪の蟇にて候   一 茶
Makari idetaru wa   kono yabu no   gama nite sōrō

"I make My Appearance,
I, the Toad,
Emerge from My Thicket!"   Issa

Issa is making fun of the toad, but in doing so, expresses part of the essential nature of the toad, its special nature, which is in some marvellous way the nature of all things, the Buddha-nature.

The form of this is 7, 5, 7. This heaviness and cumbersomeness of form is perhaps used as expressive of the gait of the toad as it crawls pompously and ponderously out of the undergrowth. The language is that of Nō, or Kyōgen.

月 の 句 を 吐 て へ ら さ ん 蟇 の 腹   蕪 村
Tsuki no ku wo   haite herasan   gama no hara

> The toad;
> Spitting out a verse on the moon,
> Its belly will subside.   Buson

Buson's treatment of animals and insects is the reverse of that of Issa. In Issa the human is brought down to the animal; our lowest common denominator is the touch of nature that makes the world kin. In Buson the animal is brought up into the human world, into the poetical world. At a banquet held at Chijitsutei, 遅日亭, Buson was asked to make a verse. Listening to the full, plethoric voice of the toad in the shadows of the summer garden, he imagines its swollen belly and feels a similar kind of congestion in himself. If only he could give vent to a verse about the summer moon that is shining overhead, he would feel the relief of the Aristotelian purgation of his passions.

蟇 ど の ゝ 妻 や 待 ら ん 子 な く ら ん   一 茶
Gama dono no   tsuma ya matsuran   ko nakuran

> Mr. Toad,
> Your wife is waiting,
> Your children are wailing.   Issa

Issa watched the toad crawling away, and thinking the toad's wife and children must be waiting for him, used the words of Yamanoue Okura, 山上憶良, 660–733, when he was serving his country as ambassador to China:

憶良らは今はまからむ子なくらむ
そのかの母も吾を待つらむぞ

> Okura must now depart;
> The children will weep;
> The mother will be waiting,
> Waiting for me.

The poetical point lies in the overflow of feelings towards the toad. If the toad is used as a symbol or illustration or comparison, there is no poetry here. And further we see once more the fact that only when we are in a certain subjective state can we perceive an objective fact, in other words, true, poetic, religious subjectivity and objectivity are one and the same thing.

雲を吐く口つきしたり蟇   一 茶
Kumo wo haku   kuchitsuki shitari   hikigaeru

> The toad! It looks as if
> It would belch forth
> A cloud!   Issa

Issa expresses here, though in a seemingly fantastic way, the grotesque, slightly sinister appearance of the toad, in particular, of its mouth.

Another verse by Issa, of the same tenor as the above:

霧に乗る目付して居る蟇
Kiri ni noru   metsuki shite iru   hikigaeru

> It looks as though
> It would ride on the mist,—
> This toad!

Shiki has the following verse:

宵闇や月を吐出す蟇の口
Yoiyami ya   tsuki wo hakidasu   gama no kuchi

> Early dusk;
> The mouth of the toad
> Exhales the moon.

古壁の隅に動かず孕蜘   子 規
Furukabe no sumi ni ugokazu harami-gumo

> In a corner of the old wall,
> Motionless,
>   The pregnant spider.   Shiki

Movement has meaning, but stillness has more, because we do not know how the thing will move, or where. Spiders are sinister when they wait without motion. When they scurry across a web or run for their lives, they are only one of us.

When things do not move, they acquire energy that is latent and mysterious. The stillness of the spider concentrates in itself the age of the wall, the remoteness of the corner, above all the nature of the spider, which is secret and dark, especially now the mother spider is big with child.

蜘蛛の子は皆ちりぢりの身すぎ哉   一 茶
Kumo no ko wa mina chirijiri no misugi kana

> The spider's offspring,—
> All scatter,
>   And make their livelihood.   Issa

The important thing about such a haiku as this is not to allow the mind to make the spider a symbol of anything human. The young spiders all separate, and, though all children of one mother, are henceforth strangers, even enemies to one another. This is a law of life, a law even of insentient things. But if the law and the example are taken separately, the law is abstracted from reality, and the spiders' scattering is meaningless. They must be taken as one by the mind, otherwise the meaning, that is, the poetry, will disappear.

よべの雨馬蘭に殖えぬ蝸牛   召 波
Yobe no ame baran ni fuenu katatsumuri

> With last night's rain,
> Snails have increased
>   On the aspidistras.   Shōha

At first sight this may seem a simple statement of fact, only meteorological, botanical and sociological in its scope. But haiku has a far wider range than this. It includes all science, all fact within it, and goes beyond it, pointing with no uncertain finger to the ground of being, the living tie that binds all things together in one. When we attempt to explain it, we say it is a mystery, but to the poet there is a region beyond wonder, where the commonplace and the wonderful are not distinguished, where the thusness of things is bright with a light that never was on sea or land, and yet is oddly there. The bright drops of water on the deep green leaves of the aspidistra, the pale, translucent, faintly banded shells of the snails and the delicate flesh of their feelers,—here there is an interpenetration of substance and mind in which life flows unimpeded through the poet and through the things equally.

朝やけがよろこばしいか蝸牛　　　　　一　茶
Asayake ga　yorokobashii ka　katatsumuri

> A red morning sky
> For you, snail;
> 　Are you glad about it?　　　　Issa

> A red sky in the morning
> Is the shepherd's warning,

but the delight of the snail, I suppose, says Issa. The snail almost certainly does not see the redness of the sky or deduce from it the probability of rain. But in exactly the same way, and for the same reason. Issa does not see the insensitiveness of the snail or consider the probabilities of its foreseeing the fall of rain. He is not divided from the snail. He feels and thinks as a snail would if it were human. This is the nature of a poet.

Verses of similar spiritual origin are the following:

手傳つて虱を拾へ雀の子
Tetsudatte　shirami wo hiroe　suzume no ko

> Little sparrow,
> Help me
> 　Pick off these lice.

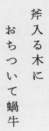

斧入る木に
おちついて蝸牛

Ono hairu ki ni
ochitsuite katatsumuri

The axe bites into the tree,
But the snail
Is calm and serene.

Snail
by Baishitsu, 梅室, 1768–1852
The verse by the artist

御祭りに赤い出立のとんぼかな
Omatsuri ni   akai dedachi no   tombo kana

> The dragon-fly,
> In red clothes,
> Off to the festival.

年寄と見てや鳴く蚊も耳のそば
Toshiyori to   mite ya naku ka mo   mimi no soba

> The mosquito also,
> Humming close to my ear,
> Must think I am old.

These instinctive utterances spring from the depths of Issa's mind; there is nothing more profound than this simplicity.

柴の戸や錠の代りにかたつむり   一 茶
Shiba no to ya   jō no kawari ni   katatsumuri

> A brushwood gate;
> For a lock,
> This snail.

Issa

In this simple verse, a whole world of ideals, a whole philosophy of life (in the poetic sense) lies revealed. Every house must have a garden, and every garden a garden gate. This one is made of the lightest and cheapest materials, brushwood. But how shall we lock the gate when we go away for the day, leaving the house empty? A snail put across the gate and gate-post will be enough with poverty of life, elimination of unessentials, trust in one's neighbours, and above all the humour to see the absurdity of both sides; the rich man with his well-guarded mansion, burglar-traps and so on, the poet in his self-inflicted poverty and inconveniences. The snail is used both as an absurd-looking creature and to point to the ridiculousness of all locks and bolts and gates and doors. But unless you see the loveliness of the snail and the pathos of both rich and poor, you are still far away from the world in which Issa lives through this haiku.

This verse by Issa, 1763–1827, seems to be an improvement on one of Bonchō, died 1714, a disciple of Bashō:

あばらやの戸のかすがいよなめくぢり
Abaraya no   to no kasugai yo   namekujiri

> The slug,
> A clamp on the door
> Of a tumble-down house.

The slug lies across the gap between one plank and another.
It looks like an iron clamp or clench used for holding beams
together. The colour and shape of the slug make it similar to
the clamp, but the poetic point lies in the expression of the
weakness of the ramshackle hut, held together by such a thing
as this soft-bodied slug.

この雨の降るのにどつちへでいろ哉   一 茶
Kono ame no   furu no ni dotchi e   deiro[1] kana

> Where can he be going
> In the rain,
> This snail?   Issa

Unless we remember that this verse is by Issa we cannot
get the proper meaning, or indeed any poetical meaning at all.
Issa spontaneously thinks of the snail as a human being, just
as Christ looked upon human beings as though they were
charming and lovable little snails. His feeling is one of surprise
that the snail should be going somewhere when it is raining
so heavily. Why doesn't he put off visiting his relatives or
going shopping, until the rain stops? There is a similar verse
by Buson:

蝸牛何思ふ角の長みじか
Katatsumuri   nani omou tsuno no   naga mijika

> A snail,
> One horn short, one long,—
> What troubles him?

The snail rests on the leaf, a beautiful creature, its trans-
lucent shell pearled with morning dew, its head delicately lifted,

[1]Issa notes that the snail, *katatsumuri*, is called *deiro* by the
villagers.

but strangely enough, one horn is long, the other shortened,
as if hesitating in its mind about something.   This is hardly
poetry, but the delicacy and tenderness of the poet, felt in the
verse, express the softness of the snail in body and mind.

夕月や大はだぬいでかたつむり　　　　　　一 茶

Yūzuki ya   ōhada nuide   katatsumuri

Under the evening moon,
The snail
Is stripped to the waist.　　　　　　Issa

To enjoy the cool of the evening the snail has "stripped
himself to the skin," that is, has come out of his shell to the
fullest extent.   This is Issa's usual "anthropomorphism" or, if
you like, lycanthropy, but expresses in addition some peculiar
characteristic of the soft, tender, almost human skin of the snail.

古郷や佛の顔のかたつむり　　　　　　　一 茶

Furusato ya   hotoke no kao no   katatsumuri

My old home;
The face of the snail
Is the face of Buddha.　　　　　Issa

Issa returns to his native place, and the insensible softening
of his feelings, the resurgence of the mind of his childhood is
seen in the snail's gentleness and meekness, which again shines
in the calm and tranquillity of the Buddhist images.

かたつむり酒の肴に這はせけり　　　　　　其 角

Katatsumuri   sake no sakana ni   hawasekeri

The snail;
We made it creep along,
As relish to our wine.　　　　　Kikaku

Issa has a similar verse to this, in which the summer shower
which unexpectedly falls is used as an accompanying dish to

the wine that is being drunk; it is probably an imitation of Kikaku's verse.

夕立やはらりと酒の肴ほど
Yūdachi ya hararito sake no   sakana hodo

A sudden summer shower,—
Enough to be a relish
To our wine.

蝸牛そろそろのぼれ富士の山   一 茶
Katatsumuri   sorosoro nobore   fuji no yama

O snail,
Climb Mount Fuji,
But slowly, slowly!   Issa

Issa may have meant this, as commentators explain it, as a contemptuous reference to themselves, meaning, "little by little, you may attain something if you persevere long enough." I wish to take it differently, however, as of universal application. If you are a snail, be a snail. And if as a snail you climb, follow your snail nature, your Buddha nature, and climb slowly, slowly!

足もとへいつ來りしよ蝸牛   一 茶
Ashimoto e itsu kitarishi yo katatsumuri

When did it come here
Close by me,
This snail?   Issa

The slower things move, the more their mystery and inevitability are perceived. Moonlight, the tides, such things never fail to arouse in us the spirit of wonder when unseen of us they creep over the ground in silence.

蓑虫はちゝとも啼くを蝸牛　　蕪村

Minomushi wa　chi-chi to mo naku wo　katatsumuri

The *minomushi*,
"Chi-chi," it says,—
But the snail?

Buson

The *minomushi*, or straw-coat insect, is the "old clothes man" that spins a kind of cocoon round itself and sticks it onto twigs and dead leaves. Japanese people suppose it to chirp, saying "chi-chi, chi-chi", which means "father," and it thus represents filial piety and love of parents. The snail however has no cry: it is silent, and all the more meaningful.

どれ程に面白いのか火取むし　　一茶

Dore hodo ni　omoshiroi no ka　hitorimushi

How much
Are you enjoying yourself,
Tiger-moth?

Issa

The Japanese for "tiger-moth" is *hitorimushi*, "light-taking insect." Poets seem to have understood this in the sense of "light-extinguishing insect," as may be seen from the following verses, all by Issa:

消してよい時分は來るなり火取虫

Keshite yoi　jibun wa kuru nari　hitorimushi

The tiger-moth
Came just at the time
For putting out the light.

兩三度うろうろ下手な火取虫

Ryōsando　uro-uro heta na　hitorimushi

Two or three times
It hesitated, the unskilful
Tiger-moth.

庵 の 燈 は む し さ へ と り に 來 り け り
Io no hi wa   mushi sae tori ni   kitarikeri

> Even the insects come
> To extinguish the light
> In my hermitage.

木 が く れ や 火 の な い 庵 に 火 取 虫
Kogakure ya   hi no nai io ni   hitorimushi

> The tiger-moth comes
> To a lamp-less dwelling,
> Hidden among the trees.

夏 虫 の 死 ん で 落 ち け り 本 の 上   子 規
Natsumushi no   shinde ochikeri   hon no ue

> Summer insects
> Fall dead
> Upon my book.   Shiki

We may compare this verse and the following, by Shōha, to Hardy's *An August Midnight*.

夏 虫 や 夜 學 の 人 の 顔 を 打 つ
Natsumushi ya   yagaku no hito no   kao wo utsu

> Summer insects
> Strike the face
> Of the midnight scholar.

飛 鮎 の 底 に 雲 ゆ く 流 れ か な   鬼 貫
Tobu ayu no   soko ni kumo yuku   nagare kana

> A trout leaps;
> Clouds are moving
> In the bed of the stream.   Onitsura

Fish move through the air. Clouds swim in the stream. Compare this to the following verse from the *Zenrinkushū*:

雨 中 看 果 日 、 火 裏 酌 清 泉 。

Perceiving the sun in the midst of the rain;
Ladling out clear water from the depths of the fire.

It is strange how birds draw us to the sky, fish to water, men to God. In the following verse by Shiki, we see the same thing as in Onitsura's.

一群の鮎目をすぎぬ水の色
Hitomure no   ayu me wo suginu   mizu no iro

A school of trout
Passed by:
The colour of the water!

鮎くれてよらで過行夜半の門   蕪 村
Ayu kurete   yorade sugiyuku   yowa no mon

Presenting the trout,
I did not go in, but went on:
The midnight gate.   Buson

This verse has been praised for its brevity and condemned by implication for its obscurity, but when one is used to it, it does not seem so excessively brief or obscure. As it is usually understood, however, it is literature rather than poetry. We feel keenly the good manners and culture of the Japanese in the first two lines, but it is the third which is the point of the poem. The friend going late at night to give the trout, knocking at the gate, making his salutations, being asked in and declining on account of the lateness of the hour, saying good-bye and departing,—all this is leading up to the final scene, the gate standing there silent in the silent night. What appeared to be a small narrative or drama turns out to be a picture in black and white, a single gate standing there.

Sampū, Bashō's disciple, has a verse the words of which may have suggested themselves to Buson:

手をかけて折らで過行く木槿かな
Te wo kakete   orade sugiyuku   mukuge kana

Stretching out my hand,
I did not break it off, but went on,—
The Rose of Sharon.

Taigi, a contemporary of Buson, uses a similar technique in the following verse:

な折りそと折りてくれけり園の梅
Na ori so to   orite kurekeri   sono no ume

"Don't break it off!" he said,
Then he broke one off and gave it me;
The plum-tree in the garden.

Evidently the poet was going to break off a branch of the plum-tree in his friend's garden, without asking him. Catching him in the act, his friend asked him not to do it. Then repenting of his selfishness, he broke off a branch himself and gave it to the disconsolate poet. (The original of this verse is of course much more obscure than the translation.)

夕暮は鮎の腹見る川瀬かな   鬼 貫
Yūgure wa   ayu no hara miru   kawase kana

In the evening,
The bellies of the trout,
Seen in the shallows.   Onitsura

During the day, the trout remain in the same place, but as it grows dark, they go up the river. When they reach the shallow rapids, they move to and fro, and their silver bellies show clearly in the dusk. This is a sight, and this is a verse, of which one can never grow tired, can never become satiated. It has the simplicity and unaffectedness of nature itself.

けふの日も棒ふり虫よ翌も又   一 茶
Kyō no hi mo   bōfurimushi yo   asu mo mata

Today's day also,
And tomorrow again, wasted,—
Mosquito larvae.   Issa

The mosquito larvae squirm and wriggle up and down in the water today; they will do the same thing tomorrow, and the next day. As always, Issa sees his own life in that of other

creatures, and their life in his. This haiku is Issa's version of
Macbeth's words:

> Tomorrow, and tomorrow, and tomorrow,
> Creeps in this petty pace from day to day.

しづまれば流るゝ脚や水馬　　　　　　　　太　祇
Shizumareba nagaruru ashi ya mizusumashi

> The whirligig;
> When it stops skating,
> The legs float away.　　　　　　　Taigi

The *amembo*, the pond-skater, seen skating in summer, has
a long slender body, long legs, and wings at certain times.

When for a moment it ceases its perpetual gyrating and
figure-skating, the current pulls his legs along and the whole
posture of the insect becomes asymmetrical. This is all there
is in the verse; it is nothing but a minute observation, but we
feel in and through it just as much of the power of nature,
law, inevitability, as in the rising of the sun or the procession
of the seasons. The same applies to an even simpler verse by
Shiki:

川上へ頭そろへて水馬
Kawakami e kashira soroete mizusumashi

> The whirligigs,
> All pointing their heads
> Upstream.

朝風の毛を吹見ゆる毛虫かな　　　　　　蕪　村
Asakaze no ke wo fukimiyuru kemushi kana

> The morning breeze
> Seen blowing the hairs
> On the caterpillar.　　　　　　　Buson

The meaning of the original is slightly different from that of
the translation. It is that the morning breeze is *seen* in the
hairs of the caterpillar which it is blowing. The poet does not

feel, or does not notice the wind blowing, but sees the hairs quivering, sees the wind in this fact. And the poetical meaning of the verse is precisely here. It is the *faithfulness* of the hairs to the wind, of the wind to the hairs, that strikes the poet, though not in the abstract, intellectual form. And this is a source of deep satisfaction, which comes welling out of our hearts in the pure and innocent joy of seeing the hairy caterpillar on this windy morning.

植 物 TREES AND FLOWERS

蜘蛛の巣は暑きものなり夏木立   蕪 村
Kumo no su wa   atsuki mono nari   natsu kodachi

> Spiders' webs
> Are hot things,
> In the summer grove.   Buson

This instantaneous judgement is a non-intellectual one. It is
merely putting into words the physical sensation immediately
experienced, but in so doing we are told something of the nature
of summer, of the woods in summer, of the character of the
spider and its web.   Above all, we realize something of the
inexhaustible nature of hotness, as the web clings to our nose
and eyebrows and ears.

先づたのむ椎の木もあり夏木立   芭 蕉
Mazu tanomu   shii no ki mo ari   natsu kodachi

> I look first of all
> To the pasania tree there,
> In the summer grove.   Bashō

This verse comes at the end of Bashō's 幻住庵記, *Record of
the Visionary Life Hermitage*, 1690, which closes, after speaking
of Hakurakuten and Toho, with the words:

> 賢愚文質の等しからざるも、いづれか幻の
> 栖處ならずやと思ひ捨ててふしぬ。

> The literary abilities of the wise and foolish are
> not the same, but, "Is this not, in either case, a
> phantom dwelling place?" I reflected, and laid
> me down there to rest.

This is a very innocent-looking, not to say apparently unin-
teresting verse, but the more we study it, the more unexpected
depths it reveals.   First, there are a large number of sources
which might have suggested the verse.   In the *Heike Monogatari*,
chap. 15, we find the following waka by Yorimasa:

のぼるべき便りなき身は木の下に
しひを拾ひて世を渡るかな

> Never to rise higher,
> I go through the world
>   Beneath the trees,
> Picking up
> Pasania[1] acorns.

In the *Manyōshū*:

岡のこの向つをに椎まかば
ことしの夏の蔭にならむか

> Were pasania acorns
> To be sown
>   On yonder hill of Kataoka,
> Would it not give shade
> In summer, this year?

There is a waka of Saigyō:

ならびいて友をはなれぬこがらめの
ねぐらに頼む椎の下枝

> The marsh-tits,
> That side by side
>   Never part from one another,
> Desire the lower boughs
> Of the pasania for their nests.

In the *Genji Monogatari*:

立ちよらん蔭と頼みし椎が本
空しき床になりにけるかな

> The pasania
> Desired by me,
>   And whose shade I approached,—
> It has become
> A vacant sleeping-place.

All or any or none of these may have been at the back of

---

[1] "Shii" also means "the Fourth Rank," which he reached but was not satisfied with.

Bashō's mind when he came for the first time to live in the hermitage called Genjū-an. Around him were trees in the heat of summer, and among them a pasania. It is to this great tree that he commits his spirit. The pasania is to be his dwelling place. The verse is thus an expression of Bashō's natural piety.

法談の手まねも見えて夏木立   一 茶
Hōdan no   temane mo miete   natsu kodachi

> Seen preaching,
> Gesturing,—
> From under the summer trees.   Issa

As Issa walks under the shade of the pine-trees, in the distance he sees, through an opening in the trees, pious old men and women of the village in the temple sitting round the priest, reverently listening to his sermon. What he is saying is inaudible to Issa. At that moment, the priest lifts his hand and makes some gesture illustrating his remarks. There, in the warm summer glade, Issa feels once more the never-ending, poignant, discordant harmony of Nature and man. Man is somehow out of place in

the brotherhood of venerable trees,[1]

yet they are meaningless without at least his absence.

木啄も庵はやぶらず夏木立   芭 蕉
Kitsutsuki mo   io wa yaburazu   natsu kodachi

> Even the woodpecker
> Will not harm this hermitage
> Among the summer trees.   Bashō

Bucchō was one of Bashō's teachers of Zen when in Edo. This verse was composed at the temple of Unganji 雲岸寺. The passage in *Oku no hosomichi* in which the poem occurs is quoted in Volume I, page 35.

---

[1] Wordsworth, *Sonnet composed at—Castle*.

人聲に蛭落るなり夏木立   一 茶
Hitogoe ni   hiru ochiru nari   natsu kodachi

Hearing someone speak,
The leech fell down
     In the summer grove.   Issa

This kind of leech lives in trees and bushes. When people
or animals pass by, it falls on them or attaches itself to them
and sucks their blood.

The leech could not, of course, actually hear a voice, but Issa
expresses unhesitatingly his childish, animistic, unintellectual
conviction of a causal relation between the sound of a voice and
the blood-sucking will-to-live of the animal. The leech itself is
neither repulsive nor charming; it is something much more
important, much more poetic; it is interesting. It belongs to
that web of nature in which when one part is touched the
whole trembles. Issa's verse is no more true, and no less, than
the words of Christ:

Not a sparrow falls to the ground but your Heavenly
Father knoweth it.

花か實か水に散り込む夏木立   蕪 村
Hana ka mi ka   mizu ni chirikomu   natsu kodachi

Was it a flower or a berry,
That fell into the water
     In the summer grove?   Buson

Sitting by a pool in the forest glade, the poet heard a slight
noise; something fell from the boughs above into the water and
sank at once. Was it some small flower, or was it a seed or
a berry, that now lies hidden at the bottom of the water? No
one knows, no one will ever know. It is as mysterious and as
eternally unknown as life itself; it is life. The fact, and the
ultimate meaninglessness of the fact,—these two things make
up life. As human beings we feel a kind of inquisitiveness:
are all the things that happen the flower or the fruit of the
universe? If this feeling of curiosity is weak enough, if it is,
that is to say, the spirit of poetic wonder, then the falling of

a leaf or a twig contains in it all existence. The slight sound, the ripple on the water that spreads fainter and fainter, the trees that stand as if eternal in silence above, the poet in his quietness,—there is no connection between any of them, nor any division. There is another verse by Buson which is very similar in its meaning:

いづこよりつぶて打ち込む夏木立
Izuko yori tsubute uchikomu natsu kodachi

> The summer grove;
> Struck by a small stone
> Coming from somewhere.

By the same author, with even simpler materials:

動く葉もなくおそろしき夏木立
Ugoku ha mo naku osoroshiki natsu kodachi

> Not a leaf stirring:
> How awesome
> The summer grove!

田の中やたゞ四五本の夏木立   子 規
Ta no naka ya tada shi go hon no natsu kodachi

> In the midst of the fields,
> Four or five trees,—
> A summer grove!   Shiki

When we say "a summer grove," we think of a mass of trunks and foliage, but here there are only a few trees left in the middle of the rice fields to make a shade for the toilers to rest in. It is the sparseness, the absence of things that has its meaning in this verse. The significance of things, the significance of no-things: of these two haiku chooses rather the second. In the following verse, also by Shiki, it is the absence of human beings that gives meaning to the hum of insects, the warm breeze, the earth that rises to the sky in the form of tree-trunks, the leaves with their myriad shapes and tones.

夏木立入りし人の跡もなし
Natsu kodachi   hairishi hito no   ato mo nashi

> Entering the summer grove,—
> And not a trace
> Of him remains.

夏木立入りし人の跡もなし   子 規
Natsu kodachi   hairishi hito no   ato mo nashi

> There is no trace
> Of him who entered
> The Summer grove.   Shiki

This is a re-translation of the verse quoted just before. The concentration on the wonder of the ordinary and natural is the essence of the poetic life in haiku. A man is seen entering the grove of trees; he goes from the bright summer sunshine into the twilight of noon of the trees. He disappears, and the place thereof knoweth him no more. It is as inevitable, as irrevocable, as tragic as death. All meeting is the beginning of parting. The disappearance of the man swallowed up among the leaves of nature is life experienced, endured, lived.

佛ともならでうかうか老の松   一 茶
Hotoke to mo   narade uka uka   oi no matsu

> Not yet having become a Buddha,
> This ancient pine-tree,
> Idly dreaming.   Issa

This pine-tree may be taken as a symbol of Issa himself, but it is pleasanter to think of the tree alone. It stands there, neither toiling nor spinning, in the summer sunshine, giving a sound to the breeze, a meaning to the rain, a shadow to the ground. Like every other thing, the pine-tree will one day attain to Buddhahood, but now it just stands there as though ambitionless, absent-minded, heedless.

木下闇人驚かす地蔵かな   子　規
Koshitayami   hito odorokasu   jizō kana

In the gloom under the trees,
Jizō
Gives one a start!   Shiki

This was composed at Matsuyama, after he had passed by
the crematory there. This was of course in a remote place
away from human habitation, and when he suddenly saw the
statue of Jizō there, he received an almost painful shock of
surprise. What is it that surprises us as we are suddenly aware
of the figure sitting motionless under the dark canopy of leaves?
It is the unexpected appearance of what looks like a living
creature, its noiseless existence in a world apart.   More pro-
foundly, we are struck with the *existence* of the things.   Jizō
has his world and we have ours, and suddenly they come
together with a shock of astonishment that underlies and sup-
ports the mere physical surprise that is partly caused by the
coolness.

There is another verse by Shiki in which Jizō takes his place
among the vegetation without any ulterior meaning:

道も又草茂りけり石地蔵
Michi mo mata   kusa shigerikeri   ishijizō

Even the paths
Are rank with grasses,
Among them a stone Jizō.

Here the statue takes its normal place with the other stones
and weeds, just as the tombs do in the following verse by the
same author:

墓原や墓低くして草茂る
Hakabara ya   haka hikuku shite   kusa shigeru

In the grave-yard,
Grave-stones are low,
Grasses rank.

鐘もなき鐘つき堂の若葉哉　　　子 規
Kane mo naki   kanetsukidō no   wakaba kana

A belfry,
Without a bell:
The young leaves!　　　Shiki

In his wanderings, the poet comes to what seems to be a
temple. On a piece of rising ground appears the belfry, situated
as usual at the side of the main building, and a little apart.
Climbing up to it, he finds to his surprise that there is no bell
in it. In this vacancy of mind that corresponds to the empti-
ness of the belfry, the young leaves crowd closer and greener
around him.

Again and again in haiku we find how the absence of some
expected thing or sensation stimulates the mind to perceive
afresh, under some new aspect, or for the first time, some-
thing else.

高どのゝ灯影に沈む若葉かな　　　蕪 村
Takadono no   hokage ni shizumu   wakaba kana

In the light of the mansion,
The young leaves
Are submerged.　　　Buson

From upstairs, the paper screens all thrown open, the light
of the lamps streams out into the garden down on to the young
leaves of every shape and lustre that lie like a sea beneath,
layer upon layer, wave upon wave.

三千の兵たてこもる若葉哉　　　子 規
Sanzen no   hei tatekomoru   wakaba kana

Encastled,
Three thousand warriors,—
These young leaves!　　　Shiki

The power of nature over that of man; this is felt without
abstraction, non-intellectually, in the sense that the intellect is
submerged, like the warriors, in the experience. The particu-

larity of number on the one hand, contrasts with the vague, multitudinous quantity on the other.

こがねさびて若葉にしのぶ昔かな   樗 良
Kogane sabite   wakaba ni shinobu   mukashi kana

The gold-foil is tarnished;
The young leaves take one back
          To the past.   Chora

The young leaves are timeless and can take us anywhere. It is the gold and silver ornaments on the posts and beams of the shrine which decide that it shall be to the past. The young leaves belong to Now, and to that Now belong also the days of long ago, the remote past when those young leaves waved over untarnished gold.

金の間の人もの云はぬ若葉かな   蕪 村
Kin no ma no   hito mono iwanu   wakaba kana

He is silent
In the golden chamber:
       The young leaves!   Buson

There is a contrast (which is in the nature of an identity) between the visitor who sits in his stiff, embroidered clothes, his lips tightly compressed, in the room where the sliding screens are covered with gold paper, and the pale yellow-green sun-lit leaves of spring outside. The green of the leaves and the glowing gold speak so loudly that all speech is superfluous.

淺間山煙の中の若葉かな   蕪 村
Asamayama   kemuri no naka no   wakaba kana

Mount Asama;
Through the smoke
     Young leaves appearing.   Buson

The cone of Mount Asama is quite bare of trees, but the

smoke lingers down one side of the mountain. From out of
this billowing, wreathing, heavy mass of smoke, appear the
young leaves, glittering in the sunshine. The smoke and the
leaves are seen by the poet as two manifestations of many
things.

夜走りの帆に有明て若葉かな   蕪 村
Yobashiri no   ho ni ariakete   wakaba kana

Sailing at night,—
And with dawn on the sail,
The young leaves!   Buson

The translation has obscured the connection between the sail
and the dawn and the young leaves. It might be more literally
rendered:

With dawn on the sail
That ran all night,—
The green leaves!

The white sail is most important thing on the ship; it is what
strikes the eye of the poet when he wakes from his sleep after
a night's run toward the shore. Then as he raises his head
and looks at the land, he sees a mass of foliage, young green
leaves with the just risen sun glancing upon them.

傘たたむ玄関深き若葉かな   子 規
Kasa tatamu   genkan fukaki   wakaba kana

Closing the umbrella,
The porch is deep
Among the young leaves.   Shiki

From the gate to the entrance the path is long and narrow,
overhung with the new leaves that strike against the umbrella.
The poet furls it and looks at the front entrance in the distance
deep among the trees. There is a kind of loneliness that belongs
to just those few yards between him and the door. They belong
to nature, not to men.

若葉して水白く麥黄ばみたり   蕪 村
Wakaba shite   mizu shiroku mugi   kibamitari

Young leaves come out,
　Water is white,
　　Barley yellowing.   Buson

Commentators give many explanations of this verse. It is simply a pleasure in the three colours, green, white, and yellow. The omission of the word "green" is due to the splendid technique of Buson. The pleasure in colour is perhaps the purest of all human pleasures, even more so than music, for there is almost no human emotion associated with it. Buson does something similar in the following verse:

山吹の卯の花の後や花いばら
Yamabuki no   u no hana no ato ya   hana-ibara

The mountain rose,
Then the *u* flower,
Then the wild rose.

There is a sequence of yellow, white and red.

谷路行く人は小さき若葉かな   蕪 村
Taniji yuku   hito wa chiisaki   wakaba kana

Going along the valley path,
People are small:
　Ah, the young leaves!   Buson

The poet is looking down the valley with its billowing green leaves, and the path and the people on it are so almost lost to sight, that he has "a shock of mild surprise" at their insignificance. The young leaves grow greener and more multitudinous in his mind. If we translate this verse,

How tiny the men,
Going along the valley path,
Among the green leaves!

the poetry disappears, because the point is not the insignificance of man, but the significance of nature.

不二ひとつうずみ残して若葉かな　　　蕪村
Fuji hitotsu uzumi nokoshite wakaba kana

Mount Fuji alone
Remains unburied
Beneath the young leaves.　　　Buson

This verse is not so much in praise of Mount Fuji in rising above the masses of verdure, as glorifying the green leaves themselves which cover all things but the snow-clad mountain. There is a contrast between the calm and rest of the mountain, and the luxuriance and restlessness of the leaves, but it is the young leaves that touch the heart of the poet, and make his breast expand and rejoice with them.

山畑を小雨はれ行く若葉かな　　　蕪村
Yamabata wo kosame hareyuku wakaba kana

Over the field on the mountain-side,
The fine rain clears up;
The young leaves!　　　Buson

The field is surrounded by trees and bushes, and in the drizzling rain there is little distinction between one and the other. Suddenly, however, patches of blue sky appear, a wind blows and the rain is swept away. All around the field are the different shapes and colours of the young leaves, glistening, almost dazzling in the sunshine. As it clears up farther and farther in the distance, the green leaves are seen extending in waves of a sea of green.

窓の灯の梢に残る若葉かな　　　蕪村
Mado no hi no kozue ni nokoru wakaba kana

Remaining in the branches
In the light of the window,—
The young leaves.　　　Buson

All day the mind of the poet has been full of the young green leaves. As the darkness falls, they gradually disappear in the

shadows. Only on the branches that rise in front of the window
of the room where a lamp has been lit, do the leaves remain
in sight, still shining as in the daytime.

蚊帳を出て奈良を立ちゆく若葉哉　　蕪　村
Kaya wo dete　nara wo tachiyuku　wakaba kana

Coming out of the mosquito-net,
I passed out of Nara;
The young leaves!　　　　　　　　　Buson

There is a subtle harmony here between the speed of the first
two lines and that of the third, that is to say, between the
poetic brevity of the description of his waking up, getting out
of the mosquito net, dressing, eating his breakfast, leaving the
inn, walking through the streets of Nara into the country
outside,—and the energy, the green vigour, the springing life
of the young leaves glittering in the bracing air and bright
sunshine. Whether we call this poem purely objective or purely
subjective does not matter at all; the tempo of the poet's life
this spring morning, and that of the young, yellowish-green
leaves, is the same.

A simpler example of the same thing, also by Buson, is the
following:

來て見れば夕の櫻實となりぬ
Kite mireba　yūbe no sakura　mi to narinu

Coming and looking at them,
The evening cherry-blossoms
Have become fruit.

The classical example in English literature of a description of
speed is Coleridge's of a tropical sunset:

The sun's rim dips; the stars rush out,
At one stride comes the dark.

絶頂の城たのもしき若葉かな   蕪 村
Zecchō no   shiro tanomoshiki   wakaba kana

Full of hope and promise,—
The castle on the summit,
In the young leaves!   Buson

Tho whole mountain is buried under a mass of fresh green leaves. From the top emerge the white walls of the castle, and tier upon tier of roof. It is a fortress that ten thousand enemies could not take; the green leaves are seen rising in their wild energy and shining splendour. The exhilaration of height and the historical and military associations accentuate the strangeness of seeing the green leaves rising from below.

あらたふと青葉若葉の日の光   芭 蕉
Ara tōto   aoba wakaba no   hi no hikari

Ah, how glorious!
The young leaves, the green leaves
Glittering in the sunshine!   Bashō

This has the same spirit as Wordsworth's verse:

> The Cock is crowing,
> The stream is flowing,
> The small birds twitter,
> The lake doth glitter,
> The green field sleeps in the sun.

But Bashō's verse includes another "thought." It was composed at Nikkō, and Bashō is also feeling reverence for those enshrined in the Mausoleum, in particular, Ieyasu. But the glory that was Greece, the grandeur that was Rome is not separated in his mind from the pomp of sunshine upon the burning leaves. The magnificence of Man, the sublimity of Nature, are seen as they really are, one thing.

There are passages in Traherne's *Centuries of Meditation* which strongly resemble this verse of Bashō's. (Traherne is speaking of his childhood, but Bashō's life was one long childhood.) The following is well-known:

The corn was orient and immortal wheat which never should be reaped, nor was ever sown. I thought it had stood from everlasting to everlasting. The dust and stones of the street were as precious as gold; the gates were at first the end of the world. The green trees, when I saw them first through one of the gates, transported and ravished me, their sweetness and unusual beauty made my heart to leap, and almost mad with ecstasy, they were such strange and wonderful things.

葉柳の寺町過ぐる雨夜かな   白　雄
Hayanagi no　teramachi suguru　amayo kana

Passing under the leafy willows
Of a street of temples:
An evening of rain.   Shirao

On either side of the road are ranged temples of various sects. Rain falls slowly through the dusk, dripping down from the long, leafy branches of the willow trees that stand in the courtyards and along the street. The leafy willow trees have some deep relation to the temples round them. Not only the rain and the gloom are in accord with them but the green leaves also. It is the rain that brings and refreshes the greenness. It is the grief and woe of life that makes us live. In the gloom of the temples there are lights here and there.

須磨寺やふかぬ笛きく木下やみ   芭　蕉
Sumadera ya　fukanu fue kiku　koshitayami

I heard the unblown flute
In the deep tree-shades
Of the Temple of Suma.   Bashō

Bashō visited Sumadera in the summer, and under the shades of the old pine-trees there, saw the flute that Atsumori[1] used to play in the castle before his death. This is almost identical in poetical thought with Keats' lines from the *Ode to a Grecian Urn:*

Heard melodies are sweet, but those unheard
Are sweeter; therefore, ye soft pipes, play on;
Not to the sensual ear, but, more endeared,
Pipe to the spirit ditties of no tone.

卯 の 花 の 中 に 崩 れ し 庵 か な   樗 良
U-no-hana no   naka ni kuzureshi   iori kana

The hermitage,
Having tumbled down,
　　　Lies among the *u* flowers.   Chora

U-no-hana is called the Deutzia scabra. The leaves are long
and round. In May, small white flowers bloom looking like
snow. It is often seen in the mountains and in the hedges of
country houses. It has a great variety of other names.

A hermitage of some other poet or recluse has fallen down
at last; it lies there among the *u* flowers neither with nor
without appropriateness, but just as it is. It is the thusness of
things, their just-so-ness, which gives the poet that indefinable
but unmistakable feeling of significance, (something quite beyond
intellectually perceiveable appropriateness or logically expressible
congruity,) which is the poetic flow of life becoming conscious
of itself.

卯 の 花 の 絶 間 た ゝ か ん 暗 の 門   去 來
U-no-hana no   taema tatakan   yami no mon

I will knock
At the gate in the darkness,
　　　Where the *u* flowers leave off.   Kyorai

It is a warm, dark summer night, and the poet is visiting a
friend of his very late. The gate cannot be seen, but on both

---

[1] 1169–84. At the battle of Ichi-no-tani, when the Taira were defeated,
Atsumori, then seventeen years old, was seized by Kumagai Naozane,
d. 1208. In spite of the fact that Atsumori reminded him of his son
Kojiro, he beheaded him, and sent the flute Atsumori carried to his
father, Tsunemori. He spent the rest of his life at Kurodani praying
for Atsumori's soul.

sides of it flowers of the *u* are blooming whitely. They are the
only guide to where the gate stands, and where they suddenly
leave off the gate must be, and he will knock there.

卯 の 花 を か ざ し に 關 の 晴 着 か な   曾 良
U-no-hana wo kazashi ni seki no haregi kana

> A flower of the *u* in my hat,
> I pass through the Barrier,
>   As if in my best clothes.   Sora

In *Oku no Hosomichi*, it says:

中 に も 此 の 關 は 三 關 の 一 つ に し て 風 騒 の 人 、
心 を と ゞ む 。 秋 風 を 耳 に 殘 し 、

〔都 を ば 霞 と と も に た ち し か ど
　　秋 風 ぞ 吹 く 白 河 の 關〕

紅 葉 を 俤 に し て

〔都 に は ま だ 青 葉 に て 見 し か ど も
　　紅 葉 散 り し く 白 河 の 關〕

青 葉 の 梢 な ほ あ は れ な り 。 卯 の 花 の 白 妙 に 茨
の 色 の 咲 き そ ひ て 、 雪 に も 越 ゆ る 心 地 ぞ す る 。
古 人 冠 を 正 し 衣 裝 を 改 め し こ と な ど 、 清 輔 筆
に も と ゞ め 置 か れ し と ぞ 。

Among them, this is the Barrier of the three
which remains most in the minds of poets. "Au-
tumn Wind" in my ears,

> [Leaving the Capital
> Together with the haze of spring,
>   The autumn wind
> Blows here
> At the Barrier of Shirakawa.   Nōin Hōshi]

"Tinted Leaves" in my mind,

[The green leaves
Which I saw
In the Capital,
Fall as tinted leaves,
At the Barrier of Shirakawa.

Minamoto no Yorimasa]

the green sprays were lovely to behold. The white-
ness of the *u* flowers, together with the blooming
of the wild roses, made it seem like a season of
snow as we passed through. A certain man of old
put his hat on straight and changed his robes
when passing through the barrier. This fact is
related in a book [called *Fukurozōshi*, concerning
a man Taketa no Taifu Kuniyuki, who did so in
honour of Nōin Hōshi] by Fujiwara no Kiyosuke.

The verse that follows is very obscure in the original, which
is literally, "An *u* flower put as a hair ornament, best clothes
at the Barrier." Sora means that in imitation of him who put
on his court robes and passed through the Barrier ceremoniously,
he will put a flower of the *u*, growing nearby, in his *kasa*, or
umbrella-hat, and pass through. The poetry of this verse is
diffused in time, and needs some kindness of the imagination
to feel the tradition of poetic feeling running through these
people, the poet Nōin of the 9th century, up to Sora and Bashō,
of the 17th.

卯 の 花 や く ら き 柳 の 及 ご し   芭 蕉
U-no-hana ya   kuraki yanagi no   oyobi goshi

A flower of the *u*,
And dark over it,
A willow bends.   Bashō

Oyobigoshi means a bent back, a bent loin, and the above
verse could be translated more picturesquely;

The willow-tree
Leans its dark bosom
Over a flower of the *u*.

紙燭して垣の卯の花暗うすな   鳳　朗
Shishoku shite   kaki no u no hana   kurōsuna

Under the hedge, flowers of the *u*;
Do not darken them
　　　With the paper lantern.   Hōrō

The white flowers of the Deutzia Scabra gleam in the dusk under the wall, and fill the eye with joy. If the lantern is lit, the flowers will lose their own pale light.

楠の鎧ぬがれしぼたん哉   其　角
Kusunoki no   yoroi nugareshi   botan kana

Ah, the peonies,
For which Kusunoki
　　　Took off his armour!   Kikaku

Kusunoki Masashige, 正成, 1294-1336, the pattern of loyalty to the Imperial family, committed *harakiri* with his brother Masasue after his defeat at the battle of Minatogawa. He is buried in Hino-o in Kawachi Province at Kanshinji Temple, 観心寺. It was at this place that he rested himself, taking off his armour to gaze at the peonies growing there.

牡丹咲いてあたりに花のなき如し   機　一
Botan saite   atari ni hana no   naki gotoshi

When the peonies bloomed,
It seemed as though there were
　　　No flowers around them.   Kiitsu

An occidental poet will have this experience in regard to a woman with whom he is in love. When she enters the room, all other women cease to exist for him, become soulless automata. An oriental poet personalizes the flowers in the sense that their life is as vivid and meaningful to him as that of human beings. It may be thought that *per se* the interest in flowers must be of a lower order, an inferior content poetically compared with that in human beings. But the distinction is not in the standpoint, in the world view; not in the treatment, whether it is classical or romantic; not in the culture, occidental or oriental; neither is it in the object, the material that is assimilated and spiritualized. It is *depth* alone which matters, *depth* alone which admits of comparison.

方百里雨雲よせぬぼたん哉　　　　　　蕪 村
Hōhyakuri　amagumo yosenu　botan kana

The peonies do not allow
The rain-clouds a hundred leagues round
To approach them.　　　　　Buson

This is a fancy, but there is so much imagination put into it that it expresses a truth which the fancy disengages from the mere scientific fact. That is to say, the rain-clouds and the peonies are not connected, "really," as we say. The fancy supposes that the peonies have the power to prevent the rain-clouds from approaching. The imagination, seizing on the colour and size of the peonies with the utmost violence, and regarding with defiant eye the encircling banks of thunder clouds piled up on the horizon, perceives that the peonies and the clouds *are* connected in some mysterious way; that they stand opposed as enemies.

芍薬の蘂の湧きたつ日向哉　　　　　　太 祇
Shakuyaku no　zui no wakitatsu　hinata kana

The stamens and pistil
Of the peony gush out
Into the sunlight.　　　　　Taigi

From the pale red petals of the (herbaceous) peony the golden stamens and pistil burst out into the bright sunlight. In this verse we are made to feel a power and glory of the peony which has no reference to that of man.

寂として客の絶間のぼたん哉　　　蕪　村
Seki to shite　kyaku no taema no　botan kana

In the stillness,
Between the arrival of guests,
The peonies.

Buson

The peonies seem here to be described rather negatively than positively, as "they toil not neither do they spin," but for all this, they are seen under a peculiarly dynamic aspect.

園くらき夜を静かなる牡丹かな　　　白　雄
Sono kuraki　yo wo shizuka naru　botan kana

The garden is dark
In the night, and quiet
The peony.

Shirao

In the original, "night" is put in the objective case with *wo*, and this faintly suggests a causal relation of quietness between the peony and the night.

床の間の牡丹のやみや時鳥　　　子　規
Tokonoma no　botan no yami ya　hototogisu

The darkness of the alcove
Where the peonies are;
A *hototogisu* sings.

Shiki

We usually distinguish man and nature, natural and artificial, but sometimes these man-made distinctions are unmade by man. In the above verse, the poet, sick in bed, lies looking at the peonies that are "arranged" in the tokonoma, and as he does so, hears the voice of the *hototogisu* outside in the warm summer of early evening. The darkness of the tokonoma, the deep purplish red of the peony, the liquid voice of the bird roll over him in a wave of meaning. What is outside and what is inside, the free voice of the bird and the constrained form of alcove and flowers arranged in it,—there is no distinction here.

花暮れて月を抱けり白牡丹   曉 臺
Hana kurete   tsuki wo dakikeri   shiro-botan

> Dusk on the flower
> Of the white peony,
> That embraces the moon.   Gyōdai

This is a very unusual haiku in its personification and Shelleyan
flavour. It is good as Chinese poetry rather than as haiku. The
whiteness of the flower seems to draw to itself all the pallor of
the moon.

蠟燭にしづまりかへる牡丹かな   許 六
Rōsoku ni   shizumari kaeru   botan kana

> To the candle,
> The peony
> Is as still as death.   Kyoroku

The candle burns motionless; its soul of fire does not quiver.
The peony too, not to be outdone, glows immovable, overpow-
ering the candle with its fervent blooming. They are as quiet
as the grave, in their burning life.

地車のとゞろと響く牡丹かな   蕪 村
Jiguruma no   todoro to hibiku   botan kana

> The heavy wagon
> Rumbles by;
> The peony quivers.   Buson

As Buson is looking at the peony, a great cart loaded with
some heavy goods rolls by. The peony trembles a little with
the vibration of the ground. The place and time of this verse
is vague; it is like a cut from the film of a moving picture.
Contrast the following verse, also by Buson, in which the
objective description is replaced by a subjective reaction:

牡丹切つて氣のおとろへし夕かな
Botan kitte　ki no otoroeshi　yūbe kana

> Having cut the peony,
> I felt exhausted,
> That evening.

After thinking and hesitating, and being of two minds even
when he cut the flower, he felt quite spiritless that evening,
wearied to death by such a simple thing.

蟻王宮朱門を開く牡丹哉　　　　　蕪村
Ari ōkyū　shumon wo hiraku　botan kana

> The peony,
> Opening the Crimson Gate of the Palace
> Of the Kind of the Ants.　　Buson

There is said to be a great palace of ants under the earth.
The red peony is growing by the entrance as at a huge wide-
open gate.

閻王の口や牡丹を吐んとす　　　　蕪村
En-ō no　kuchi ya botan wo　hakan to su

> The mouth of Emma
> Is about to spit out
> A peony!　　Buson

Emma, or Yama, is the god of the dead in Vedic and Brah-
manic mythology. In Buddhism, he is a King of Vaisali, who
while fighting wished to be Lord of Hell, and was reborn as
such together with his eighteen generals and eighty thousand
men, who serve him there. Three times in twenty four hours
boiling copper is poured into Emma's mouth as punishment.
His face has an expression of fury, the mouth being open. The
inside of the mouth is painted bright vermilion, thus giving the
appearance of being about to spit out a bright red peony. This
verse expresses something of the flamboyant nature of a peony,
and something of the demoniac nature of Emma, which could
not be arrived at by any separate expressions of them.

It is worthy of note that Nakamura Kusatao, 中村草田男,
takes the above verse as concerning the peony, not Emma; and
the translation should then be:

> The peony;
> Emma is about to spit it
> Out of his mouth.

廣庭のぼたんや天の一方に   蕪 村
Hiro-niwa no   botan ya ten no   ippō ni

> The peonies
> Of the great garden,—
> In a part of heaven.   Buson

Buson here has used a phrase of the Chinese poet Sotōba 蘇
東坡:

望美人兮天一方

> Gazing at a beautiful woman,—
> A part of heaven.

Sotōba uses this word *bijin* to express the perfect man of
Confucius, but popularly, and perhaps as thought of by Buson,
it is used of a woman. In the above verse, the last line brings
out the heavenly nature of the peony.

牡丹折し父の怒ぞなつかしき   大 魯
Botan orishi   chichi no ikari zo   natsukashiki

> The peonies;
> On breaking one,[1] my father's anger!
> Now I yearn for it.   Tairo

A weak point of the poem is the obvious, though it may be
inadvertent, harmony of the father's anger and the red, bursting
peonies. Compare the following by Ōemaru:

[1] The original is also ambiguous, but means, of course, "When, as a
boy, I broke one."

去年まで叱つた瓜を手向けけり

Kyonen made   shikatta uri wo   tamukekeri

The melons, which last year
I scolded him for eating,
I now offer to his spirit.

In this verse, the emphasis is not so much on the child that
is mourned, or his own changed feelings, but on the melons
themselves. It is the *function* of a thing which determines its
value, and thus all things are of equal, that is, of infinite value.
A thing is what it is in virtue of its dynamic, not its static or
chemical validity. Things are fugal in their nature. There are,
it is true, differences of tone, timbre, height, but *musically*
speaking, melons are as significant as the burning of Troy, as
the birth of Buddha.

是ほどのぼたんと仕かたする子哉   一 茶

Kore hodo no   botan to shikata   suru ko kana

"The peony was as big as this,"
Says the little girl,
Opening her arms.   Issa

The little hands, and earnest face with wide-open eyes and
parted lips,—even the huge peony is eclipsed.

扇にて尺をとらせる牡丹かな   一 茶

Ōgi nite   shaku wo toraseru   botan kana

The peony
Made him measure it
With his fan.   Issa

The way in which the peony is considered as the active source
of the measuring of itself is not merely good psychology, but
shows us how Issa looks upon the plant world and upon himself.
Compared to that of the ordinary man, human beings and plants
are much closer together in the thought-feeling world of Issa.
The flower stands there in its colour and glory. It does not
bloom to be seen, nor does it wish to blush unseen. It is not

dependent upon man, but neither is it independent of him. Its purposeless purpose is fulfilled in its blooming in solitude and silence, yet when no one is gazing upon it, it has no shape or colour or fragrance. The flower needs the mind, and the mind needs the flower for its fulfilment. Issa emphasizes the power and activity of the peony not only because we live in an ego-centric, homocentric world, valueless and unpoetical, but also because he wishes to bring out the special nature of the peony, its power and magnificence, its lofty splendour. Is this splendour in the flower? Does Issa cause the flower to be measured, or does the flower cause Issa to measure it?

てもさてもても福相のぼたん哉   一 茶
Temo satemo   temo fukusō no   botan kana

Dear, dear,
What a fat, happy face it has,
This peony!   Issa

The peony is generally taken as a symbol of magnificence, but here Issa takes it in a more homely, human way. Of all Japanese poets Issa has the greatest power to lay his hands upon the most delicate sensations in the recesses of his mind and ours.

虹を吐き開かんとする牡丹哉   蕪 村
Niji wo haki   hirakan to suru   botan kana

About to bloom,
And exhale a rainbow,
The peony!   Buson

The peony bud, when it is about to bloom, has such a suggestion of power and colour and glory, that it looks as if it might emit a rainbow. This apparent hyperbole is the only means we have of expressing the gorgeous, overwhelming nature of the coming flower.

牡 丹 や し ろ が ね の 猫 こ が ね の 蝶　　　　蕪 村
Bōtan ya   shirogane no neko   kogane no chō

The peony;
A silver cat;
A golden butterfly.　　　　　Buson

This world of luxury is in some way alien to the world of
haiku, but it exists in nature and exists in art, and cannot be
entirely omitted.　The blood-red peony in the garden, a pure
white cat, and a yellow butterfly,—that these were actually
seen together by Buson is hard to believe.　Nevertheless, he
saw these three things together in his mind's eye, just as truly
as Bertha in *Bliss* saw Pearl Fulton

stirring the beautiful red soup in the grey plate.

Another of Buson's with the same delight in richness that is
yet clear and distinct:

金 屛 の か く や く と し て 牡 丹 か な
Kinbyō no   kakuyaku to shite   botan kana

On the golden screen
A peony
Brightly shining.

山 蟻 の あ か ら さ ま な り 白 牡 丹　　　　蕪 村
Yamaari no   akarasama nari   shirobotan

The mountain ant
Stands out clear,
On the white peony.　　　　　Buson

This is not merely a study in black and white; both the ant
and the peony are alive.　That is to say, they have *depth*, depth
in the material and in the spiritual sense.　The body of the ant,
as if made of jet-black beads, stands upon the creamy-white
flesh of the petal.　The heavy, vegetable life of the great flower
contrasts with the puritannical, intensely active life of the insect.

白牡丹或夜の月にくづれけり　　　　子 規
Shirobotan　aru yo no tsuki ni　kuzurekeri

The white peony;
At the moon, one evening,
It crumbled and fell.　　　　Shiki

This is what must be called a romantic verse, in the vein of
Flecker. The moon and the peony are not the pale disc we
see in the sky, the luxurious flower of earth, but exhalations
of the poetic soul. The collapse and fall of the white peony
are not the inevitable decline of nature but the decadence of
the spirit of man. What is common to both is the mystery of
all things, though the flower is so near us, the moon so far
away.

There is in this verse, a hint at the mysterious relation be-
tween the moon and flowers. This relation does not depend
upon the actual scientific cause and effect relation but on the
(apparently) purely subjective view of the matter. The white
peony that had been blooming so silently suddenly fell soon after
the moon rose. In our feeling, the white flower is overcome
with the radiance of the moon and drops down its petals. Quite
apart from scientific explanations, we all know instinctively that
everything is ultimately the cause and effect of everything else.
This is the justification for the wildest superstition and also of
the deepest intuitions of saints and poets. In any case, the
meaning of the present verse lies in quite a different realm from
that of rational thought, embracing as it does the mutually
augmented beauty of the moon and the peony, the noiseless
inevitability of the fall of the flower, the supreme indifference
of the moon, the abjectness of the fallen petals.

牡丹散て打かさなりぬ二三片　　　　蕪 村
Botan chitte　uchikasanarinu　nisanpen

The peony has fallen;
A few scattered petals
Lie one on another.　　　　Buson

What an astounding power these two or three red petals have,
more memorable than a cathedral in the moonlight. It has the

timelessness and simplicity of Classical art with the gorgeousness
and the feeling of destiny that belongs to the Romantic age.

牡丹散て心もおかず別れけり   北　枝
Botan chitte　kokoro mo okazu　wakarekeri

> The peonies having fallen,
> We parted
> Without regret.   Hokushi

This is the poetical version of Confucius' words:

> They sought for virtue; they got virtue; what was
> there for them to regret?

and of Christ's

> Where your treasure is, there will your heart be also.

雨の日や門さげて行く杜若   信　徳
Ame no hi ya　kado sagete yuku　kakitsubata

> A day of rain;
> Somebody passes my gate
> With irises.   Shintoku

The rain, the irises, so closely related with the water, and a
human being to give both a yet deeper meaning.

蛇にげて山静なり百合の花   子　規
Hebi nigete　yama shizuka nari　yuri no hana

> The snake fleeing away,
> The mountain is silent:
> This lily flower!   Shiki

There is a rustle, and the long body of the snake is seen
gliding away in its perfection of colour and movement. Every-
thing is silent, and yet more silent. A white lily glows among
the dark green leaves.　There is a secret relation between the
quiet of the mountain, the snake and its flight, and the creamy-

white lily that has something deathly and sinister in its silent beauty. Compare the following by Kyoshi:

蛇逃げて我を見し眼の草に殘る
Hebi nigete   ware wo mishi me no   kusa ni nokoru

The snake slid away,
But the eyes that glared at me
Remained in the grass.

I remember asking a man who was about to kill a harmless snake, to spare its life. He cried, "But see how it is glaring at me!" I replied, "Aren't you glaring at the snake?" So in the above verse, it is the eyes of the poet that remain in the grass.

屋根低き物置小屋や桐の花   子 規
Yane hikuki   monookigoya ya   kiri no hana

The low roof
Of the store-house;
Flowers of the paulownia.   Shiki

The flowers of the *kiri* or paulownia have something in them harmonious with what is old, low, spread out, peaceful, monotonous. There are three other haiku by Shiki which illustrate this fact:

桐の花咲くや都の古屋敷
Kiri no hana   saku ya miyako no   furuyashiki

Flowers of the paulownia blooming;
Old mansions
Of the Capital.

日光の古き宿屋や桐の花
Nikkō no   furuki yadoya ya   kiri no hana

Old inns
At Nikkō;
Paulownia flowers.

城 跡 や 麥 の 畑 の 桐 の 花
Shiro-ato ya   mugi no hatake no   kiri no hana

> The ruins of a castle;
> Paulownia flowers,
> In a field of barley.

薔 薇 を 描 く 花 は 易 し く 葉 は 難 た き   子 規
Bara wo kaku   hana wa yasashiku   ha wa kataki

> Roses;
> The flowers are easy to paint,
> The leaves difficult.   Shiki

This is a beautiful example of indirectness, not as it is usually understood, by saying one thing and thus hinting at another, but by saying what is so and leaving the reader to feel the meaning of the words. The flower of the rose is no doubt beautiful in its pink and cream way, but the leaves with their veins and multi-shaded tones of colour, their retiring, withdrawn shape are elegant beyond the power of brush or pencil to delineate. This "difficulty" of portrayal is the same difficulty we have of describing someone we love, or the fainter hues of the sky after the sun has set. It can be done only by just saying what is so, after making sure that we have something to say.

薔 薇 を 見 る 眼 の つ か れ や 病 上 り   子 規
Bara wo miru   me no tsukare ya   yamiagari

> After being ill,
> Gazing at the roses,
> My eyes were wearied.   Shiki

It is only when we are in a state of weakness that we realize how much virtue goes out of us when we merely look at things with attention. If we are ill, or convalescing, we cannot bear to read poetry or listen to music or look at pictures. This fact Shiki expresses, and this is not poetry, but psychology. However, indirectly there is homage to the power of the roses,

whose beauty we are not equal to, except in our moments of
strength.

夕風や白薔薇の花皆動く   子 規
Yūkaze ya   shirobara no hana   mina ugoku

In the evening breeze,
The white roses
All move.   Shiki

When the wind blows, everything that can be shaken is
shaken. And even those things which do not tremble feel the
force and power of it. When something happens, it happens
to everything. As for the roses, every one sways and tosses
and trembles. All are the same in moving, though all are
different in their movement. To express it more simply and
too profoundly for the intellect to fathom, all are the same,
because all are different.

象潟や雨に西施が合歓の花   芭 蕉
Kisagata ya   ame ni seishi ga   nebu no hana

Kisagata:
Seishi sleeping in the rain;
Flowers of the mimosa.   Bashō

Kisagata was a place almost as famous as Matsushima for its
scenic beauty, and Bashō's visit to it is described in *Oku no
Hosomichi*. Just over a hundred years after this, in 1804, the
bay was turned into dry land by an earthquake. It is said to
have had ninety-nine islands and eighty-eight creeks. The *nemu*
or *nebu* is a tree of about ten feet in height. The leaves close
in the evening, like the mimosa. There is a pun here on *Seishi
ga nemu,* "Seishi is sleeping," and *nebu no hana*, "flowers of
the nebu." Seishi is the name of one of the most famous
Chinese beautiful women. There is an anecdote that once when
sleeping she was wetted by a shower of rain, and as a result,
appeared more beautiful than ever. Other women tried wetting
their faces, only to make themselves even less attractive. The

idea of introducing Seishi into a verse on Kisagata came to
Bashō from the following poem by Sotōba, 1036–1101, a great
poet of the Sung dynasty, to one of whose poems he had
referred when speaking of the melancholy beauty of Kisagata,
寂しさに悲しみを加へて, "sadness added to beauty," and from
there being many bushes of the *nebu* at Kisagata.

飲 湖 上 初 晴 後 雨

水 光 潋 灩 晴 偏 好、　山 色 空 濛 雨 亦 奇。
若 把 西 湖 比 西 子、　淡 粧 濃 抹 兩 相 宜。

DRINKING ABOVE THE LAKE; AT FIRST
CLEAR, THEN RAINY

The glittering water dancing—in fine weather, how beautiful!
In misty rain also, how wonderful the mountains!
Comparing the Western Lake to Seishi,
Both a lightly-powdered face and a heavy toilete are charming.

Bashō's verse is of a kind that is now out-moded, or at least
out of fashion, but it has a charm that does not fade. It is an
accumulation of gentle thoughts by gentle people.

起々の慾目引張る青田哉　　　　　　　一 茶
Oki-oki no　yokume hippparu　aota kana

As soon as he gets up,
The green fields draw to them
His greedy eyes.　　　　　　　　　　Issa

When the rice in his paddy-fields is beginning to form, the
farmer's whole soul is put into the growing rice. Every morning,
as soon as he wakes, the first thing he wants to see, or as Issa
rather feels, the first thing that wants to be seen by him, is
those fields.　They are to him

An appetite; a feeling and a love,
That have no need of a remoter charm,
By thought supplied, nor any interest
Unborrowed from the eye.

栂寺や實櫻落ちて人もなし   子 規
Togadera ya   mizakura ochite   hito mo nashi

Toga Temple;
The cherries lie fallen,
Nobody there.   Shiki

Between the reddish-black cherries that lie scattered on the
ground like warriors after a battle, and the absence of men in
the garden of the temple, there is a subtle connection which
may be felt but not explained.   The loneliness that the verse
expresses is however in the fallen cherries, not in the lack of
people present, and verges on Wordsworthian "quietness."

夕顔に都なまりの女かな   子 規
Yūgao ni   miyako namari no   onna kana

An evening-glory,
And a girl
Speaking the Kyōto dialect.   Shiki

The people of Kyōto have a special way of speaking.   Pro-
nunciation and intonation are different from those of Tokyo,
and also many common, everyday phrases and salutations.   The
women of Kyōto are famous for their beauty and white skin,
and there is a harmony here between the girl and the large
flowers that are blooming in the garden.   In addition, there is
perhaps a relation between the dialect of the girl and the slightly
weedy nature of the convolvulus which easily runs wild if not
carefully trained on its frame.

夕顔の中より出づるあるじかな   樗 良
Yūgao no   naka yori izuru   aruji kana

The master
Emerges from the depths
Of the evening-glory.   Chora

The "master" we may take as the poet himself.   The old man
has been tending his flowers in the early evening of summer.
He stands gazing into the huge purple flower, loses himself in

it, and then comes back to himself into the world of time, out of the infinitely deep depths into this flat colourless world of ours.

The ordinary and perhaps more natural interpretation is to take *yūgao* not as singular but plural. The old man comes out of a mass of convolvulus flowers which he has been tending; but even with this interpretation, the above remarks still hold good.

夕 顔 の 花 で 洟 か む 娘 か な   一 茶
Yūgao no   hana de hana kamu   musume kana

The young girl
Blows her nose
In the evening-glory.   Issa

The evening convolvulus is of course a large white one, as large almost as a "real lady's" handkerchief. There is nothing dirty in this poem, that is, in the mind of the girl or of Issa. It is a little odd, a little unusual, that is all. To anyone who objects to it we must say:

Have ye not read what David did, when he was an hungered, and they that were with him; how he entered into the house of God, and did eat the shew-bread, which it was not lawful for him to eat?

The Son of man is Lord also of the convolvulus. There are two other forms of this verse; one is:

夕 顔 の 花 で 鼻 か む お 婆 か な
Yūgao no   hana de hanakamu   obaba kana

The old woman
Blows her nose
In the evening-glory.

It is difficult to choose between them. Youth purifies, old age purifies,—but how differently! It is the systole and diastole of the heart of the world.

畫顔の花に干くや通り雨   子 規
Hirugao no   hana ni kawaku ya   tōriame

> Passing rain,
> Drying away
> On the convolvulus flower.   Shiki

The convolvulus (here the "day-glory") is itself a shortlived, transitory flower, and it is upon this that a few drops of the passing shower fall, and in a short time dry away.   There is here a kind of concentration of evanescence and change.

蚊の聲す忍冬の花散る毎に   蕪 村
Ka no koe su   nindō no hana   chiru goto ni

> The honeysuckle;
> With every petal that falls,
> The voice of the gnats.   Buson

Here the sense of hearing is at its most acute, poetically speaking. Of all sounds, the voice of the mosquito is the most mysterious, of deeply subtle meaning. Of all flowers, the whitish-yellow *nindō* is the most forlorn. Each time the voice of the gnats is noticed, the flowers become more remotely near. Each time a flower falls, the sound of the gnats is more profound in the heart.   (See page 802 for another explanation.)

鳥ないて山静なり夏蕨   子 規
Tori naite   yama shizuka nari   natsuwarabi

> A bird sings,
> The mountain grows quiet;
> Summer bracken.   Shiki

There is a verse in the *Zenrinkushū* which reminds one of the first two lines of the above poem:

風定花猶落、　鳥鳴山更幽。

The wind drops, but the flowers still fall;
A bird sings, and the mountain is more full of mystery.

入相の聞處なり草の花　　　　　一　茶
Iriai no　kiku tokoro nari　kusa no hana

> Just where I hear
> The sundown bell,—
> The flower of this weed!　　　　Issa

Under the influence of music, our defence of self-protective callousness is lowered, the reason weakens, the feelings are aroused and our actions become instinctive. At such moments impressions of truth are deep indeed. We *see* things for the first time, or rather, things are carried alive into the heart through the eye, quite unawares. The face of a common flower, at the sound of the evening bell,—and the "thusness" of things, their coming into existence and passing out of existence at a single point of time, in a word, their "non-existence" is perceived without a thought of it.

夏草やつはものどもが夢のあと　　　芭　蕉
Natsugusa ya　tsuwamonodomo ga　yume no ato

> Ah! Summer grasses!
> All that remains
> Of the warriors' dreams.　　　　Bashō

In Tennyson's lines,

> Nothing in nature's aspect indicated
> That a great man was dead,

man and Nature are taken as two separate things. Bashō takes them, quite unconsciously and instinctively, as one and the same thing. The above verse comes at the end of the following passage in *Oku no Hosomichi:*

> 國破れて山河あり城春にして草青みたりと
> 笠打しきて時のうつるまで涙を落し侍りぬ。

> "The state ruined, mountains and rivers remain. In the citadel it is spring; grass is green."[1] I laid my *kasa* down and shed tears, forgetting the passage of time.

[1] From Toho's 春望。国破山河在、城春草木深。

Bashō was at this time, 1689, in Takadate where Yoshitsune was attacked by Yasuhira under the orders of Yoritomo. He fought bravely but was outnumbered, and commited suicide after killing his own wife and children, exactly 500 years before. He was thirty-one years old.

Bashō's verse expresses the same grief as Toho's for things of long ago, but does not leave us in this state of passivity and dejection. The summer grasses remind him of

> That secret spirit of humanity
> Which, mid the calm oblivious tendencies
> Of nature, mid her plants, and weeds, and flowers,
> And silent overgrowings, still survived.[1]

Bashō's short verse contains the whole of *Sohrab and Rustum*, but especially the last twenty lines, beginning,

> But the majestic River floated on,
> Out of the mist and hum of that low land.

The second half of a *gatha* by Secchō in the *Hekiganroku*, Case 61, is similar in spirit:

謀臣猛将今何在、
萬里清風只自知。

Scheming ministers and fierce generals,—where are they now?
The cool breeze of a thousand leagues alone knows.

In Memoriam breathes the same air, and a verse by Shiki:

夏草や嵯峨に美人の墓多し
Natsugusa ya   saga ni bijin no   haka ōshi

> Summer grasses in Saga;
> Graves of beautiful women
> Are many.

降らずとも竹植える日は簑と傘　　　　　芭 蕉
Furazu tomo   take ueru hi wa   mino to kasa

On Bamboo-planting Day,
Though it is not raining,
Mino and *kasa*.

Bashō

[1] *Excursion*, I, 927–930.

Bamboo-planting Day was the thirteenth day of the Fifth
Month. A *mino* is a straw rain-coat. A *kasa* is a large umbrella-
like hat made of strips of bamboo or sedge. There is a certain
propriety to be observed in spite of an absolute freedom, and
on this day, which is supposed to be wet and suitable for the
planting of bamboos, the farmer wears his *mino* and *kasa*,
without which he would not feel at ease and able to do his
work properly.

ひや汁にうつるや背戸の竹林   來 山
Hiyajiru ni   utsuru ya sedo no   takebayashi

Through the back door,
The bamboo grove is reflected
In the cold broth.   Raizan

This is the looking-glass world, the world that others live in,
the world of our childhood. Which is the real world, the one
outside the back door, or the one in the bowl we are about to
drink from? Not that we think such thoughts when we read
the above verse, but they lie near the surprise at seeing "a
world in a bowl of soup."

蓮の花さくやさびしき停車場   子 規
Hasu no hana   sakuya sabishiki   teishajō

A lonely
Railway station:
Lotus-flowers blooming.   Shiki

There are few more lonely things than a country railway
station on a summer afternoon. For two or three hours no train
arrives. It is so hot that nothing stirs. All around is rice-fields;
here and there a lotus pond. There is something strange and
exotic about the lotus-flowers down there, something that in
its remote contrast exacerbates the feeling of solitariness and
separateness from the outside world.

丈六に
なるくもも
あり
蓮の花

Jōroku ni naru kumo mo ari hasu no hana

There is a cloud too,
That will become a Buddha;
Flowers of the lotus.

Lotuses
by Boryu, 葦柳
Verse by the artist

松茸やしらぬ木の葉のへばりつく   芭 蕉
Matsutake ya   shiranu ko no ha no   hebaritsuku

Sticking on the mushroom,
The leaf
    Of some unknown tree.   Bashō

Fate is in juxtaposition. In this life we see the mystery of chance. Everything is foreordained, but however much we understand the laws of the physical world, the mystery remains as before, or increases with knowledge. A circle is round, and there is no more to be said, but the roundness itself is an unfathomable mystery and an everlasting wonder. Some branches are long, some short, and no doubt there is a reason for it. This particular leaf on this particular mushroom,—there is cause and effect we can ascribe to the whole chain of events that the mind contrives. But the leaf, the mushroom, the two joined as in holy matrimony,—the mind rests on these things and nourishes itself on them, their thusness, their meaninglessness.

わすれ草は咲けどわすれぬ昔哉   諸九尼
Wasuregusa wa   sakedo wasurenu   mukashi kana

The forget-me-not[1] is blooming;
But the things of long ago,—
    How can I forget them?   Moroku-ni

Blessed are they that mourn; for they shall be comforted.

How? When? Where? Why? The feeling of time, what Nietzsche calls "the pathos of distance," is of all man's spiritual possessions the deepest. Anguish is its invariable concomitant.

Nessun maggior dolore
Che ricordarsi del tempo felice
Nella miseria.[2]

It is no more the aim of Zen to remove grief and pain, than it is that of poetry. They are to be felt perfectly, expressed perfectly,—that is all.

[1] The Japanese is a "forget-me" flower, the day-lily.
[2] *Inferno*, 5, 121.

舟乗の一濱留守ぞ芥子の花   去 來
Funanori no   hitohama rusu zo   keshi no hana

> All the fishermen of the beach
> Are away;
> The poppies are blooming.   Kyorai

It is a hot summer day. The sea is calm, only small waves
lapping on the shore. All the fishers are out in the offing, their
white sails on the horizon. Among the yellow sandy dunes,
poppies are blooming. That is all, yet we feel some connection
between the poppies and the fishermen which is beyond affirma-
tion and negation, beyond cause and effect. This same com-
ment can be made on the following verse, also by Kyorai, where
the causal relation is bluntly stated:

湖の水増さりけり五月雨
Mizuumi no   mizu masarikeri   satsukiame

> The waters of the lake
> Have increased:
> The summer rains.

The meaning here also is not an intellectual, scientific one.
It has the feeling of unity of clouds, rain, and vast sheet
of water.

花芥子に組んで落ちたる雀哉   白 雄
Hanakeshi ni   kunde ochitaru   suzume kana

> The sparrows
> Grappling, fell down
> Among the poppy-flowers.   Shirao

There is something lacking in this delightful and colourful
confusion,—a point of rest. That is to say, the poet did not
see it, or, if he did, has not communicated it to us. Mere
movement, mere colour, is no better than simple repose and
monotony, however exquisite the skill with which they are
represented. Compare and contrast the following by Shūha.
During the spring-cleaning of a large house, someone let drop
a box of precious Chinese plates:

一函の皿あやまつや煤拂
Hitohako no   sara ayamatsu ya   susuharai

A box of china,
Smashed to pieces,
During the winter house-cleaning.

Here we feel a certain point of repose. In the very fact of choosing such a (to the persons concerned) tremendous subject, of various and conflicting emotions, Shūha shows his power, as also in the restraint of his treatment. In the original, "smashed to pieces" is literally, "made a mistake."

芥子さげて群集の中を通りけり   一 茶
Keshi sagete   gunshū no naka wo   tōrikeri

Making his way through the crowd,
In his hand
A poppy.   Issa

How delicate our world is. A smile from someone we love and life is worth living; a frown, and heaven is lost to us. In this haiku, the thought is of a man with his precious flower that he is carrying so carefully, but the emotion is that of all humanity.

Issa had previously written, 喧嘩の中を通りけり, "Making his way through the quarrellers," but he felt rightly that this was too strong, too flamboyant, taking away the colours of the poppy.

善盡し美を盡してもけしの花   一 茶
Zen tsukushi   bi wo tsukushite mo   keshi no hana

The epitome of goodness,
The extreme of beauty,—
Yet, a poppy flower.   Issa

There are few flowers that wilt more quickly after being plucked than the poppy. There is an almost unique combination of great beauty and almost moral comeliness, with a frailty and tenderness of feminine character. Shiki has some verses expressive of the impermanence of the poppy:

芥子の花餘り坊主になり易き
Keshi no hana　amari bōzu ni　nariyasuki

　　The flower of the poppy,—
Too easily
　　　It turns priest.[1]

芥子咲て其の日の風に散にけり　　　　　子 規
Keshi saite　sono hi no kaze ni　chiri ni keri

A poppy bloomed,
And in the wind of that day,
　　It scattered and fell.　　　　　　　　Shiki

The poetical point lies in the words "of that day." The poppy
and the wind, so different-seeming, the one gay but fixed, the
other colourless but free, are brought together by time, by this
particular day. The petals of the flower of the poppy fall and
scatter after only a few hours of splendour. But there is not
even a feeling of inevitability; only the poppy blooming, the
wind blowing, and the fall of the flower.

ちるときの心安きよけしの花　　　　　　越 人
Chiru toki no　kokoroyasuki yo　keshi no hana

　　The poppy flowers;
How calmy
　　　They fall.　　　　　　　　　　　　Etsujin

This may be compared to Christ's

　　　　Consider
The lilies of the field,—
　　How they grow!

In the one, it is the sense of fate in life; in the other, the feeling
of life in fate. Etsujin's verse is Shakespeare's

　　　　Ripeness is all.

But it is deeper than this, because it reveals to us not only

[1] With close-cropped head. This verse is little more than a senryu.

nature in general, the nature of Nature, but also the nature of
the poppy, its poppy-nature, the poppy-nature of all things.

麥 の 穂 を 力 に つ か む 別 か な   芭 蕉
Mugi no ho wo   chikara ni tsukamu   wakare kana

> They clutched convulsively
> The ears of barley,
>   At their parting.

Bashō

In their intense grief of parting, they clutched involuntarily
the ears of barley that grew either side of the path. In actual
fact, on the 11th of May 1694, when Bashō was 51, he set out
on a journey for his native place. His friends and disciples said
good-bye to him from the suburbs of Edo. This was his last
journey, dying the same year on the 12th of October in Osaka.

Another example of the keenness with which Bashō felt his
partings with his disciples and friends may be taken from *Oku
no Hosomichi*, towards the beginning:

行 く 春 や 鳥 啼 き 魚 の 目 は 泪
Yuku haru ya   tori naki uo no   me wa namida

> Departing spring,
>   Birds crying,
>   Tears in the eyes of the fish.

This verse is preceded by the following passage:

彌生も末の七日、あけぼのの空朧々として、
月は有明にて光おさまれるものから、不二の
峰かすかに見えて、上野谷中の花の梢、また
いつかはと心ぼそし。むつまじきかぎりは宵
よりつどひて、舟に乗りて送る。千住といふ
處にて舟をあがれば、前途三千里のおもひ胸
にふさがりて、幻の巷に離別の涙をそゝぐ。

On the 27th of the 3rd (lunar) Month (I set out).
In the dawn, the moon was blurred with mist, a
crescent moon whose light was fading. Mount Fuji
could be seen dimly. The far-off cherry-blossoms
of Ueno and Yanaka I felt a yearning for; when

might I see them again, if ever? Friends had
gathered from the night before, and saw me off by
the boat. When we landed at Senju, the thought
of the long journey before me filled me with ap-
prehension, and I shed tears at this parting in this
vale of illusion.

The haiku may owe something to Toho's poem, 春望:

感 時 花 濺 涙、 恨 別 鳥 驚 心。

Feeling the passage of time, the flowers shed tears;
Grieving at separation, the birds startle our hearts.

It is quite clear that Bashō knew these lines from Toho, for he
quotes from the beginning of the same poem, further on in *Oku
no Hosomichi*, already given:

國 破 山 河 在、 城 春 草 木 深。

The state being lost, mountains and rivers remain;
The spring of the castle is deep in weeds and undergrowth.

In any case, both haiku are hardly successful as poetry, but in
their hyperbole and straining after effect, we feel Bashō's painful
emotions on parting.

旅芝居穗麥がもとの鏡立て   蕪 村
Tabishibai   homugi ga moto no   kagamitate

The travelling theatre;
They have set up their mirrors
Under the ears of barley.   Buson

There being no proper place for the actors to perform, a field
of barley has been laid waste, and they are sitting there in the
hastily-constructed booths painting their faces before the mirrors.
Not all the barley has been cut, and around them ears of barley
wave in the summer breeze. Nature and art are very close in
this verse.

麥刈りに利き鎌もてる翁かな   蕪 村

Mugikari ni   kiki kama moteru   okina kana

The old man
Has a marvellous sickle
For cutting barley.   Buson

There is some faint touch here of the magic sword, the tool
with a spirit in it which raises it far above the ordinary. This
comes, no doubt, from the genius of him who uses it, but it
seems to reside still in the weapon, awaiting a master hand to
bring forth its latent power. The old man, from his age, seems
to have some secret affinity with the marvellous sickle, and as
he goes to the field people glance with a peculiar feeling at the
sickle he carries so carefully.

雨に折れて穂麥に狭き小徑かな   丈 草

Ame ni orete   homugi ni semaki   komichi kana

Bent over by the rain,
The ears of barley
Make it a narrow path.   Jōsō

In old-fashioned novels, we often have the situation of a man
or a woman who realizes only at the end of the book, and
usually when it is too late, who it was that he or she had loved
for many years without knowing it. So a great many haiku
tell us something that we have seen but not *seen*. They do not
give us a *satori*. an enlightenment; they show us that we have
had an enlightenment, had it often,—and not recognized it.

秋

AUTUMN

The fall of the year is not merely the fall of the leaves but the fall of the vital powers in all natural things including man. We feel it in ourselves and are thus and thus only able to see it in things outside.

The Milky Way is most clearly seen and deeply felt in this month, but it is the moon that is the soul of autumn. The sun we take for granted, but the moon, in its remote nearness, its silent-smiling light, deepens the mystery of our own life. The wind of autumn also has a different voice from that of any other season; we can hear perhaps the rustle of death in it.

It seems difficult not to write well on scarecrows; these are a peculiarly Japanese subject. The crying of insects in autumn was always a cause of poetical feeling, in Chinese and Japanese poetry.

The beauty of leaves and flowers, and the powerful, esoteric scent of the chrysanthemums make them the chief flower of the season.

時 候 THE SEASON

草 花 を 畫 が く 日 課 や 秋 に 入 る   子 規
Kusabana wo   egaku nikka ya   aki ni iru

Entering autumn,
The painting of flowering plants
A daily task.   Shiki

During his illness, Shiki often passed the long day in bed
drawing and painting flowers that his friends and mother and
sister brought him.   Autumn is in every way the best season
for such things. From one point of view Shiki is here describing
his own monotonous life, the rise and fall of the fever, long
hours gazing out of the window, correcting and selecting other
people's haiku until the brain reels. From another point of
view, Shiki is expressing an aspect of autumn not yet seized,
its paintableness, its picturesqueness, its quiet colourfulness,
not very different from that which Keats portrays in his *Ode
to Autumn*.

七 月 や 先 づ 粟 の 穂 に 秋 の 風   許 六
Shichigatsu ya   mazu awa no ho ni   aki no kaze

The Seventh Month;
First to the ears of millet,
The wind of autumn.   Kyoroku

This is the seventh month of the Lunar Calendar, what now
corresponds to August.

Kyoroku does not mean that the autumn wind blows on the
ears of millet before anything else, nor that by accident he
noticed it first by the waving of the ears.   He means that the
wind which blows every day is only the wind of autumn when
it blows over the ripening fields of millet. When this has
happened, and the poet has perceived it for the first time, the
wind is then the wind of autumn, whenever and wherever
it blows.

病人に八十五度の残暑かな   子　規

Byōnin ni   hachijūgo-do no   zansho kana

> For the sick man,
> A "lingering summer heat"
> Of 85 degrees.   Shiki

The poetry of this verse lies in the tragic parody of the polite nothings of a conventional Japanese epistle. When Japanese people write letters, even to their near relatives and close friends, they always begin with a formal reference to the weather as it should be according to the old calendar. Thus in early autumn there will be a reference to the heat that lingers on when autumn has begun. Shiki takes the expression and refers it also to the high temperature that his consumption has brought him. There is a grim humour here that reminds us strongly of Heine.

家々に朝顔咲ける葉月かな   蓼　太

Ieie ni   asagao sakeru   hazuki kana

> Round every house
> The morning-glory blooms,
> In the month of leaves.   Ryōta

The only special point of this verse is the name given to the eighth month according to the Lunar Calendar, August, the Leaf-Month. It is also called 木染月, Tree-dyeing Month, 月見月, Moon-gazing Month, 雁來月, Wild-goose-coming Month. In addition, the morning-glory has the same function as the rain in the following verse from Stevenson's *A Child's Garden of Verses*.

> The rain is raining all around,
> It falls on field and tree;
> It rains on the umbrellas here,
> And on the ships at sea.

次 の 間 の 燈 も 消 え て 夜 寒 哉　　　　　子 規
Tsugi no ma no　tomoshi mo kiete　yosamu kana

The light in the next room also
Goes out;
The night is chill.　　　　　Shiki

The cold of autumn, of an autumn evening is not the biting, bitter thing of winter, but a melancholy chilling of the spirit. Despondency and gloom settles on the mind with a gently irresistible power, and everything becomes tasteless and meaningless; yet there is a taste in this tastelessness, a meaning all its own.

朝 寒 や 小 僧 ほ が ら か に 經 を 讀 む　　　　子 規
Asazamu ya　kozō hogaraka ni　kyō wo yomu

Morning cold;
The acolyte intones the sutra
Cheerfully.　　　　　Shiki

The autumn melancholy is not the deep grinding despair that winter brings; it is in Shiki's mind something more of sentiment, something vague; other verses of his:

大 寺 に ひ と り 宿 か る 夜 寒 か な
Ōdera ni　hitori yadokaru　yosamu kana

Lodging alone
In a great temple;
The night was cold.

小 坊 主 の ひ と り 鐘 つ く 夜 寒 か な
Kobōzu no　hitori kane tsuku　yosamu kana

The acolyte
Rings the temple bell by himself;
A cold evening.

大 寺 の と も し 少 き 夜 寒 か な
Ōdera no　tomoshi sukunaki　yosamu kana

In the great temple
Lights are few,
The night is cold.

須摩寺の門をすぎゆく夜寒かな

Sumadera no　mon wo sugiyuku　yosamu kana

> Passing by
> The gate of the Temple of Suma;
> The evening is cold.

One more similar to Shiki's verse at the top of page 891, in its indirect directness of the expression of cold:

や〻寒み燈による蟲もなかりけり

Yaya samumi　hi ni yoru mushi mo　nakarikeri

> It is colder;
> No insect
> Approaches the lamp.

秋たつや何におどろく陰陽師　　　　　　　蕪　村

Aki tatsu ya　nani ni odoroku　inyōshi

> The beginning of autumn;
> What is the fortune-teller
> Looking so surprised at?　　　　　　　Buson

To the fortune-teller, as to the poet, the seasons, and especially their beginning and ending are of the greatest significance. As Buson passes along the road this first day of autumn, he sees a fortune-teller with an anxious-looking client. The fortune-teller puts his head on one side and is saying something. Buson has expressed this in a rather hyperbolic way. Man and fate and the progression of the seasons are expressed in this verse lightly and humorously.

初秋や餘所の燈見ゆる宵の程　　　　　　　蕪　村

Hatsuaki ya　yoso no hi miyuru　yoi no hodo

> The beginning of autumn;
> A lamp from someone's house is seen;
> It is not quite dark.　　　　　　　Buson

The relation of autumn to lamps and candles, to lights of any kind, is a most remarkable and significant thing. The point of

this verse is in the last line, but it would remain unnoticed
were it not for that vague feeling within, that corresponds to
"the beginning of autumn" without. There is melancholy, but
it has something steady in it, quite different from that of a
spring evening.

張りぬきの猫に見えけり今朝の秋   芭 蕉
Harinuki no   neko ni miekeri   kesa no aki

> It is seen
> In the papier-maché cat,
> This morning of autumn.   Bashō

The toy cat sits there in the light of the early morning sun
that shows up the scratches and worn edges on it. The passing
of time, the decay of nature, the lessening energies of men are
all seen in this inanimate, meaningless plaything.

貧乏に追ひつかれけりけさの秋   蕪 村
Bimbō ni   oitsukarekeri   kesa no aki

> Overtaken
> By poverty,
> This autumn morning.   Buson

This does not refer to someone who has become suddenly
poor. This poverty is a continuous thing, a chronic disease. It
is only that this morning there is something in the air, some-
thing autumnal that increases the feeling of strain and struggle,
the hopelessness of it all. Poetically speaking, there is a harmony
between poverty and autumn, which is brought out by the discord
with morning.

ふみつけた蟹の死骸や今朝の秋   子 規
Fumitsuketa   kani no shigai ya   kesa no aki

> The dead body
> Of a trodden-on crab,
> This autumn morning.   Shiki

This is a remarkable poem, such that haiku only is capable
of being. All the summer the yellow and red crabs have been
scuttling to and fro, sideways and backwards, so many, that in
walking we can hardly avoid treading on them. But this morn-
ing of autumn, on opening the door, a crushed crab is seen lying
on the path outside, and instantly we perceive its appropriate-
ness, its inevitable rightness to the time and the season. D. H.
Lawrence says in a letter:

> We went for a walk this evening through the woods,
> and I found a dead owl, a lovely big, warmbrown, soft
> creature, lying in the grass at my feet. It sticks in my
> mind curiously—as if something important had died this
> week-end—though what it can be I don't know.

仲秋や芋畑に出て我家の燈　　　　　　酔　佛
Chūshū ya　imobatake ni dete　wagaya no hi

Mid-autumn;
Going out to the potato field,—
The lamp in our house.　　Suibutsu

The middle of autumn has a different meaning from that of
the beginning and end. It is less poignant, though less resigned;
more composed and meditative. When the poet goes out of his
cottage to see how the potatoes are doing, night is already
falling. There is little twilight in Japan, and the field is soon
quite dark. Over there is a square of yellowish light, his own
house. It is not a happy thing nor a sad one; it is simply so.
I am here in the dark among the unseen potato plants and over
there is my house. I am here and yet I am nowhere, every-
where. The house is so near, and yet it is infinitely distant.
Compare Buson's verse on page 896. There is a poem by Haku-
rakuten, similar in feeling as well as in incident:

浦中夜泊

闇上江堤還獨立、　水風霜氣夜稜稜。
回看深浦停舟處、　蘆荻花中一點燈。

ANCHORED AT NIGHT IN A CREEK

I climbed upon the river embankment, and stood
  there in the darkness;
The river breeze and frosty air chilled me.
When I turned and looked where the boat lay deep
  in the creek,
Among the flowers of reed and lespedeza, was one
  point of light.

この秋は何で年よる雲に鳥　　　　　芭 蕉
Kono aki wa　　nan de toshiyoru　kumo ni tori

This autumn,
How old I am getting:
Ah, the clouds, the birds!　　　Bashō

This was written towards the end of September, while on a
journey, his mind full of thoughts of old age and death. Fran-
cisco de Quevedo expresses this state in a sonnet ending,

Y no halle cosa en que poner los ojos
que no fuese recuerdo de la muerte.

But Bashō does not remain in this state of the first two lines.
In the third line he reminds himself of his own true nature,
that of the clouds and birds, the clouds which form without joy
and dissolve without pain, the fowls of the air that God cares
for. But the clouds and the birds are not extraneous things.
They are part of his own true self; and this is the meaning of
Bashō's return to nature, a return to his own nature. What a
difference there is between Bashō's aspiration and the feelings
of Burns in,

How can ye chant, ye little birds,
And I sae weary, fu' o' care![1]

Burns recoils back from things upon his own false individual
self. Bashō's stream of despondency flows out into the bound-
less ocean of life.

---

[1] The Banks of Doon.

笛 の 音 に 波 も よ り 來 た る 須 磨 の 秋   蕪 村
Fue no ne ni   nami mo yorikitaru   suma no aki

To the sound of the flute
The waves also approach;
Suma in autumn.   Buson

This was composed by Buson at the temple of Sumadera.
The flute is the same which Bashō heard,[1] the silent flute of
Atsumori called "Greenleaf," 青葉. All things are moved by
number, by music, and the waves approach and recede in accord
with the "spirit ditties of no tone."

Byron has some somewhat similar lines in *Stanzas for Music*,
speaking of a woman's voice:

> When as if its sound were causing
> The charmed ocean's pausing,
> The waves lie still and gleaming.

秋 深 き 隣 は 何 を す る 人 ぞ   芭 蕉
Aki fukaki   tonari wa nani wo   suru hito zo

Deep autumn;
My neighbour,—
How does he live?   Bashō

Bashō is lying in bed ill, death not far away. Suddenly the
silence becomes unbearably profound, and he thinks, with no-
thing to prompt it, with no apparent reason, of his neighbour.
What is he living for? What is he living by? Is he really
alive? Is he too living in that spiritual world

Beyond the light of the morning star,

but also and only, no more and no less, this material world?
The thought of his neighbour comes with a sudden clutch of
the heart, as though with the sound of a trumpet, and the walls
of Jericho between mind and mind are about to fall. There is
a verse by Buson similar to this, not so profound, but pleasantly
objective:

[1] See page 854.

此二日砧聞へぬとなりかな
Kono futsuka   kinuta kikoenu   tonari kana

> Unheard, these two days,
> The fulling-block
> Of my neighbour.

Another of Buson's which also illustrates his more picturesque
and objective attitude, is the following:

凩や何に世わたる家五軒
Kogarashi ya   nani ni yowataru   ie goken

> The winter tempest;
> How do they live,
> Those five houses?

Yet another, closer to Bashō's verse in appearance but worlds
away in meaning:

壁隣ものごとつかす夜さむかな
Kabetonari   mono goto tsukasu   yosamu kana

> Next door, the other side of the wall,
> Rattlings and rustlings,—
> How cold the night!

十月や餘所へも行かず人も來ず   尚 白
Jūgatsu ya   yoso e mo yukazu   hito mo kozu

> It is the Tenth Month:
> I go nowhere;
> No one comes here.   Shōhaku

When we consider the poetical life of the writer, there are
associations which beautify this lack of a subject. But the
point of the poem is not in these outskirts but in the very
centre of the will. "I go nowhere." Why does he go nowhere?
"No one comes here." Why does no one come? It is all in the
will of the poet himself. And we may ask one more question.
Why should absence have a deeper meaning than presence, no
one and nowhere than someone and somewhere? In truth, the
"no one" of the poem is a being as real as ourselves:

"I see nobody on the road," said Alice.

"I only wish I had such eyes," the King remarked in a fretful tone. "To be able to see Nobody! And at that distance too! Why, it's as much as I can do to see real people, by this light."

枯枝に烏の止りけり秋の暮　　　　　　芭 蕉
Kare-eda ni　karasu no tomarikeri　aki no kure

Autumn evening;
A crow perched[1]
On a withered bough.　　　　　Bashō

There is a perfection of unity among the objects of this verse and the "mood" of it, a peculiar union of the expressed objective and unexpressed subjective that justifies its universal acceptance as a masterpiece and a historical milestone of Japanese culture.

Kare-eda means either "withered branch" or "withered tree"; or "bare of leaves," though not withered. Here is a picture by Bashō himself, which shows a tree, not with bare branches (which would make the season winter, rather than autumn) but with the whole tree lifeless and withered. The loneliness of autumn is thus intensified by the deathly immobility and colourlessness of the scene.

The subject itself is of course not new, especially for Chinese and Japanese artists. In prose and verse also we may find frequent references to it. In the 93rd section of the second part of the *Saikontan*, we have the following:

如桃源犬吠、　桑間鶏鳴。　何等淳龐、　至於寒潭
之月、　古木之鴉、　工巧中、　便覺有衰颯氣象矣。

"A dog barking in a village of peach-trees, cocks crowing among the mulberries,"—what artless simplicity! But when we take "The moon in the cold tarn, a crow on a withered tree," we feel in this cleverness an air of dreary lifelessness.

The author of the *Saikontan*, Hung Ying Ming, is said to have flourished during the Wan-li Era 1575–1619, about seventy years

---

[1] "Perched" is of course the past participle.

枯えたにからすの
とまりけり秋の暮

Crow on a Withered Tree

by Bashō

before Bashō's time, 1644-94. It seems then that he would have criticised that verse for something artificial in it, and we can see some justification for this. It is certainly not the simple picture of an autumn evening that at first sight it seems to be.

There is a waka by Sadaie, 定家, 1162-1241, which may have had some influence in the creation of the verse, and it shows the tendency, a baneful one, towards the dreary and desolate, as being supposedly more poetical than the bright and cheerful.

見渡せば花も紅葉もなかりけり
浦の苫屋の秋の夕暮

> Looking over the bay,
> Spring blossoms and autumn leaves
> Are as nothing,
> Compared to those thatched huts
> In the autumn twilight.

There is the same tendency in the English romantic poets, for example in Keats, and Shelley:

> The sedge has withered from the lake,
> And no birds sing.
> There was no leaf upon the forest bare,
> No flower upon the ground.

Nevertheless we must say that Bashō had taken another step towards his inwardly felt but not yet explicit ideal of haiku, in assimilating to it the essence of waka and of Chinese poetry. This verse was published in the *Azuma Nikki*, 1681, when Bashō was nearly forty. In this Diary are to be found other verses on the subject of an autumn evening, the best of them, perhaps, being by Yūsui:

秋淋しため息やつく遠寺の鐘
Aki sabishi   tameiki ya tsuku   tōdera no kane

> Lonely autumn;
> A sigh—ah! The sound
> Of a far-off temple bell.

In the first version, as it appears in the Diary, we have:

枯枝に烏のとまりたるや秋の暮
Kare-eda ni   karasu no tomaritaru ya   aki no kure

a still longer form of 5, 10, 5. The meaning is practically the same, but the later version is more severely objective in tone. This haiku represents Bashō's first step in breaking away from the Danrin School, and the setting up of his own, indeed, the creation of what we now call "haiku."

飯時や戸口に秋の入日影　　　　　　　　　　樗　良
Meshidoki ya　toguchi ni aki no　irihi kage

At meal-time, in autumn:
Through the open door,
The evening sun.　　　　　　　　　　　　Chora

Meal-time in the evening, autumn; the long shadow, the open door, and the sights and sounds and smells of harvest—at such a moment we are nearest to the life of man. The pulse of the season beats slowly and surely in us. Eating, after harvesting the rice, brings us as close as we can be to material things. The long, level rays of the evening sun give us a feeling of the passing of time, uniting us to all those who have gone before us, and to those who will come after us.

此道や行く人なしに秋のくれ　　　　　　　　芭　蕉
Kono michi ya　yuku hito nashi ni　aki no kure

Along this road
Goes no one,
This autumn eve.　　　　　　　　　　　　Bashō

This is not sentimentality, nor is it stoicism. There is an unutterable feeling of "loneliness" which is quite ordinary loneliness with something profounder and not undesirable in its inevitability. In the same way, this road along which Bashō travels alone is the way of Poetry, which, to this day, how few there are that tread! When we realise that the Way and the way are one, not two, we do not find any double meaning in this verse. To express the matter euphuistically but none the less truly, the way we walk along the way is the Way.

What is the quality of the emotion that we have as we walk

along the lonely autumn road, along the Way? Both Beethoven
and Nietzsche said it was a feeling of Joy:

> Doch alle Lust will Ewigkeit,
> Will tiefe, tiefe Ewigkeit![1]

But the Japanese poets find it otherwise. They say with Landor,

> There is a gloom in deep love, as in deep water, there
> is a silence in it which suspends the foot, and the folded
> arms and the dejected head are the images it reflects.
> No voice shakes its surface, the Muses themselves ap-
> proach it with a tardy and a timid step, and with a low
> and tremulous and melancholy song.[2]

門を出れば我も行人秋のくれ   蕪 村
Kado wo dereba   ware mo yukuhito   aki no kure

When I go out of the gate,
I also am a traveller,
In the autumn evening.   Buson

In this verse Buson is following Bashō's sentimental vein
rather than his own calm attitude, that of the spectator and
artist.

山門をぎいと鎖すや秋の暮   子 規
Sammon wo   gii to tozasu ya   aki no kure

Shutting the great temple gate,
Creak! it goes:
An autumn evening.   Shiki

As the monk shuts both ponderous doors, massive and gloomy
as those of the *Inferno* or of *Paradise Lost*, the hinges groan.
They make this strident noise every day of the year, but this
evening of autumn the sound has a meaning it has at no other
time. Like the stridulation of the cicadas, there is something
of the meaning of autumn, its dryness, its feeling of the heavi-

[1] *Am Mitternacht.*
[2] *Pericles and Aspasia.*

ness of old age and grief, of oncoming death, of unbearable
loneliness.

一人來て一人を訪ふや秋のくれ   蕪 村
Hitori kite   hitori wo tou ya   aki no kure

One came,
And visited someone;
An autumn eve.   Buson

This has the same astounding simplicity and depth as the
words of the Bible or Shakespeare:

The Lord is my shepherd; shall not want.

Fear no more the heat o' the sun.

If you cannot see the poetry of these, their deep meaning, that
is like man Friday, who, with far better eyes, could not see
the ship that Crusoe saw, because he did not know what to
look for:

Behold, I have set before thee an open door.

かぎりある命のひまや秋の暮   蕪 村
Kagiri aru   inochi no himaya   aki no kure

In a short life,
An hour of leisure,
This autumn evening,   Buson

The Japanese feel the impermanence of things persistently
even if not deeply, and this autumn evening Buson feels the
value of the tranquil time, in contrast to the limited life be-
stowed upon him. His life is time, and this evening eternity.

秋の暮烏もなかで通りけり   几 湫
Aki no kure   karasu mo nakade   tōri keri

An autumn evening;
Without a cry,
A crow passes.   Kishū

How well this illustrates that which is neither silence nor speaking! In the relative world, a bird must either sing or be silent, but in the world of poetry, either may be something which is neither. Its song or its soundlessness may have a meaning beyond these opposites. That is to say, the world of poetry is not the absolute, whatever that may be; it comes into being when the absolute and the relative are one. As the poet stands there in the autumn evening, a raven flies by without haste. It utters no sound, and this very fact seems to draw the soul out of him, to take away her breath. Somehow or other, at that moment, a depth is opened up within and without her, and as Blake said, "No man can see truth without believing it."

淋しさのうれしくもあり秋の暮　　　　　　　蕪 村
Sabishisa no   ureshiku mo ari   aki no kure

An autumn eve;
There is a joy too,
In loneliness.　　　　　　　　　　　　　　Buson

Sometimes, rarely, we feel like the bird,
Too blest with anyone to pair,[1]

or like the child:

This happy Creature of herself
Is all-sufficient; solitude to her
Is blithe society.[2]

But this feeling of Buson's is not so much deeper, as richer than what Wordsworth is speaking of. It is something that belongs to maturity rather than to youth.

[1] Wordsworth, *The Green Linnet*.
[2] *Characteristics of a Child Three years Old*.

をさな子やひとり飯くふ秋の暮   尚 白
Osanago ya   hitori meshikū   aki no kure

The little girl
Eats her evening meal alone
In the autumn evening.   Shōhaku

This has the prescript, 母におくれける子のあはれを, "The pathos of a child whose mother has died and left her behind." The little girl has not long ago lost her mother; she is quite helpless. Someone, probably a relation, has given her her food, and being "busy about many things" has left her to eat by herself. The melancholy of youth, of loneliness, is all in harmony. But over and above this is our realization, instinctively, poetically, that we are all young, all orphans; we all eat in complete solitude; the melancholy of the four seasons bathes us in its pitifulness.

And deeper even than this is our perception of the pathos of eating. *We eat to live.* We are but a step from starvation, a hair's breadth from death. And the obliviousness of the child to her own pathos, the self-forgetful state in which she is while eating, induces in us the same state of unself-consciousness. This is the realm of pathos (in the sense that All Is Pathos) to which this verse leads us with such gentle hands.

After all this, we turn with relief to Shiki's objective, unsentimental, almost non-human, and yet satisfying verse:

人もなく子一人寝たる蚊帳の中
Hito mo naku   ko hitori netaru   kaya no naka

Nobody there;
A child asleep
In the mosquito net.

秋の夜や旅の男の針仕事   一 茶
Aki no yo ya   tabi no otoko no   harishigoto

An autumn evening;
A man on a journey
Sewing his clothes.   Issa

This is probably Issa himself, but if we take it in this sense, the verse becomes too sentimental. The reason for this is probably the hard fact that a man may sew on his own buttons, or cook his own food just as well as a woman, and there is nothing pathetic, intrinsically, in the picture the verse brings before us. Even if we take it to be an expression of loneliness, the loneliness here is the common or garden variety, and it still remains mere sentimentality. Issa has written very few such verses, and this one may be given here as showing what haiku is not, and what Issa did not really intend to do.

をさな子や笑ふにつけて秋の暮   一 茶
Osanago ya   warau ni tsukete   aki no kure

> The young child,—
> But when he laughed,—
> An autumn evening.   Issa

This child was the boy, 金三郎, Kinzaburō, a year old, left by Issa's first wife Kiku, 菊女, when she died in 1823; four or five young children had already died. A prescript says, 母のなき子の這習ふに, "A motherless child learning to crawl."

The baby is just beginning to crawl on the tatami. In the midst of his herculean efforts to advance an inch or two, he suddenly looks up and laughs—with his dead mother's laugh:

> O Death in life, the days that are no more!

Is it not too heartrending for poetry? Down it must go in black and white like all the rest. And in the last line, autumn has come, evening has come, the world rolls on, life and death in endless succession. Life is suffering.

月もあり黄菊白菊暮るる秋   子 規
Tsuki mo ari   kigiku shiragiku   kururu aki

> There is the moon;
> And white and yellow chrysanthemums;
> Autumn draws to its close.   Shiki

Surprisingly little is needed for happiness, for the good life, for the way of haiku. A great deal of wisdom, and the moon and chrysanthemums white and yellow,—and autumn is passing, life is being lived.

燈せば燈に力なし秋の暮   子 規
Hitomoseba   hi ni chikara nashi   aki no kure

Lighting the light,
It has no strength;
An evening of autumn.   Shiki

We may take this, if we wish, as a purely subjective view of the light of the lamp. It is autumn, when everything is losing its strength, and even the lamp, which might be expected to remain the same throughout the year, seems to be weaker and gives a feeble light.

But this "seems to be" is only the antechamber to poetry. Poetry is what is, not what seems to be. In the seeming itself we are to discern with joy something that is not merely inward, and bilious or sanguine or melancholy. In our various moods we are to see, and know we see, something outward which corresponds to, which also is that which sees. Thus the purely scientific question of the intensity of the light does not arise, and philosophy cannot clip an angel's wings. In this quiet autumn evening, as we light the unwilling yet willing lamp, the autumnal aspect of the lamp is seen. Without the sinking of energy in nature, without the ebb of life in us, this could not be done.

雨戸越す秋のすがたや燈のくるひ   來 山
Amado kosu   aki no sugata ya   hi no kurui

The shape of Autumn
That has passed through the shutters,—
The candle's twisted flame.   Raizan

To see the twisted flame of the candle as the spiritual form of Autumn is worthy of the imagination of Blake, but the *this-*

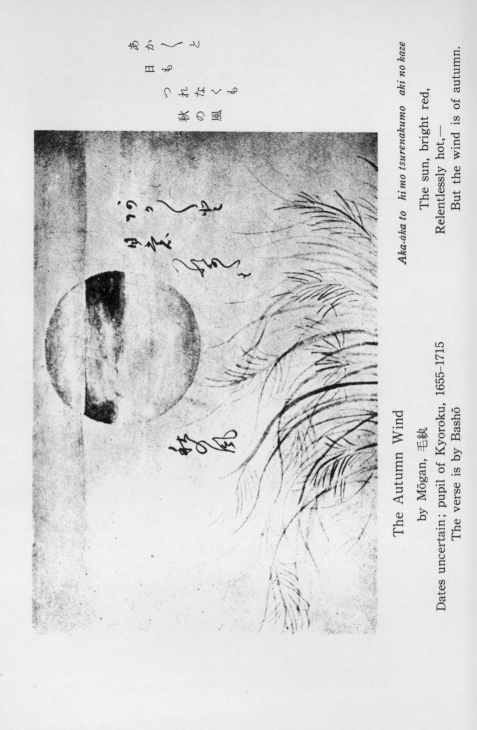

あかあかと日はつれなくも秋の風

Aka-aka to himo tsurenakumo aki no kaze

The sun, bright red,
Relentlessly hot,—
But the wind is of autumn.

The Autumn Wind
by Mōgan, 毛紈
Dates uncertain; pupil of Kyoroku, 1655–1715
The verse is by Bashō

worldliness of the Japanese poet enables him to avoid Blake's symbolical eccentricity and mystical personification.

父 母 の 事 の み 思 ふ 秋 の 暮 　　　　蕪 村
Chichi haha no　koto nomi omou　aki no kure

It is evening, autumn;
I think only
Of my parents.　　　　Buson

As we grow older, and perhaps only then, we realize how little we did of all that we might have done for our parents. When death has taken away the opportunity, we feel the value of the saying,

Honour thy father and mother.

Confucius says, of a son,

子曰、父母在、不遠遊、遊必有方。
While father and mother are living, he should not go far away. If he does travel, it must be to a particular place.

子曰、父母之年、不可不知也、一則以喜、
一則以懼。（論語、四、十九、二十一。）
The age of mother and father should never be unknown, both for anxiety and for happiness.

There is a haiku of Bashō that expresses more passionately what Buson felt.

故里 や 臍 の 緒 に 泣 く 年 の 暮
Furusato ya　heso no o ni naku　toshi no kure

Weeping over my umbilical cord
In my native place,
At the end of the year.

Japanese usually keep the umbilical cord; Bashō, revisiting his home after many years, wept on seeing his which his mother had treasured up, a symbol of the spiritual blood of life and love which had flowed so long from her to him.

So each new man strikes root into a far fore-time.[1]

小言いふ相手は壁ぞ秋の暮   一 茶
Kogoto iu   aite wa kabe zo   aki no kure

An autumn evening;
The only sharer of my complaints,
The wall.   Issa

Issa married for the first time at fifty two years of age. At
the age of sixty one, after giving birth to five children, all dying
young, his wife also died, thirty seven years old. The above
verse dates from this year, as also the following:

小言いふ相手もあらばけふの月
Kogoto iu   aite mo araba   kyō no tsuki

If only she were here,
My complaining partner,—
Today's moon.

Issa is lying in bed, a feeble oil-lamp behind him, staring at
the wall between him and which his wife had lain for nine
years. A toothless, white-haired bridegroom, she served him
with duty and love up to the day of her death. The wall
remains, a mud wall with not only the previous tenant's marks
on it, but their own; cracks and stains, fly-spots, smears of
mosquitoes, and the blood of bed-bugs. The wall alone remains,
mute, yet speaking; implacable, yet faithful; dead, yet alive.

中々に人と生れてあきの暮   一 茶
Nakanaka ni   hito to umarete   aki no kure

An autumn evening;
It is no light thing,
To be born a man.   Issa

According to Buddhism, to be born a man is a very fortunate
thing, but this dark, gloomy evening of autumn, Issa wonders
whether this is so. Our pains and griefs are many. Those joys

[1] Arnold, *Empedocles on Etna.*

we have are precarious. To love others is the greatest of
happinesses, but those we love,—we know

> That Time will come and take my love away.
> This thought is as a death, which cannot choose
> But weep to have that which it fears to lose.

The "wrackful siege of battering days" takes everything;

> How with this rage shall beauty hold a plea,
> Whose action is no stronger than a flower?

愚案ずるに冥途も斯くや秋の暮   芭 蕉
Gu anzuru ni   meido mo kaku ya   aki no kure

> As it seems to me,
> The Region of the Dead is like this:
> An autumn evening.   Bashō

This is an early verse of Bashō's, expressing the deathly,
unpoetical loneliness so near to and yet so far from that other
loneliness in which we are solitary but not alone, "because the
Father is with us," that is, we are not ourselves, but are the
very pain and loss that are felt.

牛しかる聲に鴫立つ夕かな   支 考
Ushi shikaru   koe ni shigi tatsu   yūbe kana

> At a voice
> Shouting at the ox,—
> Snipe rise in the evening.   Shikō

The sun has sunk behind the western hills. All is quiet over
the fields. A farmer on his way home suddenly shouts at the
ox he is leading. At the sound some snipe rise from the thicket
close at hand.

In the quietness of the autumn evening this unexpected
occurence brings out the sound that lurks in silence, the move-
ment in stillness. We feel at the same time the deep, though
apparently accidental relation that exists between all things.
The ox wishes to stop a moment, and a snipe rises into the air

with a whirr of wings. A Japanese poet of two hundred years ago notices this thing, and an Englishman today feels its deep meaning.

飛んで來る餘所の落葉や暮るゝ秋   子　規
Tonde kuru   yoso no ochiba ya   kururu aki

Fallen leaves
Come flying from elsewhere:
Autumn is ending.   Shiki

This "from elsewhere" which is literally "of elsewhere," gives us a feeling of the wildness, the unpredictability, the infinity of nature. It is the close of autumn, and the leaves fall and are blown hither and thither without discrimination, erratically, yet inevitably. They fly from one place to another, whirl up in the sky, at random, yet their resting place is determined from before the beginning of time.

長き夜を月とる猿の思案かな   子　規
Nagaki yo wo   tsuki toru saru no   shian kana

The long night;
The monkey thinks how
To catch hold of the moon.   Shiki

All the long night, the monkey is meditating on the problem of how to grasp the moon that hangs there just beyond the branches. An animal psychologist may doubt whether a monkey is capable of entertaining the thought even for a moment, though children sometimes ask to be given the moon. The aim, the object of this verse, is something different from the apparently solid things we see around us. It is the no less real world of those flights of the mind, those gossamer-like thoughts, those faint respirations and exhalations of the soul of man when it lives a quiet and silent life by itself, happy with its own created playthings.

長き夜や障子の外をともし行く   子　規

Nagaki yo ya   shōji no soto wo   tomoshi yuku

The long night;
A light passes along
Outside the *shōji*.   Shiki

The poet had at last fallen asleep when suddenly his eyes
opened. Outside the paper screens, a light is moving; someone
is passing by with a lamp or lantern in his hand. Who it is,
why he or she is passing, where they are going, will never be
known. The poet realizes once again the mystery of life, the
way in which we are separated from one another not only by
ages of time and vast realms of space, but by moments, and
by the thinness of a paper screen.

長き夜や思ふこといふ水の音   五　竹

Nagaki yo ya   omou koto iu   mizu no oto

The long night;
The sound of the water
Says what I think.   Gochiku

The poet lies sleepless. Schopenhauer says,

> Sleep is a morsel of death borrowed to keep up and
> renew that part of life which has been exhausted by
> the day.

The thoughts of Japanese, like those of Europeans and Amer-
icans, are so impregnated with the feeling of the passing of
time, the origin of all cosmic pessimism, that they too can
hardly perceive the simplest thing apart from a feeling of
sadness, a vague overshadowing of the emotion of time and the
transitoriness of the world that surrounds its momentary ex-
istence. Spengler's words may thus be applied to haiku poets:

> The Pure Present which so often aroused Goethe's
> admiration in every product of the classical life and in
> sculpture particularly, fills that life with an intensity that
> is to us perfectly unknown.[1]

[1] *Decline of the West*, Introduction.

くゝり目を見つつ夜長き枕かな　　　　貞　徳
Kukurime wo   mitsutsu yo nagaki   makura kana

Staring, staring
At the gathers of the pillow:
Long is the night.　　　　Teitoku

A Japanese pillow is stuffed with various things, for example bran, or the husks of some grain. It is sausage-shaped and tied at both ends.

The poet lies awake, not in a daze, not thinking of other things, but in a state of unconscious concentration. His eye chooses, for no apparent reason, such an unimportant thing as the gatherings where the end of the pillow is tied. These seem, when he comes to himself, to have had some inexpressible meaning, somehow connected with the length of the night. Those particular threads in that particular pattern, matter extended in space in that particular formless form, the utter ununderstandableness of it all,—is felt as a counterpart to the meaningful meaninglessness of the passage of time. Space the expanding, boundless, lonely. Time the irreversible, implacable, fatal.

山鳥の枝踏みかゆる夜長かな　　　　蕪　村
Yamadori no   eda fumikayuru   yonaga kana

The copper pheasant on the bough
Shifts from one foot to the other;
Long is the night.　　　　Buson

Buson is not of course describing something he has seen. It is, like so many of his historical verses, the result of a kind of imaginative creation that has no special name in English. It is both imaginative and imaginary, and though not the product of experience, is also not fanciful. It corresponds to the Imaginary Conversations of Landor and others, or rather, it is of the same nature as the work of oriental artists, who do not paint an actual landscape, or a remembered one, but from all the elements of their past experience of nature create forms of earth and sky that correspond to their feeling of the aesthetic fitness of things. There is for both poetry and art the danger of becoming fanciful, and in the manner of Doré or Swinburne of falling into exaggeration, artificiality or vagueness, but few of Buson's verses are open to this objection, whether it is in unseen aspects of nature, or events of the historic past; his poetic insight is strong enough to see things of long ago or far away as present to the mind's eye. A modern example by Shuōshi;

> ぜすきりしと踏まれ踏まれて失たまへり
> *Zesukirishito fumare fumarete usetamaeri*

> Trodden on, trodden on,—
> The picture of Christ
> Is worn away.

This refers to the pictures of Christ that had to be trampled on by people to show that they did not belong to the proscribed Christian religion.

> 長き夜や千年の後を考へる　　　子規
> *Nagaki yo ya chitose no nochi wo kangaeru*

> The long night;
> I think about
> A thousand years afterwards.　　Shiki

The length of the night is expressed through the long thoughts of the poet. It is the length of the night which leads his mind out into eternity. It is the far distant time which shows the meaning of this never-ceasing, incessant march of the moments.

Another verse of Shiki in which it is the past that gives significance to the present moment of infinite length:

> 長き夜や孔明死する三國志
> *Nagaki yo ya kōmei shisuru sangokushi*

> The long night;
> Reading the *History of the Three Kingdoms*,
> Up to the death of Kōmei.

The *Sangokushi* is a historical work in sixty-five volumes covering the struggles of the Kingdoms of Gi, Go, and Shoku between 220 and 280 A.D.

行秋の草にかくるゝ流かな   白　雄
Yuku aki no   kusa ni kakaruru   nagare kana

The stream hides itself
In the grasses
Of departing autumn.   Shirao

Tall grasses waver everywhere, and through them, almost
hidden in them wanders a small stream, unwanted and unnoticed.
Autumn also is thus departing; like the stream, coming from
nowhere and going nowhere, covered in the wild confusion of
grasses that themselves must go away, no one knows whither.

行く秋を尾花がさらばさらばかな   一　茶
Yuku aki wo   obana ga saraba   saraba kana

The pampas grass
Waves good-bye, good-bye,
To departing autumn.   Issa

This verse may be called entirely fanciful, even a lie, because
the grass is merely moving in the wind. But somehow or other
we do not believe this. It is not merely that we trust the poets
more than the intellectual Gradgrinds of the world; we feel
ourselves saying good-bye in the pampas grass, we sway with
it, and will not be put to the question, for we know that all
flesh is grass.

天 文 SKY AND ELEMENTS

秋晴れてものゝ煙の空に入る   子 規
Aki harete   mono no kemuri no   sora ni iru

A fine day of autumn;
Smoke from something
Rises into the sky.   Shiki

There is a mystery in smoke, that is one of the pleasures of
smoking tobacco (I suppose). As it rises into the autumn sky,
its faint blue colour, the colour of infinity and eternity, draws
our minds up with it. But there is mystery too in its origin.
What is it that burns unseen? Who is it that burns it?

椎の木を伐り倒しけり秋の空   子 規
Shii no ki wo   karitaoshikeri   aki no sora

Having felled
A pasania tree,—
The sky of autumn.   Shiki

When even a small tree is cut down, we feel once more the
presence of the sky above us; how much more so when it is
a great pasania tree, with all its attendant danger, the slowly
reeling trunk, the crash of boughs, the silence following. At
this solemn moment, the sky of autumn above us draws our
souls out of us with its purity and distance. There is the same
feeling of relief, of a weight being taken off the mind, in the
previous verse.

木によれば枝葉まばらに星月夜   子 規
Ki ni yoreba   edaha mabara ni   hoshizukiyo

Leaning against the tree,
Branches and leaves are few:
A night of stars.   Shiki

This verse is of a great simplicity. Shiki goes to the trunk

of the tree and looking upwards, sees the starry sky through
the remaining few leaves and bare branches. As the boughs
are almost leafless, the stars are seen in all their bright multi-
tudes. It is interesting, and indeed of profound significance to
notice that the tree is necessary for the seeing of the sky and
its stars. (*Hoshizukiyo* seems to mean "a night of stars, bright
as a moonlight night.")

禪寺の門を出づれば星月夜 子 規
Zendera no   mon wo izureba   hoshizukiyo

> Coming out of the Great Gate
> Of a Zen Temple,—
> A night of stars. Shiki

The point of this lies in the fact that it is a temple of the
Zen sect. The austerity and simplicity of the furnishing of the
temple, the altar and the hall; the feeling that Zen has some-
thing which can never be expressed in words or symbols of
any kind, and yet is expressed through and in spite of them,
—this predisposes the mind to looking at a sky in which a
million worlds and suns are scattered like grains of sand, with
an intimacy and lack of fear of those infinite spaces that is
strangely pleasant. This is a verse that can have its appeal
and significance to only a few people. To come out of a Zen
temple after having undergone some spiritual training of a
rigorous, solitary, and apparently meaningless kind,—the whole
world is changed in a marvellous way. Within oneself and
without, all things are as they are, and this "as they are" is
a seed of joy that blossoms in shining stars.

眞夜中やふりかはりたる天の川 嵐 雪
Mayonaka ya furi kawaritaru ama-no-gawa

> It is deep midnight:
> The River of Heaven
> Has changed its place. Ransetsu

While he was asleep, the whole universe has utterly changed.

The River of Heaven (The Milky Way) has wheeled round, and now stretches across the sky in a different direction. It is the "deep midnight" which gives the River of Heaven its limitless meaning. A feeling of *sabishisa*, "loneliness," spreads through all space, pervades all worlds, and he himself shares in it. How different from Pascal's

Ces espaces infinies m'effrayent!

荒海や佐渡によこたふ天の川   芭 蕉
Araumi ya sado ni yokotō ama-no-gawa

A wild sea!
And the Galaxy stretching out
Over the Island of Sado.   Bashō

In 銀河の序, *Introduction of the Silver River,* Bashō writes:

日既に海に沈んで、 月ほの暗く、 銀河半天
にかゝりて星きらきらと冴えたるに、 沖の方
より波の音しばしば運びて、 魂削るが如く、
腹ちぎれてそゞろ悲しび來れば。

The sun had already sunk into the sea, the moon darkly sombre. The Silver River stretched out over half the heavens, the stars flickering bright and clear. From the offing, the sound of the waves was now and then wafted hither. Lóneliness oppressed me; a grinding feeling of wretchedness, a feeling as if my bowels were being torn asunder.

It appears that the place of the poem was the province of Echigo. Bashō was standing on Cape Izumo looking over the sea towards the Island of Sado, fifty odd miles away.

This haiku is justly admired for its expression of vastness and sublimity in so short a compass. And it is paralleled, in a kind of inverted way, by the simplicity of the materials with which all this grandeur and majesty are created. Goethe says:

—— die Welt konnte nicht bestehen, wenn sie nicht so einfach wäre. Dieser elende Boden wird nun tausend

Yahre bebaut, und seine Kräfte sind immer dieselbigen.
Ein wenig Regen, ein wenig Sonne, und es wird jeden
Frühling wieder grun.

うつくしや障子の穴の天の川   一 茶
Utsukushi ya   shōji no ana no   ama-no-gawa

How lovely,
Through the torn paper-window,
The Milky Way.   Issa

There is nothing affected here, no thought of "though it is
through a hole in the paper." It is simply the irregularity of
outline of the picture of the stars that shine and twinkle in
the Milky Way. There is no hint of the poverty, not to say
squalour in which Issa was living and always lived.

片側は山にかかるや天の川   子 規
Katagawa wa   yama ni kakaru ya   ama-no-gawa

One end hanging over
The mountain,—
The Milky Way.   Shiki

Shiki here gives us a feeling of nearness and remoteness.
The Milky Way is brought down to earth, and one end is hung
over the hill, but by this we feel drawn to the other side of
it, to the unseen beyond.

霧時雨富士を見ぬ日ぞおもしろき   芭 蕉
Kirishigure   fuji wo minu hi zo   omoshiroki

A day of quiet gladness,—
Mount Fuji is veiled
In misty rain.   Bashō

Contrary to his expectation, Bashō had no feeling of frustra-
tion or disappointment when Mt. Fuji was invisible the whole
day long on account of rain. The mental picture, the spiritual

Mt. Fuji was so vividly before his eyes that the absence of the actual mountain was felt as an advantage. There is a similar experience in Keats' lines;

> Heard melodies are sweet, but those unheard
> Are sweeter.

曙や霧にうづまく鐘の聲   芭 蕉
Akebono ya   kiri ni uzumaku   kane no koe

> The voice of the bell
> Eddies through the mist,
>   In the morning twilight.   Bashō

The sound of the bell has taken to it the form of the mist, lingering here, hurrying there, trailing and swirling through the damp air. Compare Onitsura's verse, Vol. II, page 420.

朝霧や畫に書く夢の人通り   蕪 村
Asagiri ya   e ni kaku yume no   hito-dōri

> The morning mist
> Painted into a picture:
>   A dream of people passing.   Buson

On the white expanse of bright morning mist are drawn the vague, dreamy outlines of passing people. Buson felt the artist's pleasure in mist and haze that reveals in hiding:

朝霧や村千軒の市の音
Asagiri ya   mura sen-gen no   ichi no oto

> A village of a thousand eaves:
> Sounds of the market
>   In the morning mist.

霧深し何呼ばりあふ岡と船   几　董
Kiri fukashi   nani yobariau   oka to fune

> In the dense mist,
> What is being shouted,
> Between hill and boat?   Kitō

In this verse we feel the absence of subject, verb, and object
in actual life. Who shouts, what he shouts, who hears it and
answers, and what he says,—these things are all unknown,
unknowable. There is a hill, shrouded in mist, and a small
boat, invisible. There is a sound of voices calling and answer-
ing, that is all.

川霧や馬打入るる水の音   太　祇
Kawagiri ya   uma uchiiruru   mizu no oto

> The river mist;
> Urging the horse into the water,
> The sound of it.   Taigi

We may take this as either morning or evening. Taigi rides
his horse into the water. He can see nothing but the horse's
head in the white haze round him. The sounds of the water
as the horse wades in are peculiarly musical and significant,
since sound is the only avenue of sense left to him. Even
when the horse stands still, the swift current makes a subtle
gurgling sound past the horse's legs.

風に乗る川霧輕し高瀬船   宗　因
Kaze ni noru   kawagiri karushi   takasebune

> Riding on the wind,
> A light river mist,
> And through it a vessel.   Sōin

The *takasebune* is a flat-bottomed vessel that can go up the
higher shallows, 瀬, of the river; also written 高背船, a deep
vessel with high sides.

The swiftness of the ship (not mentioned in the original) is

in peculiar harmony with the wreaths of mist that hover over
the river. This verse is similar to Bashō's on the Long Bridge
of Seta, this volume, page 689; and Buson's on the Korean boat,
Vol. II, page 412, but has a simplicity lacking in both.

人を取る淵はかしこか霧の中　　　　　蕪 村
Hito wo toru　fuchi wa kashiko ka　kiri no naka

The deep place in the river,
That engulfs people,—
Is it over there in the mist?　　　　Buson

There is something childlike in this verse that is not typical
of Buson, but belongs rather to Issa. There is also something
in it of Goethe's *Der Fischer,* a feeling of dread and yet of
attraction towards the unknown:

Halb zog sie ihn, halb sank er hin,
Und ward nicht mehr gesehn.

朝霧や杭打音丁々たり　　　　　　　蕪 村
Asagiri ya　kuize utsu oto　chō-chō-tari

In the morning mist
The sound of striking a stake,
Smack! Smack!　　　　　　Buson

Someone is driving in a stake. It is misty and he cannot be
seen. There is something about this noise of the mallet on the
stake which, perhaps *because* it is inexpressible in words, causes
Buson to be unable to forget it. He therefore gives us the
simple sound onomatopoeically, *oto-chō-chō-tari.*

ありあけや淺間の霧が膳を這ふ　　　　一 茶
Ariake ya　asama no kiri ga　zen wo hau

The dawning of day:
Mist of Mt. Asama
Creeps o'er the table.　　　　Issa

The way in which we grasp things of the past, present, and future, of far and near, in one activity of the mind, is brought out in this verse. The mist that lingers outside, and faintly clouds the bushes and stones nearby, and reaches even into the room and hovers over the breakfast table, is the mist of Mt. Asama, a great volcanic mountain continually pouring out smoke and lava. The far-off and invisible is brought before us. There is a kind of blur, a mist of identity, but at the same time a morning clarity of difference.

蜻蛉や狂ひしづまる三日の月　　　　　其角
Tombō ya　kurui-shizumaru　mikka no tsuki

The dragon-flies
Cease their mad flight
As the crescent moon rises.　　Kikaku

This verse expresses that kind of see-saw we find in nature. A sword can hardly be blunt and sharp at the same time. When one meaningful thing departs, another takes its place. In addition to this there is the mysterious (because obvious) relation between the dragon-flies and the crescent moon. There is the contrast, the rustling, darting creatures, and the silent sickle above the darkened mountains in the still faintly flushed sky.

待宵や女あるじに女客　　　　　　　蕪村
Matsuyoi ya　onna aruji ni　onna kyaku

The moon-awaiting evening;
The woman who lived mistress of the house
Had a woman visitor.　　Buson

The "moon-awaiting evening" is the evening of the fourteenth day of the Eighth Month.

There is something mysterious in this verse, the woman visitor and the hostess whispering together on the evening when the moon is awaited. Buson remembered perhaps the passage in the *Heike Monogatari,* in the chapter on the Fujigawa River:

中にも副將軍薩摩守忠度は、 或宮腹の女房
の許へ通はれけるが或夜おはしたりけるに、
此女房の局に、 やんごとなき女房客人來て、
小夜もやうやう更け行くまで歸り給はず、 忠
度軒端に佇みて扇を荒くつかはれければ、 彼
女房、 野もせにすだく蟲の音よと、 優に口ず
さみ給へば、 扇をやがて遣ひ止みてぞ歸られ
ける。

Meanwhile Satsuma no Kami Tadanori, the second
in command, used to visit a certain princess's
daughter. One night when he went to her house,
a visitor was there, a lady of high rank, who did
not go back even though it grew late. Tadanori,
standing under the eaves fanned himself noisily,
and the Princess sadly hummed,

> Over the moor, the sound
> Of crying insects——

He then stopped fanning himself and went away.

But Buson's verse has a secret meaning that only the two
women know, and they will never tell it.

砕けても砕けてもあり水の月　　　　聴　秋
Kudakete mo　kudaketemo ari　mizu no tsuki

> The moon in the water;
> Broken and broken again,
> Still it is there.　　　　Chōshū

The astounding persistence, the faithfulness of things, their
law-abidingness, is felt in deep contrast to the waywardness
of life. Here we have Nature and Destiny; law, the unchanging,
and life, the lawless. And yet it is only the reflection of the
moon in the water, broken into pieces by some passing wave.

水の月もんどりうつて流れけり　　　蓼　太
Mizu no tsuki　mondori utte　nagarekeri

> The moon in the water
> Turned a somersault
> And floated away.

Ryōta

The brevity of the whole, the vivid concreteness of the second line, and the hyperbole of the third, takes one's critical breath away. Mark the poet's sublime indifference to literal fact (the stone falling in the water, disturbing the reflection of the moon, the ripples on the flowing water) and deep fidelity to his impressions. Poetical faith is identical with religious faith, requiring the same spiritual elements, ·experience, susceptibility, courage.

月早し梢は雨をもちながら　　　　芭　蕉
Tsuki hayashi　kozue wa ame wo　mochinagara

> The moon swiftly fleeting,
> Branches still holding
> The rain-drops.

Bashō

There is a description of such a scene in 敷島紀行, *The Record of a Journey in Shikishima,* which took place in 1687; the above verse was written during this year.

> あかつきのそらいさゝかはれ間ありけるを...
> 月のひかり雨の音たゝあはれなるけしきのみ
> むねにみちていふべきことの葉もなし。

> The sky of dawn had cleared a little...In the light of the moon, the sound of the rain-drops was deeply moving; our breasts were full, but no words could express it.

涼しさのかたまりなれや夜半の月　　　貞　室
Suzushisa no　katamari nare ya　yowa no tsuki

> The moon of midnight;
> A solid mass
> Of coolness?

Teishitsu

This is ancient verse, and perhaps too indirect and intellectual for modern taste, but it is interesting as an example of the way in which the haiku poets often confuse sense-perception. Here there are three things, the shape and colour of the moon; the coolness of the evening; the visually perceived hardness and solidity of the moon. They are seen-felt as one thing.

世 の 中 の も の ゝ 影 よ り け ふ の 月   南 崖
Yo no naka no   mono no kage yori   kyō no tsuki

From the shades
Of all things on earth,—
Today's moon.   Nangai

Light and darkness, the thing and its shadow, are contraries. Logically they are of equal power, but their life-direction is different. Light comes out of darkness, not darkness from light. Rōshi says:

故 有 之 以 爲 利 無 之 以 爲 用。   第十一章
The use of things becomes possible because of that of non-existence.

天 地 萬 物 生 於 有、 有 生 於 無。   第四十章
All things in Heaven and Earth spring from Existence, and Existence from Non-existence.

名 月 や 疊 の 上 に 松 の 影   其 角
Meigetsu ya   tatami no ue ni   matsu no kage

The bright moon;
On the *tatami*
The shadow of the pine-tree.   Kikaku

There are some extremely simple things (and their number is perhaps limited), which have an inexplicably profound meaning. The present poem gives us some of them. The moonlight, the pine-tree and its shadow, the straw mats,—these are the most elemental of things, yet they suffice.

落栗の音を雨月の窓下哉   芋　錢
Ochiguri no   oto wo ugetsu no   sōka kana

Rain over the autumn moon:
Beneath the window,
    Chestnuts pattering down.   Usen

There is a well-known verse of *In Memoriam* which resembles
this but with an added subjective element that gives weight,
but not necessarily depth:

    Calm is the morn without a sound,
      Calm as to suit a calmer grief,
      And only thro the faded leaf
    The chestnut pattering to the ground.

吹く風の相手や空に月一つ   凡　兆
Fuku kaze no   aite ya sora ni   tsuki hitotsu

Companion of the tempestuous wind,
A single moon
    Rolls through the sky.   Bonchō

Could it be proved that wind, like water, has some profound
relation with the moon, this poem would gain nothing, rather,
it would lose in mystery and power. The relation which poetry
is concerned with is not that of causality, but of destiny, that
is to say, it belongs to the realm in which things are free.

名月になにを急ぐぞ帆掛船   貝　錦
Meigetsu ni   nani wo isogu zo   hokakebune

Under the autumn moon,
Why shouldst thou hasten so,
    O ship with swelling sail?   Baikin

This resembles Bridges' *A Passer-By,* but has more mystery,
more passion in it. The first two lines of the English poem
are worth all the rest, but even these are, to Japanese taste,
a little overloaded:

Whither, O splendid ship, thy white sails crowding,
Leaning across the bosom of the urgent West...

名月や御煤の過ぎし善光寺   一 茶
Meigetsu ya   o susu no sugishi   zenkōji

After the cleaning,
Zenkōji Temple:
The bright autumn moon.   Issa

Spring-cleaning a great temple (here, the autumn spring-cleaning) is no easy task. For days the whole place has been in confusion, monks rushing hither and thither, their gowns flying; sweeping and hammering and dusting have caused the religious atmosphere to be lost entirely. Now all is quiet. Over the towering roofs of the temple the moon is shining with a holy light. The poet's feeling is one of renewed purity, and as he gazes at the moon, the great shining disc draws him out of himself into the true realm of this "Virtue-radiance" Temple. But in this mystical atmosphere, the spring-cleaning also has its place. It humanizes the moon and the temple. Nature and religion are at one with humanity.

芋を煮る鍋の中まで月夜かな   許 六
Imo wo niru   nabe no naka made   tsukiyo kana

Even to the saucepan
Where potatoes are boiling,—
A moonlight night.   Kyoroku

The moon is reflected in the water of the saucepan, but the poet goes beyond the fact that the moon of highest heaven is in the saucepan together with the potatoes. It is not merely the moonbeams but the whole autumn night, the wind in the pine-trees, the darkness, the radiance,—all are in the saucepan.

月天心貧しき町を通りけり   蕪 村
Tsuki tenshin   mazushiki machi wo   tōrikeri

The moon in highest heaven,
I pass through
    A poor quarter.   Buson

Compared to Issa's verse on page 944, what a gain of objec-
tivity, picturesqueness, "poetry,"—but what a loss of power!
In Buson's poem the sordid elements are lifted up into a
poetical lunar world of light and beauty.

Noteworthy is the onomatopoeic melody of ma, ma; ri, ri;
ki, ki; n, n. It clothes the poor quarter with its own verbal
softness and radiance.

青鷺のギャッと鳴きつつ今日の月   嵐 雪
Aosagi no   gyatto nakitsutsu   kyō no tsuki

The heron
Is screeching
    Under today's moon.   Ransetsu

The round, soft, lovely moon is shining over the marshes.
The heron suddenly begins to fly off somewhere, screeching,
and its harsh voice is felt to be somehow or other in harmony
with the scene, far more so than any "moan of doves in im-
memorial elms." Discord has a deeper harmony than harmony
itself. A somewhat similar, but purely pictorial contrast is
seen in the following by Chora:

嵐吹く草の中より今日の月
Arashi fuku   kusa no nakayori   kyō no tsuki

Today's moon
Rises from among
    The tempest-tossed grasses.

名月や煙這ひゆく水の上   嵐　雪
Meigetsu ya   kemuri haiyuku   mizu no ue

Under the bright autumn moon,
The smoke goes creeping over
The surface of the water.   Ransetsu

This verse is extremely simple, but there is a distant con-
nection between the light of the moon and the smoke of the
fire; the level, waveless surface of the water and the smooth
disc of the moon. The smoke moves but is silent, the moon
shines and is silent.

水鳥のつつきくだくや浪の月   随　柳
Mizutori no   tsutsuki-kudaku ya   nami no tsuki

The water-fowl
Pecks and shivers
The moon on the waves.   Zuiryu

Suppose we explain this as meaning that the water-bird pecks
at something on the still surface of the water, and the reflection
of the moon is shattered and broken,—this is still interesting,
but something has been lost. The poem says that the water-
bird pecks the moon, not its reflection. It is here that we are
to have the courage of our poetical convictions, and see the
moon being pecked and smashed by this little bird.

雲をりをり人を休むる月見哉   芭　蕉
Kumo or iori   hito wo yasumuru   tsukimi kana

From time to time
The clouds give rest
To the moon-beholders.   Bashō

There is something quiet and calm in this verse, something
that breathes a patience that does not feel itself so, a patience
with the clouding over of the moon that only the pure in heart
can acquire from gazing at the moon, the patience that nature
itself has. Wordsworth expresses it formally in,

All that we behold
Is full of blessings,[1]

and most profoundly, in what sounds like a description of
Bashō:

He is by nature led
To peace so perfect that the young behold
With envy what the old man hardly feels.[2]

The same patience is seen elsewhere in the haiku of Bashō, for
example in the verse about Mt. Fuji unseen on page 920, in
that on the autumn eve, page 901, in the one about fleas and
lice on page 792, and in that on page 961, all in this volume.

ひととせの月を雲らす今宵かな   宗　祇
Hitotose no   tsuki wo kumorasu   koyoi kana

And hast Thou clouded o'er,
This night,
The moon of the year?   Sōgi

"Thou" means Heaven, in the Confucian sense. Poetry can-
not do without some such idea, though it be clothed in poly-
theistic, monotheistic, or (as here) atheistic words. Sōgi, 1420–
1502, is one the earliest renga poets to write hokku (renamed
later haiku). He compiled *The New Tsukuba Collection,* in
which some hokku were included.

名月や池をめぐりて夜もすがら   芭　蕉
Meigetsu ya   ike wo megurite   yomosugara

The autumn moon;
I wandered round the pond
All night long.   Bashō

We may compare this verse, written at his own hut, with
two poems composed by Hakurakuten when at his official

[1] *Tintern Abbey.*
[2] *Animal Tranquillity and Decay.*

residence in Kōshu, 江州. He had a small pond made in his garden, to enjoy the cool of the evening by its side.

小池二首　其一

畫倦前齊熱。　晚愛小池清。
映林餘影没。　近水微涼生。
坐把浦葵扇。　閒吟三兩聲。

其二

有意不在大。　湛甚方丈餘。
荷側瀉清露。　萍開見遊魚。
每一臨此坐。　憶歸青溪居。

THE SMALL POND

1.

In the day-time, the front room is unbearably warm;
How refreshing the small pond at night!
The evening sun, that glows on the forest, now sinks;
Near the water is coolness.
Taking a fan of the leaf of the *hōki* I sit down;
Quietly I chant a poem or two.

2.

What I wanted was not anything big,—
A little more than ten feet square filled with water.
From the leaves of the lotus fall clear dew-drops;
Duckweed blooms, fish swim at their pleasure.
Whenever I sit and gaze at it,
I think of my retirement to the cottage in that quiet valley.

Also in a poem entitled *The White Lotus*, 白蓮, we have the line:

夜深衆僧寝、　獨起繞池行。

Deep in the night, when all the monks were asleep,
I arose and wandered round the lake alone.

There is a passage in *Walden* which gives us a hint of Bashō's state of mind as he wandered along the edge of the lake:

As I walk along the stony shore of the pond in my shirtsleeves, though it is cool as well as cloudy and windy, and I see nothing special to attract me, all the elements are unusually congenial to me. The bullfrogs trump to usher in the night, and the note of the whippoorwill is borne on the rippling wind from over the water. Sympathy with the fluttering alder and popular leaves almost takes away my breath; yet, like the lake, my serenity is rippled but not ruffled.

名月やもたれてまはる縁ばしら   梢風尼
Meigetsu ya   motarete mawaru   enbashira

Ah, the bright autumn moon!
Leaning back on the verandah post,
          And moving round it.   Shōfū-ni

It seems strange, though it is one of the commonest things in the world, that we should be impressed by certain trivial facts or objects out of all proportion to their worth as intellectually perceived. Reality is like the wind that bloweth where it listeth; it may enter, in the form of an angular wooden post, into a heart that is strained to receive the bright glories of the moon of autumn.

名月や行つても行つてもよその空   千代尼
Meigetsu ya   ittemo ittemo   yoso no sora

Autumn's bright moon,
However far I walked, still afar off
          In an unknown sky.   Chiyo-ni

There is a feeling of separateness here which is not to be denied. The poetess realizes that she and the moon are two different entities, in a different sky, in a different world. There is a waka by Kotomichi[1] which expresses that other side of truth, that "a man is a bundle of relations, a knot of roots whose flower and fruitage is the world."[2]

---

[1] 言道, 1798–1868.
[2] Emerson, *History.*

山邊より帰るわが身を送り來て
あくれば門も月も入りけり

Down from the mountain,
The moon
Accompanied me,
And when I opened the gate,
The moon too entered.

月かげを汲こぼしけり手水鉢   立 圃
Tsukikage wo   kumi-koboshikeri   chōzubachi

Scooping up the moon
In the wash-basin,
And spilling it.   Ryuho

The moon is reflected in the water of the stone washbasin
like a mirror. When the water is ladled up, the moon is held
in the ladle. When it is spilled back in the basin, the moon
is spilled back with it, and lies quivering there. There is no
other meaning, but this yet is an experience of "something or
other" which has a value that cannot be measured.

名月やはひふきすてるかげも無し   不 玉
Meigetsu ya   haifuki suteru   kage mo nashi

The bright moon;
No dark place
To empty the ash-tray.   Fugyoku

Stepping down from the verandah, the poet wanted to throw
away the tobacco ashes, and naturally looked for a dark corner
so that they should not be seen. But to his pleasant surprise,
everywhere seemed as light as day, and he was left with the
bamboo ash-tray in his hand. The verse praises the brightness
and power of the moon, but it is the impotence of the poet
that enables him to perceive it.

梨 の 木 に 寄 つ て わ び し き 月 見 か な   蕪 村
Nashi no ki ni   yotte wabishiki   tsukimi kana

Drawing near the pear-tree,—
A lonesome
    Moon-viewing.   Buson

The leaves of the pear-tree have been falling day by day;
only a few now remain silhouetted against the evening sky.
Standing beneath the tree, the voices of insects are heard here
and there. Cold dew is falling; the moon glows palely on the
horizon.

賤 の 子 や 稲 す り か け て 月 を 見 る   芭 蕉
Shizu no ko ya   ine surikakete   tsuki wo miru

The poor boy
Grinding the rice,
    Gazes up at the moon.   Bashō

This is the Japanese version of Burns' words:

For a' that, an' a' that,
    Our toils obscure, an' a' that;
The rank is but the guinea's stamp;
    The man's the gowd for a' that.

Contrast the following by Etsujin; nature is all in all:

山 寺 に 米 つ く お と の 月 夜 か な
Yamadera ni   kometsuku oto no   tsukiyo kana

At the mountain temple;
The sound of pounding the rice;
    A moonlight night.

The sound of the mortar and the roundness of the moon;
the tall trees and the temple beneath them, itself like a fungus
that has arisen from the ground; the calm autumn night, the
warmth inclining to coolness,—all these things have their own
meaning, different yet the same.

名月に犬ころ捨る下部哉   蕪 村
Meigetsu ni   inukoro suteru   shimobe kana

> The full moon;
> A man-servant
>   Leaving a puppy to die.   Buson

Buson here is raised above morality, above Buddhism, above pantheism, into a realm where things simply are. The bright autumn moon is shining, and a man-servant is taking a whimpering puppy to leave it in the thicket to die of starvation. He is much too kind and averse to killing to drown it, and avoids responsibility by allowing Nature to do her perfect work. Under the bright rays of the moon all is purified: cowardice and heroism, cruelty, kindness, and sentimentality, the half-human puppy, the half-canine man-servant. God makes his moon to shine down on the puppy alone in the undergrowth. To bring out the extremes of Buson's poetical genius, we may contrast this verse with another, of the spring moon, showing how the poet looks at it with the ears of Buddha, 六根五用:

月に聞て蛙ながむる田面かな
Tsuki ni kikite   kawazu nagamuru   tanomo kana

> Listening to the moon,
> Gazing at the croaking of the frogs;
> The surface of the rice-field.

This has the prescript, 几董が蛙合催しけるに, "For Kitō's Frog-hearing Party."

Buson's verse would be described by some as a mere literary device, an example of the figure of speech called the Transferred Epithet. But as was pointed out in the chapter on Figures of Speech in *Zen in English Literature,* a figure of speech was once a form of the imagination; it is a certain way of apprehending things, different from the normal, which demands therefore a different form of expression. Sometimes, indeed usually, we gaze at the moon and listen to the frogs, but sometimes, and oftener than we realize, we do what Buson has written.

三井寺の門叩かばや今日の月   芭　蕉
Miidera no mon   tatakaba ya   kyō no tsuki

I would fain knock
At the gate of Mii Temple,
Under today's moon.   Bashō

This kind of verse only Japanese or foreigners who have
"lived" long in Japan can appreciate. For this very reason,
we may hesitate to call it poetry. Poetry should not be too
specialist in its appeal. "A poet is a man speaking to men,"
not to Japanese.

Miidera, or Onjōji, 園城寺, a temple of the Tendai sect, built
in 858 A.D. by Enchin, was a rival of Enryakuji Temple. It
was burnt down several times and is famous rather in history
than religion.

月を松に懸けたり外しても見たり   北　枝
Tsuki wo matsu ni   kaketari hazushite mo   mitari

I kept hanging the moon
On the pine-tree, and taking it off,
Gazing at it the while.   Hokushi

When our will is so fully the will of God that we cooperate
with Him in all His activities, we can not merely remove
mountains, but hang the moon upon a pine branch, and take
it off again. The form is very irregular: 6, 9, 3.

義仲の寝覺の山か月悲し   芭　蕉
Yoshinaka no   nezame no yama ka   tsuki kanashi

Are these the hills
Where Yoshinaka awoke?
The moon is sad.   Bashō

This kind of verse has a lyrical quality (in its material) that
reminds us of the Hebrides in *The Solitary Reaper*. The thing
is sufficient in itself, but the bleakness and bareness (of the
moon, of the solitary peasant girl) is veiled by the historical
and geographical associations.

Minamoto Yoshinaka, 1154–84, defeated the Taira and entered Kyōto in 1182. Afterwards attacked by Yoshitsune, he was shot down as he fled. There are two romantic love episodes, with Tomoe, sister of one of four warriors devoted to him; and the daughter of the *Kwampaku,* Fujiwara Motofusa. Dallying with the latter was one of the minor reasons for his ultimate defeat. Two of his officers, Echigo Chūta and Tsuwata Saburō committed suicide in front of the mansion, whereupon he came out, but in vain.

While Yoshinaka was in the castle which he built, Hiuchi ga Shiro, 燧が城, he must often have seen these mountains and the moon above them. The account of Bashō's journey in these regions is given in *Oku no Hosomichi,* but no verse is found there.

一つとは思はぬ夜なりけふの月　　　蓼太
Hitotsu to wa　omowanu yo nari　kyō no tsuki

Tonight's moon!—
Unthinkable
That there was only one!　　　Ryōta

This poem praises the moon by representing the pleasant confusion of the poet's mind, his sense of the underlying mystery of origin, as he gives one name, the moon, to the source of all the impressions, the varied scenes, the poetic life, of that moonlight night. The following is on the same subject by Atsujin, 曰人, a nineteenth century poet:

立ちよれば名月もたぬ松もなし
Tachiyoreba　meigetsu motanu　matsu mo nashi

Going up to them,
Not a pine-tree
But has its bright moon.

Ryōta's verse has its feeling of wonder and mystery; Atsujin's has concreteness, particularity, movement, picturesqueness. It embraces the thought of Ryōta, that there is not one, but multitudinous moons, and in addition, we see each pine-tree of different shape and meaning, with its attendant moon.

筆とらぬ人もあらうか今日の月   鬼 貫

Fude toranu   hito mo arō ka   kyō no tsuki

> Today's moon;
> Will there be anyone
> Not taking up his pen?   Onitsura

All praise of the moon, the cherry-blossoms, the nightingale, the snow, even of God himself, is really praise of human beings, of human nature, of the Buddha-nature in us. Onitsura feels himself to be of that country, that nation which has no frontiers, on which the sun never sets, of that

> choir invisible,
> Whose music is the gladness of the world.

盗人にとりのこされし窓の月   良 寛

Nusubito ni   torinokosareshi   mado no tsuki

> The thief
> Left it behind,—
> The moon at the window.   Ryōkan

In any other poet but Ryōkan this verse might be suspected of affectation, but our knowledge of Ryōkan's daily life enables us to read this as it was written, in complete simplicity and truth. There is some comparison to be made, though the mood and the melody are different, between this verse and the last two lines of Cory's *Heraclitus:*

> Still are thy pleasant voices, thy nightingales awake;
> For Death, he taketh all away, but them he cannot take.

身の秋や月は無瑕の月ながら   一 茶

Mi no aki ya   tsuki wa mukizu no   tsuki nagara

> The autumn of my life;
> The moon is a flawless moon,
> Nevertheless——   Issa

Issa was fond of using *nagara,* 乍ら. This verse is to be completed entirely in the feelings, not by any intellectual cogitations, however emotionally suffused they may be. The intellect is to go into the emotions, not vice-versa. The intellect is to deepen and enrich, to humanize the animal feeling. Thus in proportion to the depth of our experience of life, this "nevertheless――" will have its depth of incommunicable meaning.

月見する座に美しき顔もなし　　　　芭　蕉
Tsukimi suru　za ni utsukushiki　kao mo nashi

Among the moon-viewing party,
There is none
With a face of beauty.　　　　Bashō

Comparisons are always odious, but especially so in poetry, to which they are the antithesis. But to make yet another, and bring out the differing qualities of the minds of men and women, we may put beside Bashō's verse that of the most famous woman composer of haiku, Chiyo-ni, a contemporary of Buson:

何着てもうつくしくなる月見哉
Nani kite mo　utsukushiku naru　tsukimi kana

Whatever we wear,
We look beautiful,
When moon-viewing.

Bashō's verse, however, is to be considered from another point of view also. It is said to be the third attempt of which the following verse is the first and the best.

名月や兒たち並ぶ堂の縁
Meigetsu ya　chigotachi narabu　dō no en

The autumn full moon;
Children sitting in a row
On the verandah of the temple.

Nature and poetry, art and religion; between these sit the children, perhaps those taking part in the festive procession of temple or shrine, concerned with none of them, yet the embodiment of them all:

If thou appear untouched by solemn thought,
Thy nature is not therefore less divine.

According to the *Hatsusemi*, 初蟬, and *Sanzōshi*,[1] 三冊子, while
Bashō was at Gichūji Temple, he composed the above verse,
but not being satisfied with it, he amended it to this second
attempt:

名月や海にむかへば七小町
Meigetsu ya   umi ni mukaeba   nana-komachi

The full moon:
Turning towards the sea,—
The Seven Komachis.

The last line of this verse refers to Ono no Komachi, 834-900,
the subject of several Nō plays. In her life-time she went
through so many changes that the various beauties of the moon
are compared to the seven forms she assumed.

名月を取つてくれろと泣く子かな   一 茶
Meigetsu wo   totte kurero to   naku ko kana

The child sobs,
"Give it to me!"
The bright full moon.   Issa

This is Davies'

The child
That cries aloud to own thy light:
The little child that lifts each arm
To press thee to her bosom warm.

赤い月これは誰のぢや子供達   一 茶
Akai tsuki   kore wa tare no ja   kodomotachi

Whose is it then,
My children,
This red, red moon?   Issa

Emerson has a feeling like this in *Each and All*:

---

[1] A book by Tohō, 土芳; actually three books, *Shirozōshi*, *Akazōshi*,
and *Kurozōshi*, of his comments on Bashō's verses, put together by
Rankō, 蘭更.

I thought the sparrow's note from heaven,
Singing at dawn on the alder bough;
I brought him home, in his nest, at even;
He sings the song, but it pleases not now,
For I did not bring home the river and sky.
He sang to my ear—they sang to my eye.

In Yōka Daishi's[1] *Song of Enlightenment,* 證道歌, 二十四, we read:

江月照松風吹、永夜清宵何所爲。

The moon shines over the river; the wind blows through the pine-trees;
The whole night, all is tranquil—why? for whom?

This is echoed by Secchō, 雪竇, in the *Hekiganroku,*[2] the 5th Case:

百花春到爲誰開。

The myriad flowers that come in spring, for whom do they bloom?

寺に寝てまこと顔なる月見かな   芭 蕉
Tera ni nete   makotogao naru   tsukimi kana

I stayed at a temple:
Gazing at the moon,—
With my veritable countenance!   Bashō

On a visit to Kashima, Bashō was staying at a temple, Komponji, and when the night of the full moon came, he sat there with the monks on the steps of the temple. The moon is a common Buddhist symbol for ultimate truth, but what Bashō means here is that he saw the moon of truth with the truth of himself, something perhaps that Blake saw when he looked at the sun and saw it a company of angels shouting hallelujah. There is a verse in the *Zenrinkushū* which makes us feel what Bashō saw;

[1] Died 713. Disciple of Enō, 6th Patriarch of Zen.
[2] Printed in 1125. Brought to Japan 1227. See Suzuki, *Essays in Zen Buddhism*, 2nd Series, p. 217.

水　流　元　入　海、
月　落　不　離　天。

The water flows, but back to the Ocean;
The moon sinks, but is ever in Heaven.

The "veritable countenance" comes more or less from a poem by Toho, entitled 遊龍門奉先寺, At the Dragon Gate of Hōsenji Temple, the phrase being, 令人発深省,

Causing one to come to a deep realization.

Bashō's face, as he gazed at the moon, seemed somehow different from usual, purer, more translucent; more, shall we say, like the face of the moon itself.

地　獄

夕月や鍋の中にて鳴く田螺　　　　　　　　　　一 茶
Yūzuki ya　nabe no naka nite　naku tanishi

Hell

The bright autumn moon:
Crying in the saucepan,
The pond-snails.　　　　　　　　　　　　　　Issa

See Vol. II, pages 616-7. Issa does not mean here what Keats says in his *Sonnet on Visiting the Tomb of Burns:*

All is cold beauty; pain is never done.

The beauty of the moon is just as real, just as warm, though men and animals are writhing in anguish in hells of their own or others' making. Again, the fact that the pond-snails are not actually crying, does not affect the matter at all. The whole creation groaneth to the hearing ear.

名月の御覧の通り屑家かな　　　　　　　　　　一 茶
Meigetsu no　goran no tōri　kuzuya kana

The full moon;
My ramshackle hut
Is as you see it.　　　　　　　　　　　　　　Issa

It is not ugly or pitiful or meaningless or a thing of beauty or a joy for ever; *it is as it is.*

Another form of the same feeling:

明月の小すみに立る蘆家かな

Meigetsu no   kosumi ni tateru   ashiya kana

> The autumn moon:
> Poked away in a corner,
> My thatched cottage.

橋守と語りて月の名殘かな   太　祇

Hashimori to   katarite tsuki no   nagori kana

> Talking to the bridge-guard,
> I gazed a good-bye
> To the moon.   Taigi

This verse expresses the state of mind of the poet as he stands talking to the bridge-guard, his conscious mind occupied with small-talk, but his real mind full of the moon, freely wandering in a world of light, and reluctant to part from it.

浮世の月見過しにけり末二年   西　鶴

Ukiyo no   tsuki mi sugoshi ni keri   sue ninen

> Twice more have I seen
> The harvest moon
> Of this fleeting world.   Saikaku

Ihara Saikaku died in 1693 at the age of fifty two, fifty being considered the average age of a man in Japan. This poem is his death-verse, worthy of a poet and a novelist.

家孤なり月落ちかゝる草の上   子　規

Ie ko nari   tsuki ochikakaru   kusa no ue

> A house all by itself;
> The moon declining
> Over the grasses.   Shiki

This is a picture, but like all pictures, it is not merely lines and masses of colours; the things themselves have an extra-artistic meaning which is inseparable from it. In this verse we are told explicitly that it is a solitary house, and the grasses that rise so luxuriantly increase the feeling that the house, like all other things in the world, is alone. The moon is large and bright; the house a black silhouette against the sky, the grasses with it.

我をつれて我がかげ歸る月見かな   素 堂
Ware wo tsurete   waga kage kaeru   tsukimi kana

After the moon-viewing,
My shadow walking home
  Along with me.   Sodō

The Japanese says, "My shadow took me home," but "I walk home with my shadow," or "My shadow walks home with me," what is the difference? Emerson says:

  Draw, if thou canst, the mystic line
  Severing his from thine,
  Which is human, which divine.

The Basutos believe that a man walking by the side of a river may be dragged in if he allows his shadow to fall on the water. A crocodile may seize it and pull him in with it.

入る月の跡は机の四隅かな   芭 蕉
Iru tsuki no   ato wa tsukue no   yosumi kana

The moon has sunk below the horizon:
All that remains,
  The four corners of a table.   Bashō

This is an elegy on the death of Kikaku's father, who is represented by the moon. The table is the one he always sat at. The "four corners" of the table, however, are not symbolical of anything at all. In contrast to the perfect circle of the moon, that daily deforms itself and rises and sinks, these four corners are something eternal and unchanging, not beauty, not truth, but the suchness of things.

秋雨や水底の草を踏れたる　　　　蕪　村
Akisame ya　mizusokono kusa wo　fumaretaru

In the autumn rain,
Walking on the grass
Under water.　　　　　　　　　　Buson

This was a new sensation for Buson. When we walk in the water, we tread on stones or sand or mud. On this particular day, the narrow, grass-covered country road was submerged, and as he waded along bare-footed, he found himself walking in water on grass. This peculiar experience was in accord with the autumn rain that was still falling, ruffling the surface of the water.

秋雨や我菅蓑は未だぬらさじ　　　　蕪　村
Akisame ya　waga sugemino wa mada　nurasaji

Autumn rain is falling;
Not yet have I wetted
My sedge raincoat.　　　　　　　　Buson

There is nothing "religious" about Buson; he is an artist-poet like Rossetti. But in the above verse, explicitly as elsewhere implicitly, he shows himself a true follower of the pious Bashō. Without pain accepted, discomfort desired, poetry must always be barren of its best fruits. Life is suffering, suffering is life, and a true asceticism is a necessary endeavour to lean rather on the side of pain than of pleasure. Outside, cold autumn rain is falling, while we sit snug and warm and stupid within. The raindrops are rolling on the leaf of the lotus, staining the sides of the oxen, pattering on the fallen leaves, glazing the surface of the lake. Buson is rightly ashamed of his *kasa* and *mino*, still unwetted by the rain. We think of Turner tied to the reeling mast for hours, watching the waves smite each other. Without the poet there, what is the meaning of all this confusion and woe?

二軒家や二軒餅つく秋の雨　　　　　　一　茶
Nikenya ya　niken mochitsuku　aki no ame

Two houses!
Two houses making rice-cakes:
Autumn rain.　　　　　　　　　　　Issa

There is something enigmatic in this repetition within an already microscopic compass of words. "Two houses," gives us an impression of loneliness deeper than that of "one house." There is no sign of life or joy; no activity or social amenities. But when we listen, we hear a sound of beating from both houses. Evidently they are making *mochi,* a kind of rice-dumpling. But the poem closes with another affirmation of loneliness, the autumn rain, that comes down so steadily, as if for all eternity. The sound of the rain, the sound of the beating, the dreary sound and the joyful, are both heard under their *inevitable* aspect.

口あけて親まつ鳥や秋の雨　　　　　　一　茶
Kuchi akete　oya matsu tori ya　aki no ame

Opening their mouths,
They await the parent birds
In the autumn rain.　　　　　　　　Issa

This blind instinct, this faith in nature (the nature of their parents) on the part of the fledglings touches Issa with the contrast of hope and painful reality. But hope is also part of reality.

あかあかと日はつれなくも秋の風　　　芭　蕉
Aka-aka to　hi wa tsurenaku mo　aki no kaze

The sun bright red,
Relentlessly hot,—
But the wind is of autumn.　　　　　Bashō

The sun is still hot, but the wind tells of the decline of the year. Bashō feels at one moment both seasons, and the change of one into the other.

秋風や酒肆に詩うたふ漁者樵者   蕪 村
Akikaze ya   shushi ni shi utau   gyosha shōsha

The autumn breeze is blowing;
In the wine-shop, fishermen and woodcutters
Are singing a poem.   Buson

This is a typical verse of Buson in his Chinese style. The
vocabulary, the treatment are that of Toho or Ritaihaku. We
see the red rays of the setting sun fall across the rice-fields
ready for cutting. On the long white road, a swirl of dust;
from the wine-shop, voices singing an old poem. There is
rustic culture, human pleasure, and round it all the warm cool
airs of autumn, of nature, happy with its imperceptible touch
of sadness.

あき風に散るや卒都婆の鉋屑   蕪 村
Akikaze ni   chiru ya sotoba no   kanna-kuzu

In the autumn breeze,
The shavings of the grave-posts
Fly here and there.   Buson

The grave-posts have been planed in the cemetery, and the
carpenter has left the shavings where they fell, in a heap. In
the late afternoon breeze, they fly about as though animate,
and as apparently purposeful as living things. The yellow
scrolls contrast with the dark green moss and luxuriant grasses.
It is all a strange medley of man and nature.

秋の風一茶心に思ふやう   一 茶
Aki no kaze   issa kokoro ni   omou yō

The autumn wind;
There are thoughts
In the mind of Issa.   Issa

There is always something pathetic when a poet speaks of
himself in this way. Shelley says, for example, at the end of
The Recollection:

Less oft is peace in Shelley's mind
Than calm in waters seen!

It is the using of the name in the third person that gives
the verse its peculiar significance. The autumn wind brings
"thoughts" that words can never express,—but we know what
they are.

塚も動け我泣く聲は秋の風   芭　蕉
Tsuka mo ugoke   waga naku koe wa   aki no kaze

Shake, O tomb!
My weeping voice
Is the wind of autumn.   Bashō

This remarkable verse was written on the death of Isshō, a
promising poet of Kanazawa. Isshō became an adherent of
Bashō's school of haiku, and was said to be skilful in making
poetry, and of great talent. He died on the 6th of November,
the first year of Genroku, 1688, aged thirty six. This does not
seem very young, but it must be remembered that at his age,
Bashō had written nothing that could be called poetry.

This verse, an elegy like *Lycidas* or *Adonais,* was the result
of Isshō's death, which seems to have aroused in Bashō a state
of mind in which utterly unrelated things are brought together,
or rather, are seen connected in a fashion that strongly reminds
us of ancient Hebrew poetry.

The voice of the Lord divideth the flames of fire.
The voice of the Lord shaketh the wilderness,
The Lord shaketh the wilderness of Kadesh.[1]

Contrast the weakness of Wordsworth's lines in *At the Grave
of Burns:*

Oh! spare to sweep, thou mournful blast,
His grave grass-grown.

[1] *Psalm xxix,* 7–8.

秋風やむしりたがりし赤い花   一 茶
Akikaze ya   mushiritagarishi   akai hana

The autumn breeze;
Scarlet flowers blooming
The dead girl wished to pluck.   Issa

Issa has lost his only daughter, and she cannot ask for the
flowers. But the autumn breeze blows as ever.

朝顔に吹きそめてより秋の風   樗 良
Asagao ni   fukisomete yori   aki no kaze

The wind of autumn
Blew first of all
Upon the morning-glories.   Chora

The wind, in its invisible power, the mystery of its coming,
the irrevocability of its going, has always been felt as some-
thing that manifests the Destiny of the universe. We feel this
Destiny active in ourselves and other things. The autumn
wind blows first upon the flowers of the convolvulus. Our
own destiny we see first in others; that is the natural order
of things, and it is this *natural order* which is the secret of
the above poem. Nothing can tell us which is the right order
but our instinct, an instinct of fate which runs through us,

and rolls through all things.,

This inevitability of the wind blowing first in the flowers of
the morning-glory, what Shakespeare in *Hamlet* calls "ripeness,"
is no different from that of the development of the theme in
a movement of a Mozart symphony, or that of the spacing and
line-pattern of a drawing by Claude Lorraine. The expression
of this inevitability in verse or music or art is poetry; in life,
we call it Zen.

はぜ釣るや水村山廓酒旗の風   嵐 雪
Hazetsuru ya   suison sankaku   shuki no kaze

Catching goby;
A river village, a mountain quarter,
A wine-shop flag in the wind.   Ransetsu

A man is fishing for goby at the mouth of a river, on the outskirts of a village. Up towards the higher ground is a pleasure quarter and over it flutters the beckoning flag above the wine-shop. The verse is literally:

Goby-catching: water village, mountain enclosure, wine-flag wind.

The last three come from a poem by Toboku entitled 江南春, *Kōnan in Spring,* from which the second line of seven is taken over bodily, "goby-fishing" being merely added to the beginning. If the verse is successful it is more as a *tour de force,* but it gives yet another example of the debt of haiku poets to Chinese classical poetry. The verse can hardly be called haiku, or even Japanese, but the harmony of the original is increased, and the picture is made more homely, more concrete, most of all, more pointed and particular, by the centralizing of the picture on the goby-catcher.

馬下りて川の名問へば秋の風   子 規
Uma orite   kawa no na toeba   aki no kaze

Getting off the horse,
I ask the name of river:
The wind of autumn.   Shiki

This verse sounds like part of a Chinese poem. The Japanese, however, had the genius to see that the part is sometimes greater than the whole. But a certain amount of mental and physical preparation is necessary if, for example, we are to grasp something of the nature of the autumn wind. Riding out into the country, the poet comes to a river of considerable size. He gets down from the horse, and leading him along asks a man by the river its name. He is told the name, but what strikes him is not the name or the man who tells it, but the wind that blows along the river bank, rippling the water and waving the mane and tail of the horse standing meekly there. It is the wind of autumn.

秋風や生きて相見る汝と我   子 規
Akikaze ya   ikite aimiru   nare to ware

The autumn wind is blowing;
We are alive and can see each other,
  You and I.   Shiki

This verse contains perhaps all there is in the life of man. Under the windy sky of autumn I stand here with you. These are after all the essentials of human (and perhaps even animal) existence.

肋骨のくれし拂子毛の長さ三尺もあり

馬の尾に佛性ありや秋の風   子 規
Uma no o ni   busshō ari ya   aki no kaze

Has the tail of a horse
The Buddha-nature?
  The autumn wind.   Shiki

Shiki received a mosquito whisk, a Buddhist sign of authority consisting of a handle with horse-hair attached, used to drive away mosquitoes. This particular one was very long, three feet in length. Shiki thinks of the First Case of the *Mumonkan*, "Has a dog the Buddha nature?" and asks, humorously, whether the tail of a horse also will ultimately become a Buddha, the Buddha. The melancholy wind stirs the hairs as he holds up this Buddhist symbol. He thus brings together the poetry of Japan and the religion of China, of India even.

石山の石より白し秋の風   芭 蕉
Ishiyama no   ishi yori shiroshi   aki no kaze

Whiter than the stones
Of the Stony Mountain,—
The wind of Autumn.   Bashō

This was composed at the temple of Natadera, 那谷寺, the buildings of which are situated on the boulders the mountain is covered with.

This confusion of the sensations is a kind of atavistic return to the simplicity of the undifferentiated sensitivity of the amoeba, that is nevertheless a god-like grasping of the manifold as unity. In the expression "the wind of autumn," there is perhaps a further hint of harmony, in that autumn is sometimes called in Chinese poetry, 素秋, "white autumn."

かなしさや釣の糸ふく秋の風   蕪 村
Kanashisa ya   tsuri no ito fuku   aki no kaze

Ah, grief and sadness!
The fishing-line trembles
In the autumn breeze.   Buson

This is not anguish, not a heavy grief, not lethargy, but a sensitive trembling with all that trembles. What is it that causes the line to quiver? It is our hearts that shudder in that slender twine.

牛部屋に蚊の聲よはし秋の風   芭 蕉
Ushibeya ni   ka no koe yowashi   aki no kaze

In the cow-shed,
Mosquitoes' voices are faint;
The wind of autumn.   Bashō

Outside, the cold, gusty wind of autumn is blowing, and leaves are pattering down. Inside the warm cow-shed, the air is still; the hum of a few mosquitoes that fly slowly here and there is feeble and pathetic.

秋 風 の 心 動 き ぬ 縄 す だ れ   嵐 雪
Akikaze no   kokoro ugokinu   nawa-sudare

> The moving
> Rope blind,—
> The nature of the autumn breeze. Ransetsu

In front of small eating-houses and wine-shops there is a
kind of blind over the doorway made of pieces of hanging rope.
Moving and twirling in the wind of early autumn, we see in
these insentient, indifferent pieces of rope the nature of the
autumn breeze, and our own nature as well, for it is our minds
that are moving, not the wind or the blind.

蔦 の 葉 や 殘 ら ず 動 く 秋 の 風   荷 兮
Tsuta no ha ya   nokorazu ugoku   aki no kaze

> The leaves of the ivy;
> Not one but quivers
> In the autumn wind. Kakei

This is at once the easiest and the most difficult verse to
appreciate. The poetic feeling is slight but profound. It is
simply the fact of *every* leaf stirring, a perception of law in
its perfection, the universality of nature, seen in the leaves of
the ivy, of which not one is still,—but not separated or separ-
able from them. Law can only be abstracted in thought; in
fancy, not in fact. A similar verse by Shiki, more romantic
in subject:

夕 風 や 白 薔 薇 の 花 皆 動 く
Yūkaze ya   shiro-bara no hana   mina ugoku

> In the evening breeze,
> The white roses
> All tremble.

底のない桶こけありく野分かな   蕪　村
Soko no nai   oke kokeariku   nowaki kana

There was a tub
With no bottom,
Rolling in the autumn blast.   Buson

There is some peculiar connection between the autumn tempest and the tub without a bottom. A tub or a pail with no bottom is itself a significant thing, much more so than the normal one. In fact, it is used in Zen as a symbol of enlightenment. But lying there with its uselessness so painfully patent, the wind blowing through it, the tub brings out the violent and indifferently careless character of the autumn tempest.

小皷の棚より落つる野分哉   子　規
Kotsuzumi no   tana yori otsuru   nowaki kana

With the autumn tempest,
The small drum
Falls from its shelf.   Shiki

A drum has somehow or other a connection with the wind, and when it is blown off the shelf by a blast of the "field dividing" autumn wind, we feel there is an appropriateness in it, none the less real and significant because it is apparently accidental. It is this kind of thing, or the possibility of it, the unseen relation between the air and everything it envelops, which causes the feeling of uneasiness that comes over us when the wind blows strongly:

野分の夜文よむ心定らず
Nowaki no yo   fumi yomu kokoro   sadamarazu

An autumn storm at night:
Reading a book,
My mind is restless and uneasy.

There is another verse by Shiki on the same subject, but more subtly treated. It is the unconsciously perceived increasing intensity of the wind that makes him feel ill at ease, that makes him realize the instability and fickleness of an ever-changing universe:

心細く野分のつのる日暮かな
Kokorobosoku   nowaki no tsunoru   higure kana

> As the day darkens,
> The tempest grows more violent:
> I feel uneasy.

客僧の二階下り來る野分かな　　　　　蕪 村
Kyakusō no   nikai orikuru   nowaki kana

> A visiting priest
> Comes down from upstairs:
> The autumn tempest!　　　　　Buson

The cyclones that reach Japan in August and September are of great power, and houses are blown down, roofs blown off in dozens and hundreds.

A priest is upstairs; he has been invited for the reading of the sutras in a Buddhist mass for the repose of some dead relative's soul. But the groaning and creaking of the house upstairs is so great that the priest feels rather nervous, and comes downstairs, a little shamefacedly perhaps.

If we think of this verse as an expression of the power of the tempest, in a concrete way, the poetry predominates, but if our attention is concentrated on the priest, the effect is more humorous and the haiku approaches senryū. Others of Buson in which the humorous element is rather too strong:

炭うりに鏡見せたる女かな
Sumiuri ni   kagami misetaru   onna kana

> A woman showing
> A charcoal-seller his face
> In a mirror.

ふぐ汁の我活きている寝覺哉
Fugu-jiru no   ware ikite iru   nezame kana

> Waking up,—
> I am still alive,
> After eating swell-fish soup!

The swell-fish, or globe-fish is very poisonous, but as people think it delicious, they often eat it at the risk of their lives.

心細く野分のつのる日暮かな   子 規
Kokorobosoku   nowaki no tsunoru   higure kana

> Forlorn and helpless;
> The autumn storm grows more violent,
> As day begins to droop.   Shiki

Shiki feels the inevitability of nature, its power and violence, and man's weakness before it. We see the same in the following, also by him:

此の野分更にやむべくもなかりけり
Kono nowaki   sara ni yamubeku mo   nakarikeri

> This autumn storm
> Increasing,
> Will not cease to blow.

There is a core of fear and alarm in these verses. In the following, also by Shiki, this negative attitude is replaced by the positive; it is an *Ode to the West Wind*.

狂亂の野分ありたき我が思ひ
Kyōran no   nowaki aritaki   waga omoi

> Ah, that my thoughts
> Might have the frenzy
> Of this "field-dividing" wind!

關の火をともせば滅入る野分かな   蕪 村
Seki no hi wo   tomoseba meiru   nowaki kana

> As they were lighting
> The lanterns at the barrier,
> The autumn storm subsided.   Buson

The connection between the lighting of the lamps of the barrier gate and the falling of the wind is an almost entirely accidental one, viewed objectively and scientifically. Seen subjectively or sentimentally, we may ascribe any relation to any

unrelated groups of phenomena, and we then get what is called
the pathetic fallacy. But when in the poetic or religious realm,
(a region that is not susceptible of the intellectual, dichotomous
division of related and unrelated), we are at one with the events
concerned, we feel the interpenetrative and not the causal
relation of things. It is in this state that the above verse was
written and is to be read. The lighting of the lights and the
dying down of the wind are perceived rather as the leaves and
blossoms of a flowering bush, where the relation is a vital and
not a mechanical one.

This laborious explanation of a perfectly simple and straight-
forward verse is necessitated by the cynicism and disbelief of
the intellect, that cannot but weaken our courage and faith in
our intuitions and experiences.

猪も共に吹かるゝ野分かな　　　　芭 蕉
Inoshishi mo tomo ni fukaruru nowaki kana

The autumn tempest
Blows along also
Even wild boars. Bashō

Hyperbole is rather uncommon in Japanese poetry, though
it is a prominent, even *the* prominent feature of Kabuki. In
Celtic stories it is much used; a man has more than a huge
nose,—it is several leagues long. In Indian Literature, partic-
ularly in Mahayana Sutras, hyperbole is employed quite con-
sciously to get people to give up their relative ideas of time
and space, and, as Sōshi (Chuangtse) says, become a man whom

fire cannot burn, water cannot drown, heat and
cold cannot affect, wild beasts cannot harm.

火弗能熱、水弗能溺、寒暑弗能害、禽獸弗能賊。

Another verse of Bashō's, with the same hyperbole:

吹き飛ばす石は淺間の野分かな
Fukitobasu ishi wa asama no nowaki kana

The autumn tempest
Blows away the rocks
On Mount Asama.

In the *Inferno,* Dante describes a storm in similar terms:

un vento
Impetuoso per gli avversi ardori
Che fier la selva, e senza alcun rattento
Li rami schianta, abbatte e porta fiori;
Dinanzi polveroso va superbo,
E fa fuggir le fiere e li pastori[1].

a wind
Impetuous among the diverse heats
Which strikes the forest without any stay,
Breaks off the boughs, breaks down and sweeps away;
Dust in front, proudly it goes,
And makes the wild beasts and shepherds flee.

A remaining problem is: what is it that is blown along
"together with the wild boar"? Kyoroku says:[2]

猪 の 野分 の す ま じ さ 、 臥猪 の 床 は 宵 の 程
に 吹 き ま く ら れ 松 も 檜 も く つ が へ り た る 風情
言外 に あ り 。

The fearfulness of the autumn tempest round the
wild boar! In the early evening, the wind blows
about the boar resting in his lair, and pine-tree
and cypress are overturned. The scene is beyond
description.

船頭 の 竿 と ら れ た る 野分 か な   蕪 村
Sendō no   sao toraretaru   nowaki kana

The ferry-man's pole
Has been stolen away,
By the autumn tempest.   Buson

There is a personification of nature here which belongs to
the time when everything was equally personal, when men
were seen as trees walking. The pole has been plucked away
by an unseen hand. All is calm now, and that which removed

---

[1] *Inferno,* IX, 67–72.
[2] In 篇突.

the pole has gone roaring over the hills and down the valleys
to some other realm, the pole with it.

鳥羽殿へ五六騎いそぐ野分かな   蕪 村
Toba dono e   gorokki isogu   nowaki kana

Five or six horsemen
Hasten to the Palace of Toba
Through the autumn storm.   Buson

Toba was the 74th Emperor of Japan, ruling from 1108 to
1123, when he abdicated in favour of his son Sutoku, 1124-41.
This period was one of continual quarrels and strife between
the monks of Hieizan, Miidera, Todaiji, etc. The scene of the
verse must be somewhere near Kyōto. The time is probably,
as Meisetsu says, early evening. The troublous times are
reflected in the galloping riders, and again in the strong wind
blowing. The "five or six" is typical of Buson and his love
of number, and the fewness of the knights is in harmony with
the loneliness of the season.

芭蕉野分して盥に雨をきく夜かな   芭 蕉
Bashō nowaki shite   tarai ni ame wo   kiku yo kana

The *bashō* in the gale;
I listen at night to the rain
Drip-drip into the tub.   Bashō

That evening, heavy rain clouds had rolled up from the
horizon; Mt. Fuji was invisible under them. Soon heavy rain-
drops are heard on the broad leaves of the banana-plant, and,
as the wind rises, on the shutters. Towards midnight there is
the sound of drops of water, *in* the hut; the rushthatched roof
is leaking. Bashō goes to the sodden kitchen and gets a wooden
tub to put under the leak, and gets back into bed. Outside,
the wind and rain find a voice in the labouring banana plant.
Inside, the ironically musical monotony of the drip, drip, sounds
in Bashō's heart. Inside and outside are in a harmony of
misery and desolation. Notice the unusual form, 8, 7, 5.

門前の老婆子薪貪る野分かな   蕪 村
Monzen no   rōbashi takigi musaboru   nowaki kana

> The old woman in front of the gate,
> Greedy for firewood;
> The autumn tempest.   Buson

The morning after the furious hurricane dead branches strew the paths and fields, and the old woman, her hair tousled by the remainder of the tempest that still blows, is covetously collecting them. What is so good about this verse is the way in which the violence of the autumn wind is the cause of and paralleled by the eagerness of the old woman. This is perhaps the reason why the verse is so unusually long: 5, 11, 5.

Another by Buson, not so good, but interesting, a kind of "emotion recollected in tranquillity":

市人のよべ問かはすのは[1]きかな
Machibito no   yobe toikawasu   nowaki kana

> Townsfolk,
> Asking one another about the evening before,
> The autumn storm.

妻も子も寺でもの喰ふ野分かな   蕪 村
Tsuma mo ko mo   tera de mono kuu   nowaki kana

> Wife and child
> Are eating in the temple,—
> The autumn tempest!   Buson

As the poet passes by the temple he sees a woman with her children eating a meal in the local temple. There has evidently been some kind of natural catastrophe or disaster, flood or hurricane or landslide, and these people have taken refuge in the temple. The poet feels the power of nature in the simple fact of their eating in a strange place.

---

[1] Mistake for わ.

美しや野分のあとの唐辛子   蕪 村
Utsukushi ya   nowaki no ato no   tōgarashi

How beautiful,
After the autumn storm,
The red pepper.   Buson

There is nothing more thrilling, more unforgettable than the
seeing of beauty where we never saw it before. To see meaning
in the meaningless, this is the true nature, the Buddha nature
of man.

The gale has lasted all night, but with the morning rays,
the wind drops and the rain ceases to fall. It is still cloudy,
but bright. In the garden, things are blown about and in
disarray. The earth is almost white with sand, the small
stones left on the surface of the ground after the heavy rain.
Upon this whitish, brownish surface lie the bright green stalks
of pepper with their vermilion pods.

The onomatopoeia of this verse is interesting:

utsuku*shi* ya *no*waki *no* a*to no* tōgara*shi*

The gentle rhythm suggests the calm and windless morning.
Another verse by Buson, with the same love of colour:

大風のあしたもあかしとうがらし
Ōkaze no   ashita mo akashi   tōgarashi

This morning also
After the gale,
The peppers are red.

There is a verse by Bashō very similar to these of Buson,
but with Bashō's greater particularity:

こがらしや畠の小石目に見ゆる
Kogarashi ya   hatake no koishi   me ni miyuru

The winter storm;
Small stones of the field
Are visible to the eye.

Bashō's verse is rather subdued. Buson gets more thrill out
of the mere colour; other things have changed, but the redness
of the peppers, no, this is the same as ever. Bashō sees per-
manence amid impermanence.

There is a verse by Shiki also on a similar subject:

赤き實一つこぼれぬ霜の庭
Akaki mi   hitotsu koborenu   shimo no niwa

> A single red berry
> Has fallen
> On the frost in the garden.

鴻の巣の網代にかかる野分かな　　　　蕪 村
Kō no su no   ajiro ni kakaru   nowaki kana

> The nest of the swan,
> Hanging on the bamboo fish-trap,
> After the autumn storm.　　　　Buson

Buson was an artist, but though he deeply appreciated the beauty that is to be seen often in the world of nature and sometimes in world of men, he knew that significance is what things have and what we need.　Going out after the gale, he saw the nest of a swan caught on the bamboo matting set in the river as a kind of trap for fish.

野ざらしを心に風の沁む身哉　　　　芭 蕉
Nozarashi wo   kokoro ni kaze no   shimu mi kana

> Resigned in heart
> To exposure to the weather,
> The wind blows through me.　　　　Bashō

In the autumn of 1684, Bashō at last found a chance of visiting his native place, Ueno, since a pupil of his, Chiri, was leaving Yedo for Yamato, where his native town was situated. Bashō had poor health all his life, and his disciples would not let him set out on the journey alone.　Bashō had now been in the Capital so long that he felt it to be a second home to him, and this the meaning of the following:

秋十年却つて江戸を指す故郷
Aki to tose   kaette edo wo   sasu kokyō

> Ten autumns have passed;
> I feel Edo rather
> To be my native place.

The way was long and difficult; it was sixteen years since
he had left his native place, and here in Yedo were all his
friends and pupils that made tolerable life in this world of
loneliness; he might well fall by the roadside, leaving his bones
to bleach far from both his old home and his adopted. Like
Saigyō, or Sōgi, he felt he was destined to die on a journey,
and the above verse is both a kind of elegy on himself, and
an expression of his determination to seek and accept his lot.

はつ露や猪の臥芝の起あがり   去　來
Hatsutsuyu ya   i no fusu shiba no   okiagari

> The couch of the wild boar,
> The grass, lifting up,—
> The first dew.   Kyorai

It is early morning, and the grass seems to be lifting up
again, as though it had been the bed of a wild boar during
the night. The first dew lies on the grass.

This verse has a great power combined with a delicacy of
imagination, the wild boar of the mind and the dew of the mind.

朝露や飯たくけむり草を這ふ   子　規
Asatsuyu ya   meshi taku kemuri   kusa wo hau

> Morning dew;
> Smoke from the cooking rice
> Creeps over the grass.   Shiki

This is an interesting example of how the purely pictorial,
the completely objective, the significant form alone, is a figment
of the fancy. Indeed, this verse unites the "poetic" and the
mundane, nature and man, looking and eating. We cannot
avoid looking at the smoke over the dewy grass with our

stomachs as well as our eyes. Just as the two are connected inside us, the dew and the smoke are joined outside us.

白露に四五軒の小村哉　　　子　規
Shiratsuyu ni   shi go ken no   komura kana

In the white dew,
Four or five houses,
A hamlet.　　　Shiki

Shiki here endeavours to enlarge our conception of dew. Drops of clear water lie in the lotus leaves, on the blades of grass at the ends of reeds, along the underside of fences, all near the eye. But the dew extends everywhere, it embraces the small hamlet of several scattered houses, and for a short hour is their significant element, because it is what alone unites them. This was composed at Yuda hot spring. Shiki has also made a miniature which corresponds to this landscape; it is almost a senryu:

一升の露をたゝふる小庭哉
Isshō no   tsuyu wo tatauru   koniwa kana

A small garden
Brimming with dew,—
Half a gallon of it.

武士の露はらひ行く弭かな　　　蕪　村
Mononofu no   tsuyu haraiyuku   yuhazu kana

The ends of the warriors' bows,
As they go, brushing
The dew.　　　Buson

This verse is probably not a description of something actually seen by Buson, but was "imagined" by the poet. The touch of the bows on the grasses in the early morning as the *samurai* stalk along, has that refinement of particularity, that grasp of the essential in the trivial, the perception of significance in the insignificant, that marks a poet of the first rank.

湖水納涼
すゞしさや
船に吹入るゝ
浪の露

Suzushisa ya
fune ni fuki-iruru
nami no tsuyu

The coolness!
The dew of the waves
Wafted into the boat.

Cooling on the Lake

by Chora, 樗良, 1729–81

There is another by Buson, superficially similar to this, but where the poetic imagination is much more subtle:

狩倉の露におもたきうつぼ哉
Karigura no　tsuyu ni omotaki　utsubo kana

At the hunting place,
The quivers are heavy
With the dew.

It is an autumn morning, and something suggests the idea of hunting, perhaps a story or a picture. On their backs is the sinister quiver, arrows with death in every feather. As they pass through the wood, the sun not yet risen, the dew on leaf and spray wets the quivers, which gradually become heavier and heavier. To feel the weight of a thing that has not been touched, has not been seen, that does not exist,—this is a greater power than to measure the weight of the moon, or predict the annihilation of the universe.

きくの露受て硯のいのち哉　　　　蕪 村
Kiku no tsuyu　ukete suzuri no　inochi kana

The ink-stone, receiving
The dew of the chrysanthemum,—
The life of it!　　　　　　　　Buson

Buson went to see a certain friend when the chrysanthemums were at their best. His friend set before him paper, brush, and ink-stone, and asked him to compose a verse. Thereupon Buson made the above haiku. Using the dew of a chrysanthemum as water, he rubbed the ink-stone. Thus the dry stone was brought to life, to activity, to its full capacity, by the dew received into it.

露の世は露の世ながらさりながら　　　一 茶
Tsuyu no yo wa　tsuyu no yo nagara　sarinagara

This dewdrop world—
It may be a dewdrop,
And yet—and yet—　　　　　　Issa

This verse has the prescript, 愛子を失ひて, "Losing a beloved child." This child was Sato-jo, さと女, and Issa's feelings at this time are portrayed in *Oragaharu*. He had already lost two or three children when this baby girl died.

Buddhism teaches us that this is a transitory, fleeting world to which we should not give our hearts. Only eternal things are worth our while. But this anguish we feel at the death of a child, is there anything deeper? Can an emotion of such profundity belong to a world that is merely a dewdrop world? Unconsciously almost, in his anguish, Issa is doubting one of the fundamental tenets of the Pure Land Sect, and inclining towards the Zen point of view, that this world is the eternal world; here and now we live the Buddha-life. The *Rokuso-dangyō* says:

凡夫即佛、 煩惱即菩提、 前念迷即凡夫、 後念悟即佛。

　An ordinary man is Buddha; desire and passion is enlightenment. One thought of folly makes a man an ordinary man; the next enlightened thought and he is a Buddha.

草の葉を遊びありけよ露の玉　　　　　　　嵐 雪
Kusa no ha wo　asobiarike yo　tsuyu no tama

　　Dance from one blade of grass
To another,
　　Pearls of dew!　　　　　　　　　　　　Ransetsu

Asobi-ariku means literally, playing-walk, that is gambol, frolic, sport. The point of the poem is in *yo*! the imperative, wishing things, wishing these particular things to act according to their nature, to do what they have done, and will do. Then the sparkling drops of dew fill our hearts with pleasure, and we dance too as the blades of grass lift and quiver.

露ちるやむさい此世に用なしと   一 茶

Tsuyu chiru ya musai kono yo ni yō nashi to

"I will have nothing more to do
With this sordid world,"
And the dew rolls away.   Issa

This expresses Issa's own view of the world into which he
was born, but also of the nature of the dew-drops which form
where they may stand globed until the morning sun gives
them leave to depart.

しらつゆに浄土参のけいこかな   一 茶

Shiratsuyu ni jōdomairi no keiko kana

From the white dew-drops,
Learn the way
To the Pure Land.   Issa

Just as wind is used as a symbol of the unknown comings
and goings of the spirit of life, so water is the type of our own
life, its swift, willing obedience, its bright, active desirelessness.
Above all, the dew-drop that disappears so soon, leaving not
a trace of itself behind, is our own soul, that is devoid of all
qualities, free of any kind of permanence, is the white radiance
of eternity.

蓮の葉に此世の露は曲りけり   一 茶

Hasu no ha ni kono yo no tsuyu wa magarikeri

On the lotus leaf,
The dew of this world
Is distorted.   Issa

This expresses Issa's view of life, his world-view. The dew
is of its nature perfect, but when it falls on the leaf of the
lotus, it loses its spherical beauty and lies there twisted and
deformed. This is the fundamental concept, or rather, intuition
of Mahayana Buddhism, the original goodness of man, original,
not in time, but in essence, in its nature.

露ちるや地獄の種をけふも蒔く   一 茶

Tsuyu chiru ya   jigoku no tane wo   kyō mo maku

> The dew-drops are vanishing:
> More seeds of Hell
>   To be sown today.   Issa

Issa never forgot that

> In the midst of life we are in death,

and that

> We have done those things we ought not to have done,
> we have left undone those things we ought to have done.

But Issa goes deeper into self-reproach than this. The dew-drops are disappearing, morning has begun. I must go out into the world and do things and leave things undone, from the point of view of Shin, causes of punishment in Hell, expiation in Purgatory. In Zen, they are causes of my immediately falling into Hell, instantly into Purgatory, or rather, doing things we ought not to do and leaving undone those things we ought to have done *is* Hell and Purgatory.

こぼれてはたゞの水なり紅の露   千代尼

Koborete wa   tada no mizunari   beni no tsuyu

> The dew of the rouge-flower,
> When it is spilled
>   Is simply water.   Chiyo-ni

The reddish-yellow flower is cup-shaped and holds rain or dew in the same way as the camellia. There is great "virtue" in the expression *tada no*. If we translate it "only" water, we get the feeling of disillusionment without the insight into the nature of things, into what Carlyle calls "the great Fact of existence." The poet, like the great man,

> fly as he will, he cannot get out of the awful presence
> of this Reality. Though all men should forget its truth,
> and walk in a vain show, he cannot.[1]

[1] *Heroes and Hero Worship*, 2.

白露や茨の刺にひとつゞつ　　　　　　蕪　村

Shiratsuyu ya　ibara no toge ni　hitotsu-zutsu

White dew on the bramble;
One drop
　　On each thorn.　　　　　　　　Buson

Cower says, in *The Task,*

All we behold is miracle, but seen
So duly, all miracle is vain.

Sometimes, least aware of our state of inspiration, when we
are gazing at each knot in a piece of planed wood, each node
of a bamboo, we are invaded by a sense of satisfaction, quite
inexplicable, but similar to that of solving an equation.

The objectivity of this verse contrasts with the subjectivity
of most verses dealing with the subject of dew, which is in
the poetry of all countries a symbol of evanescence. This
objectivity is confirmed by Shiki in the following passage from
A Drop of Indian Ink, 墨汁一滴:

松葉に露のたまる光景を目に見れども花の
露とばかりにては花は目に見えて露は目に見
えず、只心の中にて露を思ひやるなり、是に
於てか松葉の露は全く客觀的となり、花の露
は半主觀的となり兩者其趣を異にす。

The dew on the pine-needles is actually seen,
whereas in the case of the dew on the (cherry)
blossoms, the flowers aré seen but the dew is not,
being imagined in the mind. Thus the dew on the
pine-needles is entirely objective, but the dew on
the cherry-flowers is half-subjective. Each has its
own peculiar meaning.

A verse by Shiki, different in its ostensible subject, but
identical in its real subject, the poetical experience:

燈せば雛に影あり一つゞつ

Hitomoseba　hina ni kage ari　hitotsu-zutsu

Lighting the light,
Each of the dolls
　Has its shadow.

甘からばさぞおらが露人の露 一 茶
Amakaraba   sazo ora ga tsuyu   hito no tsuyu

> Were it sweet,
> It would be *my* dew,
> *His* dew.

Issa

In such a verse this, we have a thought, a poetico-philo-sophical thought expressed with great brevity. Whether this can be called poetry is a difficult question to answer. It is not, I think, haiku. The dew, its nature, some aspect of it, are not here grasped and expressed. It is rather the nature of Issa, of all men, their always looking for profit, whether material or spiritual, or moral. So D. H. Lawrence speaks of "the greed of giving." The true poetical world is not related to profit at all, even of a poetical kind. It sees the beads of dew, the jewels sparkling on the finger, the greed and avarice of man, in a poetic way. When we look at the verse from this point of view, the grasping of the nature of man, there is some poetry in the extremely compressed drama of Issa's verse.

何のその百萬石も笠の露 一 茶
Nan no sono   hyakuman-goku mo   kasa no tsuyu

> Pooh! What is it, either,
> A million bales of rice?—
> The dew on my kasa!

Issa

There is something very much in common between Issa and William Langland. Both had unfeigned contempt for wealthy people, who

> chosen chaffare to cheeven the bettre,
> As hit semeth to owre siht that such men thryveth.

Yet both were deeply religious and patriotic men, (and we may think of Burns also) There are many verses by Issa which prove his deep love of country, for example:

是からは大日本と柳かな
Kore kara wa   dainippon to   yanagi kana

> From now on,
> Great Japan!
> And the willow-trees!

こんな夜は唐にもあるか時鳥
Konna yo wa   kara ni mo aru ka   hototogisu

> Is there such a night as this
> In China also?—
> The nightingale singing!

白つゆに淋しき味を忘るるな   芭 蕉
Shiratsuyu ni   sabishiki aji wo   wasururu na

> Never forget
> The lonely taste
> Of the white dew.   Bashō

There is a strong resemblance between Bashō and Hardy. Both men suffered long and deeply, but not on account of their own personal affairs, which seem to have been rather on the fortunate side. It was the taste of dew, the tragic meaning of life, of the life of others that affected them so deeply. One lived in Victorian England, a time of action, the other in the Tokugawa age of prosperity and brilliance, but it was the hollowness and evanescence of things which they deeply perceived and painfully expressed. In this sense it may be said of both Hardy and Bashō, that they "did not burn, but smouldered." This is perhaps a just criticism of these two men and of this particular verse.

The Frontispiece

This comes from Bashō's *Oku no Hosomichi,* a journal of travel undertaken in the year 1689, and copied by Buson, 1715–83, with his own illustrations. The present picture seems to relate to a previous incident, the crossing of the Nakayama passes by Bashō and Sora with the help of "a stout young man with an oaken stick and a short sword at his waist." The following is a tranlation:

At Obanazawa we called on a man called Seifū, wealthy but with no vulgar tendencies. He used to go to the Capital on business occasionally and could sympathize with travellers, so he put us up for several days, and treated us hospitably.

> I sleep,
> Making coolness
> My lodging-place.

(picture)

> Creep out, O frog,
> With thy croaking voice,
> From under the silk-worm house.

> The safflower
> Calls to mind, by its shape,
> The eyebrow-brush.

> The women who feed the silk-worms,—
> Their dress takes us back
> To the remote past.   Sora

In Yamagata there is a mountain temple called Risshakuji, whose founder was Jikaku Taishi. The whole place is extraordinarily quiet. People recommended us to visit it, so from Obanazawa we retraced our steps about twenty miles. It was not yet dark when we arranged to spend the night at the foot of the hill, and we climbed up to the main temple. The hill was all boulders one upon another, the pine-trees and cypresses ancient, earth and stones old and mossy, the temples with doors closed standing on the rocks, not a sound to be heard. We crept over or round the rocks, and worshipped at the temples, our hearts filled with the mysterious silence and wonderful scenery.

> The stillness;
> The voices of the cicadas
> Penetrate the rocks.

We wanted to go down the Mogami River, so we waited for fine weather at a town called Oishida. Seeds of the older haikai schools had been sown here, and the people yearned for the poetical flowers they remembered, and softened their hearts with the sound of this Mongolian flute. However, following this course, they were hesitating whether to choose the old or the new [Bashō] school, since they had no one to guide them, so in this strange place we made one roll of linked verses, on this journey the most poetical so far.